D0060154

i am intelligent

i am intelligent

From Heartbreak to Healing—
A Mother and Daughter's Journey through Autism

BY PEYTON AND DIANNE GODDARD
with Carol Cujec, PhD

FOREWORD BY ROBERT A. FRIEDMAN, MD

YOLO COUNTY LIBRARY
226 BUCKEYE STREET
WOODLAND CA 95695

Guilford, Connecticut
An imprint of Globe Pequot Press

To buy books in quantity for corporate use
or incentives, call **(800) 962-0973**
or e-mail **premiums@GlobePequot.com**.

 skirt!® is an attitude . . . spirited, independent, outspoken, serious, playful and irreverent, sometimes controversial, always passionate.

Copyright © 2012 by Goddard Family Enterprises

All rights reserved. No part of this book may be reproduced or transmitted in any form by any means, electronic or mechanical, including photocopying and recording, or by any information storage and retrieval system, except as may be expressly permitted in writing from the publisher. Requests for permission should be addressed to Globe Pequot Press, Attn: Rights and Permissions Department, P.O. Box 480, Guilford, CT 06437.

skirt!® is a registered trademark of Morris Publishing Group, LLC, and is used with express permission.

Text design: Sheryl Kober
Project editor: Kristen Mellitt
Layout artist: Joanna Beyer

Library of Congress Cataloging-in-Publication Data is available on file.

ISBN 978-0-7627-7925-3

Printed in the United States of America

10 9 8 7 6 5 4 3 2 1

To Bert, Ernie, and Gam,
tryers who never gave up believing I would heart here heal.

To Murray and Lincoln.
Yearn I you feel your treasured worth in a peace-freed world.

—P. G.

To my two Patricks, both fathers extraordinaire.

—D. G.

To Anton, Noah, Ella, and, lastingly, Tom.
In memory of Uncle Bob,
a good egg whose life was spent in an institution.

—C. C.

CONTENTS

Foreword

Peyton Goddard first came to my office on June 25, 1996, accompanied by her parents, Pat and Dianne. At age twenty-one, she had already received comprehensive evaluations at two highly respected university hospitals, and she had been worked up by a long line of specialists, including psychiatrists, neurologists, pediatricians, endocrinologists, audiologists, speech pathologists, occupational therapists, physical therapists, and teachers. Her diagnoses included mental retardation, autism, movement disorders, epileptic aphasia, ADHD, anxiety disorders, bipolar disorder, obsessive-compulsive disorder, depression, and a sleep disorder. Peyton walked into my office with her parents on either side of her, holding her arms so that she would not strike out.

Numerous medications had been prescribed to target the symptoms associated with Peyton's diagnoses as well as her frequent, explosive outbursts of aggressive and dangerously impulsive behaviors. Her aggression and emotional dyscontrol were worsening to the point that Peyton's parents had just been advised to hospitalize their daughter in a psychiatric facility; however, they wanted to make one last effort to avoid institutionalizing their daughter. I could see it in their eyes: I was their last hope. As a medical doctor, I specialize in the practice of child, adolescent, and adult psychiatry, and have been doing so since completing a fellowship in child and adolescent psychiatry in 1990. In addition to having a clinical practice in San Diego, I am on the volunteer faculty at University of California San Diego Medical Center, where I supervise psychiatry resident physicians training to be child and adolescent psychiatrists. I am also the president and CEO of PsyCare, Inc., a group practice of more than one hundred mental health professionals with six offices throughout San Diego. But despite my credentials, I honestly had no idea how I could improve Peyton's life. Nor could I imagine what I would be able to do differently from what had already been tried.

I spent the next hour doing my best to take a history, while Peyton moved constantly about the office. She was unable to communicate by talking. Sometimes she would jump up and down in place, flapping her arms like a big bird trying to fly. At other times, she was picking up specks of lint from the floor and handing them to her father. Every so often, Peyton's eyes would dart in my direction, and I wondered if she was evaluating how I was reacting to her behaviors. I spoke to Peyton directly, and, as I did, she continued to sustain eye contact with me for just a few moments longer than what appeared to be random. "I will do whatever I can to help you," I told Peyton. "We can work together to figure out how to proceed." Peyton sustained her gaze at me even longer as we looked directly into each other's eyes for several seconds. It was enough for me to think that perhaps Peyton had understood what I had said. For the rest of the hour, as I obtained information from Pat and Dianne, I made sure to include Peyton in the discussion and assumed that she understood what we were saying, even though she was unable to acknowledge it. This was the beginning of our "therapeutic relationship," which has continued for the past sixteen years.

During my training to become a physician, I was taught that, despite the labels and diagnoses, our patients are real people who deserve to be treated with respect, patience, and compassion. I do not believe I have done anything special in working with Peyton. By treating Peyton as any one of us would wish to be treated, a space was created whereby trust was established and Peyton was able to feel safe.

For the first ten months of our working together, I understood my role to be one of "psychopharmacologist." Peyton was already being prescribed several medications in an effort to stabilize her behavior, but they were not working well. Always with a rationale, I adjusted medication dosages, but ultimately added a medication, a selective serotonin reuptake inhibitor, to target behaviors that appeared to be anxious and obsessive. Maybe, I thought, Peyton's outbursts were like anxiety or panic attacks, and this type of medication would help with her insomnia, anxiety, and obsessive-compulsive behaviors. Also, it was one class of medication that Peyton had never been prescribed. Peyton's behavior did indeed improve. She began to sleep better, the frequency and intensity of her emotional and behavioral outbursts decreased, and she was able to tune in more during our visits. Pat and Dianne reported that Peyton was calmer, and they were all reaping a modest but welcome reprieve from endless sleepless nights and tumultuous days.

A short time later, Peyton experienced a breakthrough when she was introduced to facilitated communication (FC), an assisted-typing technique in which a facilitator provides physical and emotional support so that Peyton can type with one finger on a keyboard. I was skeptical at first, wondering whether Peyton was doing the typing or Dianne, the facilitator, was the one expressing her own thoughts by directing Peyton's hand. Eventually, I conducted my own "experiments" to clarify if what I was seeing was true. On several occasions, I had Peyton's parents leave the room, while I told Peyton a specific phrase for her to type when her parents returned. Each time I did this, over several weeks, there was 100 percent accuracy in Peyton typing the correct phrase or answer to my question. There was no possible way for Dianne to know what I had asked Peyton, and it was clear that Peyton was communicating her own thoughts and feelings. Over many months, Peyton's accuracy in controlling her movements to strike the intended key on the keyboard improved steadily, and the degree of physical support required by the facilitator decreased steadily as well.

Imagine how frustrating it must have been for Peyton to hear and comprehend conversations around her and about her for decades with no way of letting people know she understood. Imagine how dehumanizing it must have been for people to treat her as "retarded" and without meaningful thought because she had no way of letting the world know that her brain was in fact perceiving and understanding everything going on around her. Now imagine this little girl, who could barely communicate, being emotionally, physically, and sexually abused by school personnel and caretakers that her parents trusted to keep her safe. Tragically, current estimates suggest that more than 65 percent of girls with developmental disabilities will be sexually abused before they turn age 18, yet few of these crimes will be reported let alone prosecuted.

Peyton's story is one of a little girl born with profound developmental disabilities that fall into the autism spectrum, who became traumatized, dehumanized, and depressed to the point that she felt her life was worthless. Seeing no hope and no way out, Peyton wanted nothing more than to die. Her parents, however, never gave up on their daughter. Despite what the experts advised, Pat and Dianne pursued every possible avenue until they found a path that led to daylight. When Peyton learned how to express herself with the use of FC, she was able to reveal her traumatic past and share with the world the struggles of living as a disenfranchised member of society.

For the next several years, with the help of Pat and Dianne, Peyton and I met weekly for therapy. We uncovered, explored, and processed Peyton's past traumas and current stresses. We developed coping strategies for anxiety, and problem solved as to how to avoid being traumatized again in the future. The more Peyton was able to express herself through typing, the more control she experienced over her motor movements. Her outbursts all but disappeared, only to reappear as a barometer of some overwhelming internal stressful memory or external stressful situation that was taking place. It wasn't always smooth sailing, and there were many setbacks along the way, but Peyton's emotional functioning and behavioral control continued to steadily improve.

Throughout these sixteen years, I have witnessed in Peyton a level of wisdom and insight into herself, humanity, and the universe that is profound and rare. In listening to Peyton, we are compelled to ask ourselves how many souls have been daily cast away from meaningful lives because we do not know how to reach them, recognize their potential, and afford them opportunities to have their voices heard? As clinicians, educators, and parents, we have to question whether our own perceptions about those who rely on us for assistance are accurate, and whether, as a society, we are doing the best we can for those who are unable to speak for themselves.

Widely considered to be the fastest-growing developmental disability, autism now affects 1 in 110 children, according to the Centers for Disease Control. And Peyton offers us rare first-person insight into the struggles of living with this disorder. However, this story is not only about autism. The battles endured by Dianne and Pat to find acceptance for their daughter will resonate with any parent. Peyton speaks for all children when she advocates for including and esteeming those who may appear different. Her message is one of treasuring all people, regardless of their abilities or perceived mental competence. As Peyton helps us understand, she deserves to be valued by others not because she is intelligent, but simply because she is a human being.

With the love and support that every person desires and needs, Peyton has found a way back from the abyss and reconnected with the beautiful spirit within her. She helps us understand what it feels like to struggle with autism, and she reminds all the people of the world that we are better together. As she says, "You and I are one in unity of creation . . . ignorance of each other will cheat us all."

Sixteen years after that first fateful meeting with Peyton, I know that to whatever degree I have contributed to helping her lead a more successful and gratifying life, she has helped me to lead a more successful and gratifying life as well. One of the many things I have learned from working with Peyton is that as medical and mental health professionals, we are far from having all the answers. The wisest in our field would acknowledge how much we really do not know. As it turns out, Peyton, now thirty-seven years old, is one of the wisest people I have ever met.

—ROBERT A. FRIEDMAN, MD
President and CEO
PsyCare, Inc.
San Diego, CA

Assistant Clinical Professor of Psychiatry
Department of Psychiatry
UCSD Medical Center
La Jolla, CA

American Board of Psychiatry and Neurology
Board Certified in General Psychiatry, 1991
Board Certified in Child and Adolescent Psychiatry, 1992

Author's Note

When my daughter Peyton was eighteen years old, four years before she learned to communicate using a keyboard, she made a vow (she calls it her IOU) that the rest of her life would be devoted to "quietly changing this worrisome world." Her early gains in speaking were lost, leaving her voiceless until age twenty-two. Though she does not speak in the first seven chapters of this book, she is fully aware of what is going on around her, and she has included her reflections on these years, which appear in italics throughout the text. In each chapter, we also include reports from doctors, therapists, and educators, which come from original documents, to show Peyton's journey from the perspective of various professionals. (Note that the names of many people and places have been changed.)

Because she seems to process language differently from most people, Peyton expresses herself in a unique style that combines poetic phrasing with her own distinctive vocabulary. During her developmental years, Peyton used fewer words than most of us to express her thoughts. Martha Leary, a trusted friend and speech-language pathologist, describes her communication style as both "less" and "more," at once spare and expansive. Peyton herself says, "I think in pictured imaginings eased by capturing words saw spiraling . . . imaginations freed." Once her voice was liberated at age twenty-two, we were amazed at the poetry and wisdom of it. She speaks in metaphors (*The whirlpool under me, in me, best operates together*), she often prefers the pronoun "I" to "me" (*I'm ready to be I*), she inverts sentence structure (*Rest these cherubs never will*), she creatively and purposefully invents language

(*Understaters utter I'm no one*), and sometimes she employs words now considered archaic, like *rasty* (meaning rancid), and *gyre* (meaning to whirl). We ask that you open your heart to hear and understand her words, which may initially appear strange. Because some of her reflections have been taken from essays she wrote and then edited for her college courses and presentations, they appear in a more straightforward, standard style.

The strategy Peyton uses to express herself is called facilitated communication (FC) or supported typing. It involves a trained facilitator offering Peyton the supports necessary for her to organize her body, overcome fear and anxiety, and focus her mind, so that she can type on a keyboard using one finger. It is a dynamic dance in which the facilitator allows Peyton to lead. The facilitator supports her with a combination of emotional encouragement ("Keep going . . . What's next?"); verbal monitoring and reminders ("Look at the keyboard . . . Is that spelled the way you want it?"); and physical touch, providing stabilization and "pull-back" resistance to her hand, wrist, or arm. This enables Peyton to inhibit frustrating, impulsive movement and achieve purposeful pointing to the letter she wants to type. Distracting movements, quick acts of impulse often swayed by emotions (her hand reaching out to pick up specks or her body getting out of the chair), often interrupt Peyton's typing. Because she must suddenly move before she can come back and finish typing her thought, it may take her several minutes to peck out a single sentence. Purposeful, independent movement is the goal she seeks. FC has been used successfully since the late seventies with many people throughout the world who have difficulties with dependable movement, including verbal speech and intentional pointing. Though skeptics have questioned the influence of the support person on the typist, the validity of FC has been confirmed through respected research studies and by the many FC users who, over time, have achieved the goal of typing independent of physical support and/ or a combination of speaking and typing. For those who continue to challenge that FC can be effective for some individuals in the face of such compelling truth, perhaps no "proof" will ever be enough. But for Peyton and those who know her, there is no controversy. Her distinctive "voice" is loud and clear.

Peyton's message to the world is simple yet profound: "All persons are vastly valuable. Treasure all because great is each." She considers this book, along with her continued advocacy, the fulfillment of her IOU.

—DIANNE GODDARD

Chapter 1

Committed

Weeds grew wherever I was pitied.
Understaters utter I'm no one.
I'm broken, moldy bread, throwaway trash, great leper.
Worthless, I fear institutions as more and more tests
pour keys locking me in.
My youth is ruptured, and tears fall that others can't read.

{PERSONAL JOURNAL: MAY 31, 1996}

Seven days, no sleep.

In perpetual motion: eyes darting, opening and closing drawers/doors, folding and refolding towels, lining items up, rearranging furniture/household items, flushing toilet, picking up phone.

Violent incidents of hitting at school and home.

Chewing on a washcloth she twists in her mouth until sopping wet.

Attempting to eat items on floor or outside: dirt, sticks, trash.

Extreme emotions—from laughter to screaming to moaning.

Expressions of anxiety: tongue darting, teeth grinding (loud enough to be heard two rooms away), difficulty swallowing.

She cannot be left alone, nor is she capable of being in public places.

Spitting out food/drink. Peyton has lost twenty-five pounds.

Pat drives as I clutch Peyton's seat-belt latch to keep our twenty-one-year-old daughter from jumping out onto the freeway. We are trekking to the hospital to meet yet another referral, a Dr. Porter, who is said to be skilled with challenging cases. This past week has come upon us like a plague. No sleep, increasingly difficult behaviors, and no ideas from doctors on medicines that might help. In the space of one week, we have consulted four doctors, and Peyton's lead physician, Dr. Tabler, has surrendered his relationship, forced to admit he is completely stumped by her challenges, which include her being mute for the last decade.

Our family is worse than a train wreck; it's more like a subway wreck. Everything seems reasonably normal on the surface, but belowground all the wheels have come off and we are upside down. In our attempts not to burden our son with specifics, do our phone conversations, assuring him that *Things are going okay,* make his heart ache more for the sweet sister of his memory? During his homecomings, he sees her smile only when they swim in interactive synchronization, like two sibling dolphins in our black-bottomed pool.

Pat and I live in fear of Peyton's insomnia episodes, which have appeared with predictable unpredictability for the past thirteen years. Nights become marathons with no relief at the finish line—dawn. Then the day hits with its "behaviors," and me always observing, studying, charting—certain that if I analyze Peyton enough, the key will be discovered to her loss of language and bodily control over the past decade. For now, the key remains hidden from me as well as our team of physicians, each of whom I keep closely informed via handwritten daily data sheets I deliver prior to each appointment.

As we fly down Highway 8, I look at my daughter's eyes, now sunken with dark shadows beneath them, like streaks of mud, and I think back to one endless night when she was twelve. Deeply slumbering after a day of challenging behaviors (and with Pat out of town), I awoke to a noise on the floor by my bed, a high-pitched giggle bordering on hysterical. Startled, I jumped up and turned on the light. Peyton was tearing pages out of a book she had brought in from her room. She was naked, but I could barely see her.

Then I was jolted fully awake by the unthinkable sight and smell: Peyton was almost entirely covered with her own feces, her arms and chest and legs smeared with it, her hands caked in it, and her hair and face—where was her face? The poop was like finger paint she had covered herself with, and I could see only her eyes peeping out from behind the brown stains. Deposits of it filled her ears, nose, even her mouth, where it encrusted her teeth. The fact that Peyton had been awake for a significant while was confirmed on our way to the bathroom as I observed Peyton's room in total disarray: all dolls off their shelves and streaked with poop, all books off the shelves, some torn, every one of them soiled with feces. The cleanup required frantic teeth brushing, shower, bath, hair wash, second shower, clean pajamas, then attempts to strip the bedding and move the books till they, along with the walls, could be wiped with Lysol, and the carpet scrubbed.

There had been occasional daytime incidents of smearing if I did not monitor her when she went to the bathroom. But this shocked me to the core. I was not angry, only silent in my sadness. Why would Peyton do this? I told only Pat and my mother, declaring that this must not happen again. But it did. Many times. Until finally I sewed one-piece pajamas that zipped up the back and buttoned over the zipper so I could lock Peyton into them. We then had a carpenter install doors on all the cabinets to lock up the movables at night. Eventually, I realized I needed to sleep with Peyton—locking us in her room—and train myself to sleep lightly.

> *My youth had harshness that porpoised me in sopping*
> *whirlpools of insanity.*
> *It fears me that I'm insane, and mysteries of my fears*
> *only I will ever know.*
> *Yowls of my heart hold no options to be heard.*

During the days when Peyton goes off to school, I try to get some rest, unless they call to say she must be picked up because of her latest behavior, like darting out of class into the parking lot at lightning speed. Because of her age, Peyton will soon "expire" from the school district. At the age of twenty-two, special-education students are no longer eligible to remain in the California public school system. In my imagination, I can see the district administrators chilling a bottle of champagne in their fridge at the central office, longing for the day when Peyton is farmed out, outsourced, so they can pop the cork on the Korbel and celebrate ridding themselves of yet another thorn in their side, this one named Peyton.

My daughter had several teachers early on who sought to understand her "atypical" behavior (which was unusual even in the disability realm), proving she could learn and progress. But as she got older and the costs of being different weighed heavier and heavier, she ran out of caring teachers. Busy keeping our failing restaurant afloat, Pat is able to spend only pockets of time with her on weekends, often with outcomes that amaze me (like, "She did okay.").

Any hope of respite is nil. Who can babysit? Only a few relatives, mostly my mother, in light of the feces-smearing. And less and less do I want to walk in both worlds. It is easier to stay home.

Surely, no one else would—could—do what I do. The only option is a rush to find the answer, the cure, before we become unable to continue. In the meantime, we make accommodations, like the custom pj's and putting locks on all the doors. Between Peyton's bed and the street there are four locks, three of which are keyed dead bolts, one with no key left in it, and one spring lock she is not able to release. She is never behind a locked door by herself, of course (no telling what we would find if she were left alone), but these precautions are necessary, as Peyton has run off before, broken away, darted out the door directly into the street, putting me into chase mode, both of us narrowly missing cars.

So now moving toward the street requires traversing a lock system comparable to the Panama Canal. Then outside there is the white picket fence, itself with latches, as a last line of defense. When Peyton walks to the car, I grip her hand firmly. These Band-Aid-type remedies have helped to keep Peyton alive and the bizarre in check. Yet I never know how to ask the real question— *What is her behavior saying?* I can only wonder what's next. I conceal the feces-smearing from Peyton's neurologist, the caring Dr. Tabler. Am I ashamed, or is it simply unbearable to speak about this to people who have no idea what my life is truly like?

Queer is equated to fear and pity. It should = love.

"Do you have Peyton's last EEG?" I ask Pat, who is nervously whistling his favorite Beach Boys tune behind the wheel.

"Relax, Dianne," he says, humming. "We've heard good things about Dr. Porter. Dr. Tabler gives him two thumbs up," he replies in his perpetual happy tone, annoying at times like this. We continue flying down the highway.

⌒

Several times during Peyton's recent bouts of insomnia, Dr. Tabler has ordered a twenty-four-hour ambulatory EEG—*ambulatory* being the key word here. For at least twenty of the twenty-four hours, Peyton never stopped ambulating, with random pacing, clapping, jumping, and pushing that filled nearly every hour of the day and night, and brought her the wild, hollow look of a psychotic. This means that after three or four days of absolutely no sleep, we would go to Children's Hospital to get our daughter hooked up to electrodes, the wires of which connected to a monitor a little larger than a Walkman, which had to remain close to the body. Up to sixteen wired electrodes were glued to Peyton's ever-moving head. Then her head was wrapped in gauze, mummy fashion, to keep the electrodes secure. Like a magician whose hands are faster than the eye, I worked constantly to keep the electrodes in place and the monitor from disconnecting as Peyton and I were Velcroed together in an endless night of sleeplessness. This kind of assignment—being tethered to a whirling dervish—is something that I approached with resolute vigilance. If Peyton reclined on the bed or slept for a few minutes, I would sit at her head, turning and readjusting the wires each time she moved. Then, after each twenty-four-hour EEG, we would reenter Children's Hospital, and I would say a prayer that The Answer would be revealed in a complete electrical assessment.

But the answer never came.

Dr. Tabler has prescribed various drugs to help Peyton with sleep, but none have worked, no matter the dosage. I'm being treated for heart palpitations, and both Pat and I have been on anxiety medication for the past three years. (Does it even help anymore, I wonder, as we hold each other tight, taking turns comforting each other, one of us regularly giving way to sobs?) After this past week, another week without sleep, Peyton's behaviors have begun to spiral out of control. A great uncontrollable force has risen up from somewhere inside her. It can and does inflict injury (or is it punishment?), and it terrifies all, even the inflictor, based on the frightened look in her eyes.

In the past, we had to watch Peyton to protect her safety; now we have to protect all those she comes into contact with—the innocent and not-so-innocent, though we do not yet know there is a difference. *Cleaning up poop pales in comparison.* The strength that inhabits this five-foot-seven, 150-pound, 21-year-old body equals my own at 51 years of age. I sometimes see an outburst coming and step in to foil its force, but mostly I am blindsided by its brutal approach. There is no Weather Channel to tune to for predictions, intensity of the wind, or where the hurricane will strike. There have been several incidents at school this year where Peyton became aggressive and lunged at her longtime aide, knocking her to the ground.

These storms are manifesting themselves at a particularly try-ing time in our lives—and not just because Peyton will soon "age out" of the school system. Pat is also struggling to keep his res-taurant, Fiddler's Green, afloat. This is the place we had opened, imagining that Peyton could work there once she had left school, filling salt and pepper shakers and folding napkins. While I take over the bookkeeping during the days Peyton attends school, Pat works eighty hours a week. Sinking deeper into debt each month, we have finally put our home of twelve years on the market. Will we make it? Will we be fortunate enough to stay healthy until (hope-fully) our son Patrick can oversee caregivers for Peyton? Will we be able to leave him with enough money to keep her out of an institu-tion? And what kind of burden will this be for him someday?

The heaviness is unrelenting. We avoid discussing the future with Patrick. I push it out of my mind with full-time, keep-busy trying. No time to physically rest is actually a useful survival strategy for me, keeping the fears at bay. I pray for the strength to be able to continue forever.

Despite the introduction of a nightly sleeping pill, Peyton's sleepless nights have continued, filled with constant obsessive-compulsive activity—cleaning, moving, stacking, picking up crumbs and putting them in her mouth, tongue twisting. And during the day she is not able to sit still to eat. In the past few months, Peyton has lost twenty-five pounds. Her intake of calories is far below her expenditure. *Is she starving herself?* I wonder. My mother (Peyton's devoted "Gam") and I take turns following Peyton around the house, putting bites of food in her mouth when we can. Avocados keep her alive. Friends drop sacks of them at our door.

There has not been one minute of sleep for Peyton in the past seven days. After spending the last six nights rearranging the few remaining movable objects in her room, Peyton was dismissed early yesterday for yowling in the school auditorium, where all of the students had gathered for a "Just Say No" presentation. Gam came over earlier than usual because of this.

A petite bundle of energy with a warm Virginia drawl, Gam worked as personnel director for various Broadway department stores in San Diego before retiring in 1985. She and Pops live just a few minutes away, and she has always been Peyton's other mother. With Gam there yesterday, I attempted to relinquish my worry about Peyton's wanderings in the house as I worked on Fiddler's payroll deadline, figuring out how to borrow from Peter to pay Paul . . . and Mark . . . and Luke. My memory shifted for a millisecond while I worked, to all the hours Peyton and Gam had spent together when Peyton was a toddler, playing dolls and having tea parties. My outgoing, joy-filled little lady would always sip the imaginary tea poured by Gam and gently cradle and coo to her dolls as if they were her own babies. (At that age, she could still speak, though her words were often unintelligible.) I wondered if Peyton remembered.

From my desk I could see Peyton darting impulsively about the house, unable to slow down and concentrate on one of the hundred puzzles she has put together so many times. Each room downstairs has an inviting, down-filled couch where Peyton always settles when she can bring herself to "nest." But she had not stopped at a couch in days. She could not bring herself to sit down, except occasionally on the floor to pick up a speck of anything and put it in her mouth.

People who feel like trash, eat trash.

Tapping numbers into my calculator, I could hear Peyton fidgeting with the kitchen drawers—open, close, open, close—rearranging the cookbooks for the umpteenth time, moving to the laundry area and folding and refolding the same hand towel, moving and centering the dining-room chairs several times, approaching the trash can under the sink (I listened to make sure she was not throwing away the car keys again). The next minute she was in the bathroom, flushing the toilet, continuously pushing the handle as Gam checked her watch and said it was time for Peyton to go to the bathroom. Peyton tried but could not, so the Depends got pulled back up until the next try, or changing. Peyton picked up and hung up the phone in the kitchen, moving not in a steady flow but impulsively rushing to each activity, sometimes tripping on something she had left on the floor, imprinting yet another bruise on her shins.

Peyton then moved toward the built-in teak television cabinet and emptied one shelf full of videos, stacking them on the carpet. Gam knew better than to touch the pile of videos, as it does not take much to provoke Peyton's wailing—fearful and painful all at once, like the cry of a prisoner held in solitary confinement. Gam cut up a large avocado, salted it, buried the midday pills in several slices, and snuck mouthfuls into Peyton during her frenzied scurrying. Peyton then began a jumping-jack routine in front of the TV, flapping her arms, clapping her dry, calloused hands, and giggling a strangely hollow laugh that bordered on crying. I did not have to be near her to know her body was hot and clammy and her heart was beating fast.

Meanwhile, five-foot-two, 110-pound Gam rested the lunch bowl on top of the cabinet and turned her head to let me know Peyton had almost finished the entire avocado. I looked up to say *Good job*, in time to see Peyton lunge at Gam with the full force of her extended arms, leveling Gam, who was thrown backward, her head striking the glass TV screen. I rushed to my seventy-three-year-old mother, who was seeing stars but assured me she was okay, just needing to rest a few minutes before trying to get up. I joined her on the floor and we looked up at Peyton, neither of us angry. Something unspoken in both of us sensed she could not control the rage. I held my mother close, and we both cried tears for the tired, tired threesome we were.

❦

Today, Pat is driving three exhausted, don't-know-if-we-can-keep-going, please-somebody-help-us zombies to meet with Dr. Porter at St. Catharine's Psychiatric Hospital. Our weary but hopeful group pulls into the parking lot, and Pat helps Peyton out of the trusty red Volvo sedan that has seen its way to countless such appointments. From the fog-laden parking lot, we enter the hospital's tunnel-like hallway, lined with white padded chairs.

While I sit down to consult with the doctor, Pat and Peyton pace the halls to satisfy her need for continual movement. It's a dance I've seen them do a thousand times, his arm around her waist, hers encircling his neck—a stroll-step resembling a slow three-legged race.

Walks I need because it is scary to stand still.
Standing still is washed in fears.
It eases me if I'm nested by your momentum.
The whirlpool under me, in me, best operates together.

As I speak with Dr. Porter, I can see Peyton through the window attempting to pick up the cigarette butts calling to her from the concrete floor. When she and Pat pause, she jumps, clapping her hands until the calluses split and bleed. Crying out, she thrusts her fingers into her mouth up to the second knuckle. As the saliva drools down her chin, Pat gently scoops it up with his forefinger before it drops onto her blue bib overalls, a daily uniform worn to prevent her from putting her hands down her pants in public. Hearing the yelling, Dr. Porter turns around to observe Peyton, and I notice an alarmed woman pulling her child by the arm to sit on the other side of the room.

There I was, awers staring at me,
ethers in their pupils horrified that I was queerly bred.
There I'm to be tied, fitted in a straitjacket.
There I'm to bleed hot, alone.

For a full thirty minutes I share the documented demise of Peyton in my most concise but comprehensive version. Over the years, we have watched our daughter gradually lose control of her own body. Though her medications have increased, her behaviors and prognoses have only gotten worse. There in the dimly lit conference room off the entry, as we occupy two of the perhaps twenty chairs, I want to believe we have reached Oz after a long and perilous journey. Is he the wizard others have promised?

Dr. Porter asks several questions but lets me continue. I am finally silenced when Pat peeks in with Peyton, letting me know what I already knew: It is getting increasingly difficult to control her. Then Dr. Porter says what no one is expecting: "I strongly recommend that you admit Peyton into the hospital for observation and treatment."

I'm standing in St. Catharine's to be imprisonered.
Rest I pray for.
Under my heart is a greed to die.
Ready I am to go to my Creator.
He loudly loves my vast values.
I'm red. Pity envelops my greedy self.
Gyres rest never. I'm greedy to greet rest.

Peyton has been hospitalized twice before: at age twelve, for a week following a seizure, and at age eighteen, for a week at the UCLA seizure clinic. In both cases, one or both of us were with her at all times, sleeping in a chair next to her, reviewing the meds given, working with the staff in support of Peyton.

When Dr. Porter suggests that Peyton be hospitalized again, I am surprised, but then honestly open to the suggestion as a possible way to solve the mystery. The doctor looks Peyton up and down for several seconds as she hops and claps in the hallway, making a low, guttural sound. His eyes narrow and he nods, saying, "We'll be able to do a complete workup on her; she'll be very comfortable, I assure you."

Ogres feed my red fears.
Each Ogre threatens that I'm a weed.
The stares of the understaters are daggers that wap me.
They are rearers of insanity in their stares.
Ready I am to date death with my sweet, sassy kiss.

The bright fluorescent lights in the admittance office fore-shadow the awakening my system is about to receive. It is nearly 5:00 p.m. now. Conditions of the stay fly at us, each new aware-ness ringing an alarm that Pat and I try to negotiate. "This is an adult psychiatric hospital. Peyton is twenty-one. No parents are allowed except for limited visits," Dr. Porter announces. But I know Peyton to be childlike in her need to be supported and pro-tected. I deafen myself to my rising heartbeat so that my head can work. "Peyton will be looked in on every fifteen minutes or so, like a suicide watch," he says.

"We never leave her alone," I protest. "She will be in danger of hurting herself."

"No parents," he insists.

"How will she be able to communicate in ways you might be able to understand?" I ask, all reasoning now off on tangents. "Maybe her aide could stay with her?" I suggest, still not certain I would be able to live with that. What about supplies? We had packed no bag, no Depends, no flip cards of plasticized photos to help satisfy her never-ending hand movements. Time is ticking faster as Pat tries to contain a fully moving Peyton confined in a small space. One admittance person calls the insurance company for preapproval before they close for the day. Another asks if we have a conservatorship (a court order granting us legal control over her care). This is something we had heard of but never pur-sued. I say no, asking what that means for today.

"It means you must assign to us all rights to treat Peyton, for the next three days. You will have no say during that time regarding her treatment," explains the administrator. My thoughts have now reached warp speed as I hear someone say, "Your insurance company is closed for the day."

Money is no obstacle here, but suddenly I think that maybe this is a sign. Then, I hear words from Pat's heart as words of purest reason: "We can do what's needed. Let's take her home."

We have no plan on where to turn next. No doctor to call tonight if events take a nastier turn. There are no more forks in the road; the known road has ended. But like Scarlett O'Hara, I think, "We'll worry about that tomorrow." When we arrive home, I give Peyton ten milligrams of Ambien, a drug that has never worked before. Within minutes, she crumples into bed and sleeps for the rest of the night.

Chapter 2

Retarded

I try to err not.
Year after year my motor madness punishes both you and me.
Each day I try to do it your way. Gyred tread tires.
What you ask, I retriever cannot do.

———

February 28, 1980
Center City Hospital
San Diego

GODDARD, PEYTON
PROGRESS REPORT

This is a five-year-old white female referred by Annemarie Stephens of speech pathology for evaluation of speech and motor delays. Her early development in terms of sitting and walking were normal. Her speech, however, was delayed, and she did not speak until after two. She has great difficulty speaking and answering questions. She cannot hop or skip, and she can barely jump. She has difficulty following commands.

Behavior was extremely infantile and she kept her fingers in her mouth most of the time. She does not speak very much, and when she does it is usually in single words. These are largely nonunderstandable.

Impressions:
Severe speech and language delay as well as motor problems, with probable intellectual function in the mild to moderately retarded range.

—Bernadette L. Ebner, MD
Assistant Professor of Neurology and Pediatrics

Even long before I was a mother, a diagnosis of mental retardation seemed to me a fate worse than any incurable disease for a child. When I was growing up in the fifties, children with this "retarded" label were not around, having been sent away by their families most likely on the recommendation of doctors, and I was silently troubled by the few cases I heard about. How would it be if my mother and I could not be together, to talk and to love each other? *Retarded.* The word pained me more than any other, including, even, *death.*

It begins with small nagging concerns. I find it curious that baby Peyton turns her head when hearing her name one day and not the next, one minute and not the next. Can she hear? I collect bells of various sizes, including a Waterford crystal bell, a golf-ball-size Christmas jingle bell, and a miniature Liberty Bell. Several times a day I sneak up on Peyton and ring a bell as she plays with her dolls on the floor. I am one minute sure my daughter hears just fine, and the next bell ringing, convinced that she must be deaf. My eyes become more eagle-like as I carry out experiments, score the results in notebooks, and deduce that the only thing predictable in Peyton's actions is unpredictability.

⟡

Pat and I live bayside in the picturesque San Diego village of Point Loma, with our sailboat *Blest* tied off in front on a private dock. Our modest Cape Cod wears Pacific blue shutters against the gray shiplap wood siding, a silhouette of a sailboat cut into each shutter. Later come the Jacuzzi and the 60-by-12-foot pool, shallow enough to aqua-exercise and deep enough to swim laps, always heated to an inviting 78 degrees.

Pat is executive vice president of the Chart House restaurant chain. He gained his consummate people skills exploring the panoramas of the world. He has surfed its oceans (aquamarine, like his eyes) off many continents. Medium build and muscular, he is a classic, good-looking Southern California guy, far too delighted with living to be called ruggedly handsome. Streaks of blond shine in his hair, and his infectious humor always begins with laughing at himself, his smile lines becoming the first wrinkles in his year-round tanned face. He is close friend to congressman and carpenter, doctor and dishwasher (the latter, his first job for the company he loves).

Prior to expanding our family, I had taught second graders in an elementary school across town. I have my sorority activities, am a member of the San Diego Junior League, and volunteer for a charity assisting abused and neglected children. In my favorite courtship story, Pat says he first noticed me out of a hundred others in a large English class during our student days at San Diego State. Sitting one row behind me, he glanced down at my neat handwriting that flowed effortlessly across my notebook. I was wearing a madras headscarf, a crisp, white collared blouse, and a thin, yellow sweater tied loosely over my shoulders. He tells people that he first noticed my flowing, dark hair and long legs, which, according to him, would complement any bathing suit he could possibly conjure up. After class, I noticed him pretending to organize his backpack while I talked to my friend Deana, but he didn't even say hello. The next time I saw him was that same weekend when I came to the Chart House with a date, and he was our waiter. Two months later we were engaged.

I paid for the wedding bands (I did not want an engagement ring), and we thriftily married at 2:00 p.m. on July 1, 1967, with champagne, cake, mints, and nuts—all of which took my father (who was between jobs at the time) a full year to pay off. We honeymooned in St. Thomas on Pat's Visa after one night at the Hotel del Coronado. It was my third airline flight ever. When we were descending at midnight into San Juan, Puerto Rico, Pat pulled out a paperback entitled *The Caribbean on $5 a Day* and began perusing for hotels. "Don't we have reservations?" I gasped. We ended up in the Old City, not the newer-hoteled Condado area, and a man with needle marks on his arms took us to our room. Pat put chairs in front of the door, but the stars in my eyes covered my fears, and I figured I was in for an adventure. I figured right.

Over the years we have come to feel somewhat important in our community, and we are satisfied—even impressed—with the number of Christmas cards we send and receive. In 1970 we became the proud parents of Patrick Jr., followed by sister Peyton four years later, on December 26, 1974. Peyton, contrary to what we expected for decades, would relish her birth date because it respectfully follows that of baby Jesus.

⤸

They look like siblings, Patrick and Peyton. They share the same genetics, the same nine-pound, ten-ounce birth weight, and the same sandy hair color and fair complexion, but it is their eyes that are exact replicas—like travertine marble with a spot of ever-changing green. I remember our drive home from Mercy Hospital, with Patrick hanging over the front seat, talking continuously to his new sister as he grasped her tiny hand. It is his turn to hold her once we enter the house, me ever-watchful, but he not needing safety reminders as he gently cradles the warm, fleshy package swaddled in a striped hospital blanket.

Patrick relishes playing with her, climbing into her crib, crawling around with her on the speckled shag carpet, searching out loose Lego pieces so she won't swallow them, showing her his GI Joe and Luke Skywalker, keeping careful watch over her in the yard, as she has a habit of climbing to the top of the toddler slide and getting stuck. When I am out of the house for a few hours, he responds to Peyton's cries promptly, whispering to her, "It's okay, Peytie, Brovie loves you," and urging Gam to feed her right away ("C'mon, Gam. You have boobs too!"). He gets rightfully perturbed when she invades his room, destroying the city of block towers he spent an hour building, or the hundred-piece puzzle he just assembled. But mostly he becomes her protector, and when the inevitable accidents occur, he hovers with empathy and helpfulness until he knows she is okay, like the time when she was five months old and tugged on a tablecloth at the San Diego Yacht Club, and her dad's hot soup spilled on her leg. The burn required a family trip to the emergency room, with Patrick again hanging over the front seat to offer comfort, and me almost requiring a dose of the Demerol given to Peyton to regain my composure.

⇌

On a warm September day, nine-month-old Peyton and I are in the yard as Patrick plays in the red, wooden sandbox his handy Pops built. I pick Peyton up off the grass that is shaded by a tall eucalyptus and stroll toward our friendly neighbor, Minton, still handsome at seventy-three. He looks into Peyton's eyes and waves to Patrick, swinging now on the tire that hangs from our prolific persimmon tree. We talk about this, our favorite month in Point Loma, and how Pat is doing on his latest Chart House project as I hear Minton's wife, Evelyn, playing a waltz on the grand piano in their large living room.

My conversation with Minton is so sweet, and baby Peyton participates with the smiles she gives to Minton like kisses she desires to share. He tells her how charming she looks in her peach-flowered sunsuit and matching bonnet. Then he, a family physician for half a century, turns to me and says, "You know, Dianne, this child smiles more than any other child I have ever known." And I realize it is the gospel truth. Peyton is always smiling: She smiled as I nursed her at my breast for eight months; she smiles with her baby dolls and books; smiles with her brother; smiled as she first crawled toward our loving arms. Glee. Delight. It is as if she has come to us from a place of joy.

Later that evening, as I prepare our dinner, I spy with envy this classic couple eating at their kitchen table, the center of which holds roses Minton picked today from his Monet-like garden in a cut-glass vase that was one of their wedding presents decades ago. A lit candle in a low silver candlestick graces the table near Evelyn, and a small 1950s tensor lamp sits on his side. I smile and think, *No wonder theirs is wedded bliss; they will probably live to be a hundred.* That they will bury two of their three children is a fact I do not know on this day.

In my room I rely on hearing my mother's healing "Hello."
In my joy she lifts me.
"You are my sweet girl. You rest in my heart perfect.
You retop my dawns in joy."

By her lulling, I'm a kitten wedded to esteem. I pot pleasure in her.
Yell I, "Try I will try to please you."

As much as I love Peyton's smile, I confess that to my measuring eye, it also means I get to check off another milestone on
the Denver Scale. The Denver Developmental Scale, with its blue
graphing of milestones, is never far from reach for easy refer-
ence. It becomes threadbare, torn at the folds, and covered with
my DNA and my aches as Peyton's early developments, which are
right on time (smiles, turns over, crawls, walks), are followed by
undeniable delays and nonachievements as tasks become more
complex (points to one named body part, throws ball overhand,
imitates speech sounds, washes and dries hands, imitates vertical line). The weight of my worry steadily increases and receives
confirmation of its worthiness in evaluations and doctors' opinions galore, and in my own notebooks of evidence, irrefutable in
black and blue ink. Only decades later do I realize the strangeness
of measuring a person on a scorecard, forgetting the soul.

My mother's sadness dazzled me in weeds of pity.
Hungry, tired looks hide my young wonderings why her sadness is
oiled by tyranny me.
Sweet Dad by journeys returning breasted her joy.
Her son was joy.
Best friends made her laugh.
I'm waster of her joy.

⤶

It is Peyton's first Christmas, and tomorrow will be her first birthday, so she is about to have a two-day crash course in opening
presents as we follow her speeding brother into the living room

to see if the cookies left out last night were eaten by Santa. Pat carries Peyton on his shoulders, dressed in red Carter pajamas that snap around the waist, accessorized with a red-and-white-gingham bib tied under her chin to catch her ever-present drooling. I watch Peyton's eyes light up as she surveys the wrapped boxes of unknown contents and the larger toys that Santa has left unwrapped and on display.

Pat puts her down on the shag carpet she navigates so well by crawling. Before diving into his own gifts, five-year-old Patrick steers her, saying, "Look, Peytie, Santa brought these toys for you," making sure she's headed in the right direction. Of all the pickings, she immediately eyes one meant for her and makes a beeline for it. It is love at first sight as Peyton meets Puddin', her first almost-like-a-real-child, blue-eyed, blinking, blonde, crying, fourteen-inch Madame Alexander baby doll. Their immediate connection is magical as Peyton, her mouth open in amazement, picks up the doll and surveys her perfect form and shiny blue irises. I watch Peyton stare deep into Puddin's pupils.

"She is your baby, just as you are mine," I whisper. "You will love her and take care of her, as I do you." And I observe with hope my precious Peyton, pushing Puddin' in the wooden stroller all morning. They are to become constant companions during the next year, as Peyton dresses and diapers her, wipes her chin, feeds her, hugs her, and puts her to bed with caring commitment.

In the years to come I search relentlessly for Madame Alexander dolls with the hunger of a collector, because I have found another toy (besides puzzles and books) that Peyton enjoys. Toys that involve pushing buttons or twisting knobs frustrate Peyton, break, or are abandoned by hands that are unable to purposely point, push, or turn the right key. Yet strangely, this little girl can put socks and shoes on her dolls, comb their hair, feed them with a spoon, and wrap them in a blanket. Pac-Man she seems unable to figure out. But Pussycat, Huggums, and Victoria (and later, Barbies, in all their plastic finery) she mothers in the loving tradition of all little girls.

In each bought blue box of dolls, I'm a mother telling them,
"I will mother you with pity never. You fill me with great joy."

At Peyton's one-year well-baby checkup, I tell Dr. Chapman about Peyton's lack of babbling and my concern about her appearing deaf at times, and he orders a hearing impedance test. Peyton and I spend the day of New Year's Eve at the doctor's, she giving "the impression of a child with mild to moderate sensory-neural hearing loss," and me scheduling the recommended brain-stem audiometry testing for two weeks later.

By eighteen months Peyton has a vocabulary of a few meaningful words—*Daddy, bye, meow, bowwow*—but she sometimes repeats these words over and over, even with no apparent stimulus, something the doctors call *perseveration*. Back to Children's Hospital we go on Halloween, for a speech evaluation to investigate her verbalizing inconsistencies. Peyton is one year and ten months, and I am at the beginning of my quest to get confirmation from anyone I can that Peyton is okay.

The report from the speech pathologist states, "We were able to confirm that Peyton's nonlanguage skills were at age level." Of course, this is based on my own reporting, maybe even my purposeful exaggeration of the consistency of Peyton's other skills in hopes of tilting the evaluation to say what I am longing for it to say. Peyton soon begins speech therapy twice a week.

I rationalize my way through mountains of worry-making partly because Pat is always so strong. And yet Pat's lack of worry makes me worry even more, as if I need to take over *all* the worrying since my foolishly optimistic husband is not going to do his share. Years later we will learn that Peyton compares us to that famous duo Ernie and Bert: Pat, full of boundless, positive energy, like Ernie, and me, obsessing about the details of the day, just like Bert.

He was my dapper dad.
He lowered me never to less.
Am I a reason for Bert's tears or Ernie's hurrah?

Where others see motor delays and deficiencies, Pat sees only his cute-as-a-bug little girl, who simply needs a bit of extra help to accomplish things.

It is in relationships that persons determine their SELF.
I'm rumbled by relating to persons who pity me.
I'm peaced by persons who esteem me.
My dad esteems me; he eases me.
Wherever I dare eat pesterers' pity,
I'm eased and saturated by my dad's love of all me.
He buttressed me, but her returning worry negated his glee.

Through the years, Pat joyfully works with Peyton on her motor skills. When Peyton was one, Pat started playing ball with her. Lofting a Nerf ball a very short distance from her, he was not dismayed when it bounced off her nose. Her hands never even left the carpet to field his soft lobs.

"No worries. Let's try a new strategy," he would say.

He started out by holding the ball and then slowly moving it toward her. It was like a dance, and they both enjoyed the new sport. The next move was to hand the ball to the other player and then wait (and wait and wait) for it to be given back. This seemed to work, although it took time because Peyton gurgled with delight and held on to the ball rather than passing it back. It didn't take long before Pat could loft the ball to her after positioning her hands and then watch her finally (usually) catch it.

After six months of "playing catch," they moved to tossing bean bags (created by me in all shapes, colors, sizes, and textures) into target receptacles: a wicker basket, a small black trash can, a cardboard box with a doll in it, a colorful salad bowl (sometimes with a lone celery stalk, which he called the "celery tree"). Pat would tape two Dr. Scholl's green insoles onto the floor to let Peyton know where to put her feet so she could focus on moving her upper body.

Our living room soon resembled a house with a leaky roof as the various receptacles sat in a semicircle, waiting to snare bean bags flying hither and yon. Peyton grabbed them like candies out of a broken piñata. With each toss, Pat dashed behind a different target and then lobbed the bag back. It took only a few errant missiles (and one broken lamp) before her lefty, righty, underhand, and overhand style settled into a respectable delivery. I marveled at their easy relationship. They played together in a constant bubble of bliss.

> *Was my dad harried by me? Was I fearful to him?*
> *Was he queer too?*
> *Or was I gin to his tonic?*
> *He is the gear that rests my gyres.*

When she is two, we see the first of seven neurologists, and Peyton has her first two EEGs in one week to rule out epileptic aphasia, a rare neurological disorder characterized by language difficulties. (This is a diagnosis I would actually embrace as other delays in motor skills become evident, despite my efforts to discount them.)

Peyton doesn't imitate patty-cake or bang things on top of her high chair as her brother had. I see her stack blocks, but not when asked to make a tower. Yet I know my baby girl is smart; she can do puzzles—difficult ones, just as her brother had. By the end of her second year she can do (first try) any form board puzzle (even up to fifteen pieces) and simple four- to six-piece jigsaw puzzles. She can do an alphabet puzzle; shape puzzles are easy for her, though she cannot name the shapes. Before age three, she can also match colors, household objects that go together, animals and where they live, and pairs of objects from many visual picture choices.

When Peyton begins attending preschool at our church three days a week, it doesn't take long for them to say they are not staffed to support her differences, so I begin attending with her, the first of countless periscoped, perched hidings, standing in a dark, cramped supply closet that connects two classrooms, peering through the high eight-by-ten-inch windowpane, waiting to be summoned. This becomes a prerequisite for Peyton's tenuous inclusion in the program: I must be invisible and watch—not help—and then remove my daughter when she fails at a task.

Four months shy of her third birthday, Peyton is still not potty-trained. She is essentially nonverbal, and in her persistent attempts at socializing, she resorts to touching others, pulling on their hands, turning their heads to face hers, trying to play interactively with peers but, instead, pestering them with her unexpected movements, like buttoning the forgotten buttons on their shirts, and bringing them book after book during quiet reading time. These movements are increasingly bothersome to

peers and adults alike, and Peyton requires support to participate successfully in activities. I feel semi-content with this negotiated arrangement, though it would be nice if the window in
the closet were one-way and at sitting level. However, I am usually not left standing there for long—in fact, less and less as the
months go by.

With this first school experience, my gut is wrenched at having to stand by and watch my daughter fail. I am forced to stay at
bay, hands tied, watching supposedly well-intentioned teachers
allow Peyton to flounder in frustration at the daily art project,
leaving her a mess of paste and paper tears. Finally, my daughter
covered in Elmer's, I am asked to come out of the closet and clean
her up, leaving Peyton in a kind of neurological—or is it emotional?—disarray that requires her to be taken home.

Questions of what to do about this guaranteed failure fall
upon me like shelves of supplies in a storeroom during an earth-
quake. The despair is as suffocating as the closet, and I become
filled with fears for Peyton's future, anxieties that harass me
every day and every sleepless night. What can I do to help Peyton?
Can Peyton—hungry to learn, as I have seen it—even go to school?
I have no one to talk to about these fears, and begin to feel more
and more isolated from the society of regular folks. The Monday
after Thanksgiving, I decide no more closet for me, and no more
church preschool for Peyton.

In order to investigate alternatives for school, I resolve to
"bring on the testing," and just before Peyton's third birthday,
we begin the intake process at San Diego Regional Center for the
Developmentally Disabled, words I see as a euphemism for *mentally retarded*. On the recommendation of her pediatrician, Peyton will undergo the Regional Center's rigorous examinations,
along with two other reputable psychological and neurological

evaluations. That Peyton exhibits deficits is not news to me, though understanding them eludes me. That Peyton harbors a unique brightness is news that testers and teachers don't seem interested in, though I commit my entire self to helping them see this fact. My life becomes dedicated to trying to teach Peyton how to show her brightness in "traditional" ways—ways the testers and teachers and I, her own mother, can appreciate.

I was mothered by a whopper worrier. She fears I'm queer, broken.

At three, Peyton can ride a bicycle with training wheels. She can swim (one of her favorite activities), skate, and even do a somersault. What I cannot deny is that Peyton has difficulty in planning her movements. She can jump spontaneously if she is excited, but as with other motor activities that are within her capacity to do, it is very difficult for her to do this on command. The same is true for kicking and throwing a ball. These skills, trivial to most, seem of immeasurable importance to those tasked with measuring them.

———

1-18-78 DOCUMENTATION MOVEMENT OBSERVATIONS— DR. MARY JANE SCHOLL, NEUROLOGY EVAL, UCSD

When presented with a group of discs mounted according to size on a shaft the child was quickly able to place the discs on but had no insight into discrimination of size. They were placed haphazardly. She could not screw the top on to the shaft.

When given a small music box which required only the turning of a lever either left or right to play it, she maneuvered it briefly for a few seconds and then seemed to lose interest. In fact, there was a picture of a baby on top of the box. She seemed more interested in this than she did in manipulating the handle.

When presented with a toy which required her to place blocks of the five primary shapes into their appropriate slots she used a trial and error method. When the correct slot was pointed out for her she was then able to place each block adequately.

When the percussion hammer was pounded rhythmically on the desk for her and then she was given it to mimic the activity, again the movement was erratic and was of little or no interest to her. Therefore she would not pursue it.

In her preschool class, Peyton did not seem to interact well with other children. But with her best friend, Hollyn (three weeks younger than Peyton, and whose mother is my childhood friend), Peyton is capable of much more: verbalizations, imagination, participatory play. I watch the girls from my ever-close perch to support occasional verbal exchanges that prompt Peyton to use her voice.

"Let's bake cookies for a tea party," suggests Hollyn one sunny spring afternoon in 1978 while playing on our deck. Peyton, who watches her every move, appears ready for action as Hollyn's slightly taller and slimmer frame reaches up into Peyton's play kitchen cupboard to find the mixing bowl and hand it to Peyton. Peyton holds the bowl while Hollyn gathers the cookie sheet and an empty box of Betty Crocker cookie mix. Hollyn's blue eyes glance at Peyton as she opens the drawer and says, "Pey, get the big spoon out so you can stir." Peyton reaches in to where Hollyn's fingers point, and retrieves the wooden spoon.

I peek out onto the deck where the girls are playing to encourage more language skills. "Hey, what are you all making today?" I ask brightly.

"Cookies," says Hollyn, and I hear *"Cookie"* from Peyton, too, and smile. Hollyn lists the steps they need to make the cookies for their dolls.

"What will you do next, Chef Pey?" I ask.

"Stir," she answers, smiling.

"Do you need an egg?" I offer.

"Yes," replies Peyton as I pull open the play refrigerator door. Peyton reaches in for one plastic egg and taps it on the side of the bowl, then lays it on the counter. Hollyn's blonde braids brush Peyton's ponytails as she pours the batter in the bowl. Hollyn lightly holds Peyton's hand and together they stir the invisible flour mixture. To me, this little girl is an angel sent from above. Hollyn doesn't seem to notice that Peyton is different from other children, doesn't see her as deficient because Peyton doesn't speak or move like other children. Hollyn never sees her as anything but a best friend, though soon they will be at very different schools and see each other only on weekends—that is, until Hollyn's increasing social interactions take her away. Yet Peyton has no invitations to take her away.

To make up for this, I focus on hunting for more Madame Alexander dolls. These dolls are limited in availability and wait lists are long, so I put myself on the call list at every specialty toy store in San Diego. When we get the call, Gam and I arrive early to stand in the line that forms outside. I am the only mother there to buy four dolls—the maximum number allotted—and then Gam goes in to buy another four. I spend as if money is no object, so convinced am I that my daughter, who may never pronounce *Yugoslavia*, needs—must have—this and all the eight-inch International Dolls, of which there are forty. But as Peyton opens each blue box offered as presents on even minor holidays like Twelfth Night, I see in her eyes less and less interest, until finally there is no excitement at all about the doll representing Spain in her red, ruffled flamenco dress, and Miss Spain lies on the floor till I pick her up, and whatever made me feel good about purchasing the entire collection drains out of me like blood.

She is pleased in her pulled-off purchases, as each pity purchase frees her worry, thinking I'm queer naught.

❧

Between her third and fourth birthdays, I methodically arrange for Peyton to undergo an onslaught of evaluations, reflected in seventy pages of reports. It is all in the name of early intervention, but it fuels my search for confirmation that my beautiful, smiling girl dressed in Polly Flinders smocked dresses with bouncing pigtails tied in ribbons—though not yet totally potty-trained or functionally speaking—is not doomed to the segregated, nowhere destination that defines *mental retardation* to me. In this year of never-ending evaluations, our three-year-old has worn those ruffled dresses and pigtails to many an assessment, and fear has filled my being. Can Peyton's intelligence be seen by those who are supposed to measure it before the guillotine of a label falls upon her? How is it that Peyton is still smiling, I wonder. Whenever I smile, it is a mask.

I purchase educational games with the intensity of an addict seeking the next fix. On our boat, in a restaurant waiting for our order to arrive, on an airplane, in a hotel room, in the car, at friends' homes, I open my bag of tricks, hoping that Peyton can interact successfully with another child in any setting, focusing on what she does well. The games have cards with pictures and words and involve matching items using increasingly intricate thought, and yet Peyton's hands move the pieces into the correct places with the ease of a child prodigy on the piano, an ease I cannot understand. These higher-level, visually oriented games seem like second nature to Peyton, and she seems to enjoy them—in fact, she gobbles them up like a favorite meal. I connect countless sets of flash cards to silver rings, waterproofing each card with clear contact paper to strengthen and drool-proof them, and Peyton seems to enjoy repeatedly flipping through the cards as a way to give purpose to her incessant hand motions.

As a former teacher, I know traditional learning patterns. Early on, I recognized my son Patrick's learning strengths were visual, as are Peyton's, but at age five, when Patrick continually wrote his name perfectly backwards, I took him for IQ testing before he started kindergarten. Yes, the psychologist confirmed, going over the evaluation with Pat and me, Patrick qualifies for the Seminar Program, classes open to only the most gifted students in the school. *Puffed up*, a phrase from First Corinthians, came to me when hearing Patrick's test score, and I put a lot of stock into that number 150. Two years later, three-year-old Peyton scores 75 on the Leiter nonverbal intelligence assessment, her first of many psychological tests. And I do not feel "puffed up."

It is October 26, 1978. Eight stone-faced administrative educators (seven of which I will never see again) sit with me and Pat around a small table at the San Diego Unified School District's Education Center on Normal Street. In the span of forty-five minutes, Peyton is certified for special education in her first Individualized Education Program (IEP). What I will remember forever is the musty smell of the old building, trying to keep my breakfast contained in my body, and one of the eight voicing "Someone needs to teach this child to point" as the tenth signature is affixed. The deed is done.

Peyton begins attending Jill Goldberger's special preschool day class at Hamlet Elementary in Clairemont. Because I do not trust Peyton's safety with strangers, I follow her onto the school bus the first morning, carrying my trusty Polaroid, which I use all the time to combine pictures with words to teach literacy skills and generate language.

"Hi," I say snappily to the unsuspecting bus driver. "I'll need to take a picture of you for Peyton's 'Who's in my Day' school assignment. Please stand up right here next to Peyton." Totally obedient, he rises and I snap the photo. After seating Peyton with a kiss, I pull out my Sharpie, returning to ask his name.

VICTOR, I write on the bottom of the photo, figuring the district will know his last name. "Drive carefully," I say, grasping my picture (as evidence, I think, for the worst-case scenario playing out in my mind). But even this is not enough for Inspector Clouseau me. For two days I shadow the bus on the freeway and side streets, all the way to the school across town. Despite my watchfulness, I realize nothing will ease my fears, so right then I commit to driving Peyton to school and speech therapy and occupational therapy for what will be the next twenty years.

~

On the fourth of July when Peyton is four, we are on our forty-foot sailboat in Glorietta Bay, near Coronado, so filled with lines of rafted boats that one can almost walk across the bay. This trip is an annual tradition for us. We all sleep below and take the dinghy periodically over to Coronado to watch the town parade and eat, usually at the Chart House, one of the many historical restorations Pat will help spearhead for the company. The bay is too cold for swimming today, except for the brazen teenagers and a few dads, so we stay put as various kids hop from boat to boat to visit and play.

Doug Peterson's daughter is here from the next boat, and the big kids have scurried to the bow. "Pey, how about you and Jamie play that new United States memory game down below?" I offer. Two voices say, "Yes." I head down the stairs, reminding Peyton to invite Jamie to "Come down," which she says to this little girl who

I hope will have a good time and be a witness to Peyton's brightness. I get the boards out and set up the cards, subtly making sure Peyton takes only one card when it's her turn to draw. Soon this new game (opened only that morning) picks up speed as Jamie matches potatoes with Idaho and Peyton slips the oil-well card on Texas, while saying "Texas." They play another twenty minutes till Jamie's brother hollers down, "Time to go, Squirt!" As she leaves the cabin, Jamie asks Peyton, "Can I come back and play later?"

"Yes," I hear Peyton say with an inflection that lets me know a smile is shining on her face. *A friend,* I think, taking a deep breath. *Priceless.* In this, our family of abundance, more and more often what the mother desires for the daughter cannot be purchased. *But it can be encouraged,* I think to myself.

Sure enough, Jamie comes back to play the next day.

⥱

Four-year-old Peyton is subjected to a few more pages of evaluations. Her communicatively handicapped–category special day class assumes normal-range intellectual functioning, which provides me with some tenuous relief as to my greatest fear, though Peyton's continued attendance in these classes will rest on her proving through IQ tests that she is of normal intelligence. Instead, reports offering carefully worded details of delays become constant looming threats.

Focusing on Peyton's language delays, I am still hoping to evade the dreaded word I cannot say out loud. Any . . . any other diagnosis I could accept, but not *retarded.* One day while driving home from school, I discover with delight that Peyton can participate in a fill-in-the-blanks type of discourse. I make statements, pausing at the blanks, and Peyton fills them in immediately: "David was absent today; he didn't come to . . . SCHOOL. He stayed at . . . HOME with his . . . MOM. Probably David was . . . SICK. Probably his mother took him to the . . . DOCTOR. Maybe the doctor gave him some . . . MEDICINE. Tomorrow he will feel . . . BETTER. Maybe tomorrow he will come back to . . . SCHOOL."

The classroom teacher is a speech pathologist, and private occupational therapy sessions twice a week for motor delays have been added to Peyton's private speech therapies. These sessions offer a poor substitute for a social life, though Peyton and her friend Hollyn still connect through their shared love of dolls. I convince myself that Peyton enjoys the therapies and attaches to the therapists. Or is it just that I am able to rest my worries for thirty minutes, briefly handing off Peyton's progress to others?

Inserted in her poised manner is boiled worry.
Was I planned? Was God joking?
When I'm looking into my memories I'm pouted by her.
My mother's heart breathes fears into me.

Compounding my worry about school is the abrupt realization that Peyton's inability to control her movement poses a threat to her very life. On a Sunday family-reunion picnic with Pat's parents in Fallbrook's Live Oak Park, I allow her to move about next to me, my arm around her waist, on a wooden park bench. Suddenly she slips through the slatted back, sliding, and then tumbling down the ten-foot drop to the I'm-not-sure-how-deep stream below. I scream, *"Pat!"* In our decade together, he has caringly, calmly, and successfully worked with me on controlling my tendency to cry out in worry, reserving my cries for a real emergency—*Like now*, I think to myself.

Pat's reflexes are sharp and swift. He hurdles over the bench, taking flight. Is it a bird, a plane, or Superman flashing by me? His speeding-bullet body fortunately does not pounce on the little girl he is trying to rescue, though I fear it will from my perch above. Bounding through the muck and brush, he reaches the embankment as her mud-covered body halts right on the river's edge. Sighs of relief ring out from thirty spellbound relatives as he carries her up the slippery slope. *Did she just lose her footing?* I wonder. We leave the party, shaken survivors in search of showers and dry clothes. How did it happen? I swear I was holding on to her.

Soon after, Peyton begins the troubling habit of walking (eventually, it will turn into running) out into the street as if totally unaware of the cars speeding by. Then one summer Saturday at the docks of the yacht club, the unthinkable happens. With the junior sailing program in full swing, we go to help eight-year-old Patrick Jr. pull his eight-foot sailboat out of the water, hose it off, and lift it into the sailboat racks. In the same concrete wash-down area there are about thirty other boats with kids in varying stages of de-rigging their mast, boom, rudders, and mainsails. Peyton seems pensive in the middle of all the activity. An errant water spray from a hose held by her teasing brother makes her move a little closer to Dad, who is lending a hand, lifting several boats into storage spaces and then helping a couple of other kids sort out whose sailboat parts went with what craft.

> *There they stare, people everywhere.*
> *They are in ugly, fried groups.*
> *Each pity cheats my joy.*
> *Under pity is the joy they are never me.*
> *They fear what they know happens to queer persons.*
> *In queer you are freed never to a real life.*
> *You are gyred, potted in back,*
> *instituted rooms even by your own parents.*
> *Red until you die.*

I notice Mary Henderson walking toward the Junior Clubhouse and begin my well-developed internal deliberating. I need to check with her about next Friday's potluck that will follow the Sabot Dutch Shoe Marathon race to Coronado. Dare I trust busy Pat to watch Peyton? She seems compelled to pick up any cup and drink from it; fasten loose buckles on life preservers worn by anyone; swiftly move to zip half-zipped windbreakers worn by anyone she can spot a mile away, nicking their Adam's apple and alarming the wearer, toddler to adult. Dare I leave it to Pat to intercept Peyton as diligently as I try to do?

"Keep an eye on Peyton," I tell Pat. "I'm just going to talk to Mary Henderson for a few minutes."

"Aye-aye, Captain," replies Pat, completely in his element.

> *I'm dazzled by the sad looks in laser retinas*
> *that pierced my sweet girl self,*
> *four-year-old queer girl in a flowered, sweet sundress.*
> *There I saw guns fired.*
> *Dazes of pity cut into my breast that ply real right*
> *out of my sad, breaking heart.*
> *Bastard stares operated lines of fast-felt, whirling bullets.*
> *I'm in war wrapped, POW.*

When I return to the boat-cleaning area ten minutes later, Pat is heartened that Patrick has done a yeoman's job in pulling all his parts together and stowing them properly. I survey the scene, in search of Peyton. *Cautious* and *careful* are traits I inherited from Pops, my reliability-engineer father, but my vigilance came from being a mother.

I try to use restraint when I ask, "Where is Peyton?"

It hits Pat like a jibbing sailboat boom, and his jolly demeanor immediately shifts to panic. "I don't know!" is his petrified cry.

Miraculously, before I can mobilize every two-legged person within shrieking range, our friend Nick Frazee comes up from the docks, holding Peyton by the hand.

"Does this sailor belong to you?" he asks, smiling.

Peyton looks up to see us still frozen in disbelief, and Pat pulls her into his arms.

> *Quiet I utter thank you, nick of time Nick.*
> *I'm wondering why the posse yearns I'm returned.*
> *Was peace possible for our fortunate family?*

Despite his worry-free nature, I notice that Pat does not sleep well that night, or for several nights to follow. Could we be having the same dream? We are frantically searching for our daughter before she falls into the water between the hulls of two beautiful but unsympathetic yachts, trying to grasp something to keep her afloat, wondering why her loving parents have not yet come to save her.

꩜

As she has for the past three years, Peyton's speech therapist Annemarie Stephens sits on the floor in her small, carpeted office the following week and accepts all of Peyton's verbalizing with smiles of joy. There are attempts at structured-speech drills; sometimes Peyton's mouth says the appropriate word spontaneously; sometimes she imitates the word after demonstration; sometimes she repeats a word or phrase as if unable to stop herself. But sometimes no words come out, no matter what Annemarie asks or what cues she offers, like holding up a ball and saying, "This is a ___."

I sit in on the sessions so I can practice the same activities with Peyton at home, not knowing why there is such unpredictability in activating her voice—why she is able to complete a fill-in-the-blank sentence one minute, but then offers no reply when I hold up a ball and ask, "What is this?"

> *Wee ones wither up in fear greeted by pity of*
> *relentless sweet-nary stares.*
> *Each day each deterred cherub dares try.*
> *Motor messages eddy, easing never.*

Annemarie's approach is play therapy with Peyton, and each day at the end of the session, she draws with colored pencils a quick picture of Peyton in her snazzy outfit and writes several sentences about all the great things Peyton said and did that day on a page from a stenographer's notebook. Annemarie tears out the page for Peyton, and she proudly shows it to me as we leave. I keep the pages. These are happy reports.

Upon Annemarie's recommendation, on the last day of February 1980, I take Peyton to see pediatric neurologist Bernadette Ebner, for evaluation of speech and motor delays. The wait is long in the lobby, and the appointment is short. The white-coated resident enters the examining room, announcing, "Dr. Ebner is running behind on clinic rounds," as he adjusts the papers on his clipboard.

Dr. Ebner comes in a short time later, her dark hair pulled into a tight bun and her large, red-rimmed glasses sitting on the tip of her nose. I feel a chill in her perfunctory "Hello" as she gets right down to the business of neurology. It is clear to me that Dr. Ebner is not a parent herself. She does not spend more than ten minutes with Peyton, and does not attempt to engage her directly. The resident takes notes from the questions she asks me while she taps Peyton's knees and twirls a tuning fork about her head, which Peyton reacts to only when Dr. Ebner touches it to her skull.

"Touch your nose," she tells Peyton. Peyton does not.

"But Peyton can point to the body parts on her dolls," I interject.

Dr. Ebner does not comment, and continues with her questions. "Is she fully potty-trained?" she asks, ready, I sense, to doubt any explanatory answer other than "No." She picks up a rubber ball from the basket in the corner, holds it up for Peyton to notice, says "Catch" as she tosses it to Peyton, and watches it bounce off her chest and dribble to the floor. She then asks about skipping and fastening buckles and copying and following commands, as the resident records all the negative answers. (It will be years before I realize that these questions have nothing to do with intelligence.)

Peyton scores well on head circumference and cranial nerves, but everything else is measured as *deficient*. Except for the mention of putting puzzles together, Dr. Ebner's questions do not allow for Peyton's brightness to be noted. And she is in a hurry. Other patients are waiting for her. I wonder if time constraints keep her from asking, "What are Peyton's strengths, her favorite things to do?" So I blurt out, "Peyton loves dolls, books, and puzzles up to twice her age level," unsure whether Dr. Ebner cares to hear it.

Each sad cherub is dazzled by stares of reporters that dare declare,
"I've found another idiot."
Rest these cherubs never will.
Their tread of joy ends and tread of tears begins.
Hearts break.
Idiots fresh are made by idiotic exams measured in rear
thinking idiotic questions.

After only ten minutes, Dr. Ebner is quick and clear with her impressions, which are recorded in black and white in the starkest report I have ever seen. In a minute, my worst fear is confirmed by one sloppily typed two-and-a-half-page report: "Probable intellectual function in the mild to moderately retarded range." Clearly to Dr. Ebner, it does not matter who is on the receiving end of her matter-of-fact stab. Though I have been preparing myself for the confirmation of my fears, the wound inflicted by this report beheads me, filling me with a sorrow deeper and wider than I had ever imagined possible. I carry my daughter, who now wears a scarlet letter R on her pink Lord & Taylor dress, out the door.

It is in the heart the break occurs.
If your Peyton is breaking your heart, thesis she is perfect-not,
rest is impossible for you or your Peyton.
Both hearts break.

Driving Miss Peyton is usually a time of facilitating chatter, but today I say nothing on the ride home. I hope Peyton will not see the slow stream of tears under my sunglasses, but I let them come anyway as I push the Raffi cassette in the tape deck to answer Peyton's repeated "Radio on, radio on" request.

The rush to deliver a sentence was unfair, as Dr. Ebner clearly had not wanted to hear all of the evidence. I think about this as I fix dinner that evening, waiting for Pat to come home. I am barely able to speak when he arrives. We eat dinner quietly and clean up the kitchen. I help Patrick with his third-grade homework while Pat and Pey practice bowling with plastic balls on the dark peach rug in her room.

As we climb the stairs to our room and slide into bed, Pat finally remarks, "You were quiet tonight. How did your day go?"

"The new neurologist has ordered some more tests," I say, trying not to cry, but I cannot keep my chest from rising in increments to a level I can release only with sobs. Pat's arms encircle me, and I say the dreaded word out loud. "She says Peyton is retarded."

Pat holds me tighter and lets my tears flow on his cheeks for as long as I need. He offers no rebuttal. But when my sobs finally begin to slow, he says in my ear, "We'll figure it out together." A kind of tired relief fills me, and I am able to fall asleep.

~

The following week, Pat is in Boston for an East Coast management meeting. Patrick Jr. was feverish all last night, so I call Dr. Chapman early for an appointment. He can see us at 10:30 a.m. I miss being able to call my preferred babysitter, Gam, since she works on weekdays. So again my cousin Connie gets a last-minute call to babysit. She is twenty-one and no longer the bubbly little girl I sewed a Mary Poppins costume for when she was Peyton's age. An adorable little girl, Connie has grown to be an introvert with few friends. Her mother, Gam's sister, Bette, told us about a shoplifting incident a few years ago involving two glamour magazines, but Connie (Peyton's godmother) seems to be on the straight and narrow these days. She saunters into the house, smiling on just one side of her mouth, hand in the back pocket of her too-tight bell-bottom jeans.

"Be safe," I call as Patrick and I rush out the door.

Each time, wearing the appearance that she came to like me,
Connie repels my presents.
I try to hold her hand. She says sassy, "Go away, pest."
Was sweet nil in me?
Wap—I feel paper hit my lip. I yowl.
I think I am hated by her. Why?
I'm a beast seeded by her waps that I quietly saw as my fault.
Real in me recedes. Am I real?

When I return, I find Peyton in her brother's room looking at his books since hers are kept high on a shelf for their own protection. I pay Connie, who answers my "How did things go" with a quick head nod and "Fine" as she leaves. Returning to Peyton I notice her intently studying the Brer Rabbit book called *The Wonderful Tar Baby Story*. I sit down beside her and read her the story.

"Look, Peyton. That sneaky Brer Fox tries to catch Brer Rabbit by making a doll out of tar. Brer Rabbit goes right up to her and says, 'Mawnin!' But the Tar Baby *ain't sayin' nuthin'*. 'Is you deaf?' asks Brer Rabbit. But the Tar Baby *ain't sayin' nuthin'*. 'I'm gonna learn you how to talk to respectubble folks,' says Brer Rabbit. And then look what happens next. He hits the Tar Baby with his fist!"

I was looking in Brer Patrick's books where it sowed
the passage of Tar Baby.
Sweet seeds never she was fed.
She was I. I was her.
I read her story with joy that I'm not the only queer one.
Made of trash, covered in lime like me,
she is a trick of pimping falsers.
She was nurtured never, sad, muted, ired by hits, but can't cry.
Was I a trick too?

Chapter 3

SEGREGATED

The heartbreak eats me up.
I'm greeted not as child of the deity,
but as putrefied child of no one human.

———

June 17, 1983

Dear Pat and Dianne,

Please believe me when I tell you Peyton's very best asset is you. Your belief in Peyton's ability to change and progress will be the cornerstone for any professional who will work with Peyton. That Peyton has made progress of any kind is a result of you first believing that she CAN. KEEP THAT FAITH.

When I began with Peyton I was frustrated. Her case is not a straightforward one—it is not possible to treat Peyton while on "automatic pilot." The problems and solutions are much too complex and simultaneously simple. Peyton's case demands thinking as you treat. Having the time to see her each day gave me the chance to break through my frustration as a therapist, because I had the time to try and work through a variety of solutions. Because of Peyton I am a better therapist now than when I began with her. She stretched my talents as no other child has done. A thank-you to Peyton for weathering through my days of uncertainty and "Well . . . let's try it this way."

Sincerely,
Lauren Hart, MHS, OTR
Occupational Therapist

It is Easter week 1980, our last night in Hawaii, but only until next year, we hope. Pat has arranged for us to eat at former senator Andy Anderson's new waterfront restaurant, since Andy and the architect, Joe Lancor, are Pat's good friends. Joe is also Pat's right-hand man in designing so many of the unique Chart House restaurants. So just before sunset, we hop into a taxi at our Royal Hawaiian Waikiki hotel, speed past Ala Moana Beach Park, and turn left into Kewalo Basin, arriving at the most spectacular island restaurant I have ever seen. Andy knew we were coming, and the premier, pivotal-view table (if the restaurant were a ship, it would be on the bow) is waiting for us. We walk past the koi ponds and lush indoor tropical gardens, splattered with white and red plumeria and orchids, Patrick Jr. forging ahead and Peyton in tow, both with hair sun-streaked from our week in the islands. Joe designed the floor-to-ceiling windows to slide open and expose the dining room to sea and sky, nothing but nature between us and Diamond Head in the distance.

As we sit down, five-year-old Peyton in her booster chair, I open my bag of tricks, pulling out a sticker book of matching tasks first. Peyton begins sorting words and pictures while Patrick Jr. studies the fishing boats returning to their marina slips and the surfers dancing across the waves in the dying sun. There are more fresh fish offerings on this menu than we have ever seen, and I order one I cannot pronounce, though years later I will still taste its perfection. And we drink and eat succulent fruits of the ancient kings.

Since Peyton must keep her body moving—her legs walking, or her hands shuffling in a focused tabletop activity—we dance our customary restaurant foxtrot. When Peyton starts squirming, Pat takes her to explore the restaurant's koi ponds while I set up the next activity to keep her occupied. I see an older couple smile sympathetically at Pat as they walk by and hear a set of junior-highish twins at another table whispering and giggling at the passing girl who can't stop saying the same phrase: "Daddy fish . . . Daddy fish . . . Daddy fish . . ." I refrain from shooting them a dirty look, pretending not to hear. What do I care about ignorant gawkers?

> *Each pity staring person rips my self.*
> *Was it queer to queer be,*
> *or is it pity whirling that equates to queer wars I'm feeling,*
> *realizing pure I'm not?*
> *Jeers of the limed-looking lady demand I stop repetition.*
> *I yearn for my lip retortures to be swept away too.*
> *"Be quiet, please," she duly says with her stares.*
> *News is I care about them—the ones who stared at pitiful*
> *tar baby, leper me.*

Our dinners out have an expiration time of one hour, maximum, the amount of time Peyton can last before the final walk must be made to the exit. Fortunately, tonight we make it to dessert, and the restaurant photographer catches our fortunate family in a glossy print at that picture-perfect spot. I will look at it a quarter of a century later and be utterly amazed to see only three of us smiling.

❧

Back at home, I have bought into the conventional wisdom that segregating Peyton into special-education classes will allow her to gain the skills necessary to someday rejoin her peers in general education. Realistically speaking, segregation is the only option offered. The legal right to choose inclusion—"separate is not equal"—although established in the civil rights era with *Brown v. Board of Education*, is not even thought of for those with disabilities. Segregation is the only known road, and we never ask for proof that it will lead back to rejoining the community.

I swore off roller coasters after just one ride (back when I was trying to impress Pat while we were dating), but these days I am endlessly riding the roller coaster of the grief cycle: shock, denial, anger, bargaining, depression, testing. Many times I cannot admit to myself that it is grief over a loss, or recognize where I am on the graph in its repetitions infinite. Often I tell myself there is no loss because the testers are wrong. I sometimes feel like the consummate actress, only later understanding that I was fooling myself alone and certainly not my daughter.

You were utterly sad.
There I'm dared fastened to your sad.
We seed each other's fears.

With Peyton now in her special-needs preschool class, I decide to give up on psychologists and neurologists for a while. I gave the evaluators their chance, and didn't like or believe what they said, so I have refused to have Peyton tested until her mandatory three-year review. That buys me some time, and I commit myself to early intervention, combined with home lessons, in a race to bring Peyton up to speed. To me this is an era of progress. Peyton is making great gains in reading and speaking, though her speech is often unintelligible to other people. She is, with reminders, potty-trained. She is doing well; therefore, I am doing well.

We settle into a comfortable schedule—comfortable to me, at least. Patrick Jr. is now a fourth grader at Francis Parker School, where most of our friends send their children. Although we were happy with the gifted program in the school district, we felt reluctant to have Patrick segregated into the elite Seminar Program.

Also, I can focus more on Peyton's education with Patrick firmly planted at a respected private school, where many of my college friends teach.

While I'm driving the car pool home from Patrick Jr.'s school one day, the neighborhood kids, including Hollyn, squish into the backseat of the beige Buick station wagon. Though attending a different school now, Hollyn still treats Peyton tenderly, offering her cookies from her lunchbox and showing her the key chain she pulled out of the prize box today. With all the other kids dropped off, I hear Hollyn ask Patrick out of the blue, "How come you're so nice to your sister? My brother fights with me all the time."

Patrick hesitates, then answers. "I do fight with her . . . sometimes." But I know he really doesn't. To him, hurting Peyton must seem unfair, and even at age nine, he is too chivalrous to attempt it.

Later that night as I tuck him in, I ask, "Do you wish your sister were like other sisters—for Peyton's sake, and for your sake?"

"Yes," he replies quietly.

"We'll keep on helping her," I tell him, knowing my response is lacking. Somehow a dozen better responses escape me at this moment, including, "It's okay to feel that way." And I realize as I fall asleep next to my "Mr. Right" that Pat and I have already made an unspoken commitment to parent our two children as only children in many ways, sharing one-on-one time individually with each, willingly content to be separate from each other. Because this is our choice, we will never see it as a sacrifice, though we begin to pay a price when it comes to opportunities for intimacy.

⤚

A typical day for Peyton and me begins by driving across town to school, where her teachers (who are all both speech therapists and credentialed teachers) welcome my help in the classroom several mornings a week. I cherish my teaching times with the children. It gives the teachers a chance to know Peyton better, and me a chance to reinforce the class lessons at home. There will be nine classroom-teacher changes and four school changes (not counting summer school) for Peyton during her seven years of communicatively handicapped classes, ages four to ten. Annual changes in teachers and schools are not uncommon in special education, but Peyton has more than her share.

Realizing that Peyton's progress is directly related to her teacher, her longtime occupational therapist Lauren Hart urges us to insist on a new placement when we see Peyton stagnating. "Peyton does not have time to waste," she says. I will over the years seek her professional counsel at pivotal crossroads, and if her Jiminy Cricket size and character had not reminded my conscience of what I knew was right, would I have settled for the crumbs we were thrown? I shall always shudder in horror to wonder.

Challenging the administration for changes means I have to keep Peyton home while the district drags its heels to find the next teacher. Each one of these interruptions is like a megaphone announcement from district administrators that they do not have a placement for her, and just as soon as psychological testing can confirm the diagnosis of mentally retarded, she will be thrown into the briar patch of private placement. As I soon learn, the ever-changing "away" of special education doesn't get closer to community over the years; it gets farther and farther away, until, as Peyton says years later, no one ever hears about the crimes committed there on the evening news.

In Peyton's classrooms, I become the perpetual room mom. Three of the teachers have pregnancies, and I organize showers; Pat and I take each class on a boat trip out on the bay and organize games and a picnic afterward; Pat plays Santa for at least five Christmas parties we arrange; and I can always be counted on to drive on the occasional field trip. Peyton has either speech or occupational therapy after school each day, with two different speech therapists, and six different occupational therapists over more than a decade. I welcome the long, productive days. Even after her lessons at home, Peyton's playtimes must be structured by me or Pat to ensure success. Without support, her activities erupt in frustration, with her often calling out, "Help me, help me." Mothering her dolls, doing puzzles, and flipping through books fill her alone time. Television holds little interest for her, though we often turn on *Sesame Street*.

> *I'm cast out of Union with creation.*
> *Wepter, I'm party not welcomed.*

In 1981 Pat is invited to serve on the board of directors at the San Diego Yacht Club. But these days, there are few invitations for Peyton, and once Hollyn moves to Washington, D.C., for several years, Peyton has no friends waiting to play with her on week-ends. For the rest of the family, our invitations increase with our growing involvement in the community. But with schools and therapies across town, Peyton has diminished presence in her own zip code; most seven-year-olds do not relish inviting some-one to their birthday party whom they seldom see, especially someone who needs to be accompanied by a parent.

My own social invitations—luncheons, volunteer projects with friends, charity events, and trips with Pat to exciting Chart House destinations—begin to present problems, not joy. Should I go through the hassle of getting a sitter if Gam has to work? Her size six shoes are hard to fill, and I cannot imagine using a stranger from a professional sitter service, even one touting experience with "special-needs" children, since Patrick Jr. is often busy now and not home to report on how Peyton is treated.

My cousin Connie remains the trusty fallback since she is family, the closest of family, living only a half-mile down the road. Feeling sorry for her with only her cats as friends, I sponsored her to join the historic ZLAC Rowing Club when she was fourteen, but she was not able to make friends, and her mother, Bette, complained about the petty, snotty girls there. So, no doubt out of pity for her, and hoping to involve her, Connie remains our number-one babysitter when Gam cannot come. Her personality does not sparkle, but I am confident that Connie will keep Peyton safe till I get home.

I'm terrored by return of torturer Connie. Retortured I was easily,
eagerly errored each time entered Connie.
There she came, pity filled I. I wet my bed.
She'd rip me out of great bed.
I'm fraught with fears as she heaped hits on my head.
Get freed, run away.
She reset the bed, saw I'm wet, therefore I'm hit again.
She would heat up red in her verses by yelling teases,
"Retard. You are trash." Holy errorer hell.
Each real in mired me pointed to popping fears that I'm pity.
Pity eats up treasures eking out reality.

Though I am surrounded by many friends in the community, I begin to feel strangely separate. I wonder why these caring friends, lips loosened by several cocktails, say to me, "You are such an incredible mother. I could *not* do what you do," or "God only chooses really special people to parent really special kids like Peyton." I protest, but not out of humility. Do they really think that God made Peyton suffer because He knew I would be able to handle it? Do they mean it as a compliment? Because it doesn't feel like one.

Swallowing the saliva of hopelessness, I seek out other mothers in my situation, but they are nearly impossible to find. At the library I find a solitary book on childhood aphasia called *A Different Drum: A Mother's Story of Her Courageous Fight to Rescue Her Son from a Tragic Handicap,* by Constance Cameron. I devour the book like a born-again Christian feeds on the Bible. Sitting on my corduroy couch, I read it over and over, keeping it until the overdue fines exceed the book's purchase price. I read how the boy played using repeated movements, reminding me of how Peyton brushes Puddin's hair continuously until the doll gets bald spots. I read how the mother figured out, as I have with Peyton, how important it is to teach the correct way to do something new the first time (as opposed to trial-and-error approaches), and never to teach two similar concepts at the same time. Hungry for someone who understands, I imagine Ms. Cameron in my living room, the two of us infusing our veins with a strong cup of Folgers, sharing each other's joys and challenges . . . and ideas about how to help the children we love.

Then, at a parent meeting for the communicatively handicapped program, I finally meet a family like ours. Their daughter Emily is sixteen and, hallelujah, they live nearby in Point Loma. I regret a missed opportunity to connect with them that night, especially the mom, so when I see her in the Food Basket a month later, I make a beeline toward her with my cart, bumping past others to catch up.

"Please, could we arrange a visit? It would mean so much to me," I say, offering my scribbled name and phone number on a gum wrapper. Sadly, she never calls. Later, I hear they have divorced and Emily has been sent to an institution.

~

Sitting in an audience of about fifty people in July 1981, I feel like a dried-out sponge, and the words of this speaker—Dr. Jon

Eisenson, a specialist on childhood aphasia—are like water I soak up in my thirst for understanding. This is my first professional conference in search of answers. *Aphasia* is a word the doctors have suggested in evaluating Peyton, and in these days before the Internet, information is scarce. Almost everything Dr. Eisenson says, I can recognize in Peyton, and this helps me feel a little less alone. For years, I will ponder one of Dr. Eisenson's topic questions: "Do we teach to a child's strengths or weaknesses?" It makes sense to me when Eisenson describes how the repetition of single words reflects difficulty organizing verbal behavior. This knowledge empowers me, and I learn that if I repeat a word that Peyton has said spontaneously, then she can avoid getting "stuck" on it and move on to say a second word, even though she may be unable to put the two words together on her own. Every day after school, I sit with Peyton on the sofa to work on reading phrases or verbalizing from pictures. When Peyton says, "Read," I repeat, *Reeeead* with a rising inflection and this unlocks Peyton's voice to say a full phrase: "Read the book," much to my glee.

In our neighborhood, I sign Peyton up for a Brownie troop with girls she has not interacted with since church preschool, and I attend with her. I also teach Peyton's Sunday school class for two years at our church while Pat sits next to Peyton to support her participation. In all situations, we are there to swoop Peyton up or sweep her aside whenever her constant attempts at connecting with others are viewed as scary or inappropriate—like placing Brownie beanies on any uncovered heads, or buttoning all undone buttons on others' Brownie shirts and sweaters. (Now whenever I buy a new shirt for a Goddard, I cut off the tags, along with any buttons one would not like buttoned under any circumstance, thereby saving our jugular veins.)

During these years, I have traded psychologist evaluations for my own ever-present trying. I sometimes wonder what is behind my need to constantly be present, help, participate. Am I trying to shore up Peyton's successes or cover up her failures? Do I want to make up for the feelings of being second-class citizens that segregation brings, feelings I don't even fully understand, feelings that we are not totally worthy of belonging to the community? Which is worse, I wonder—not being invited to the party, or being pitied when we're there?

"I'm trying to combat this *mentally retarded* label," I sob to Dr. Hagen, director of Children's Hospital Speech, Hearing and Neurosensory Center, and one of Peyton's more-compassionate doctors, "but I don't know how to prove that their evaluations do not reflect her abilities." His simple statement gives me something to cling to today and hopefully tomorrow: "Peyton is not a cup that is only capable of being three-quarters full; she is a whole cup desiring to be filled."

Like other mother-daughter teams, Peyton and I approach each September with shopping trips to the mall to try on new outfits for school, Peyton having the final say about what she likes, since she chooses her clothes each day and dresses herself with minimal support. We purchase the newest Barbie lunchbox and coloring supplies, but as Labor Day approaches, I become unsettled by worries of how the new teacher will feel about Peyton. In September of 1981, that new teacher, Mrs. Mincer, is quick with her judgment that her class is not the right fit for seven-year-old Peyton, and that in her world of special education, Peyton is just "too special."

I get the call to pick Peyton up early on the first day. When I am summoned to the office to retrieve Peyton before lunch on the third day, I ask to speak to Mrs. Mincer. Waiting in the office, I help Peyton get started on a puzzle from her backpack while I read the pinched-cursive note of dismissal: "Peyton's unwillingness to stay in her seat on task disrupted the entire class agenda again today. She refuses to complete any task, even hand washing, independently. I have told her this is not acceptable."

I look up from the note as a no-nonsense Mrs. Mincer enters and declares abruptly, "I cannot operate my class with a student who does not cooperate." Her attitude of *Peyton doesn't fit* startles me in its "end-of-discussion" finality. I know I cannot pierce this inflexibility.

"I understand," I reply simply, turning to Peyton. As we gather up the puzzle pieces, my mind completes that thought: *I understand that I cannot allow you to "teach" Peyton.* I call the district specialist for a meeting the minute the still-unopened Barbie lunchbox enters my kitchen thirty minutes later.

There are only two kinds of students in this confused world.
The first kind was encouraged early by great teachers. They were
never tugged in wasted ways of futile, eager-not teachers.
Fearlessly, they came to school and they quested joy and affection
each day, hurt never by embarrassment and rejection.
They desired and got full of golden data and wisdom.

The other kind ultimately had no pleasing reasons to go
to places of learning.
They never plot opportunities to learn and oppose the horrible hill
of being tugged never to learn. Eagerness opposed by rigid teachers
killed their jolly, enthusiastic attitudes.
I know from experience that it is hell not to hurdle anything.
Things only flop in failure.
Radically they appear trying to cope with embarrassment,
fear, and horror each day.
They are each unprepared for life.

The district responds by demanding that Peyton be tested. Though I had put a "cease and desist" order on all testing of Peyton, I must submit this time, since a three-year review is mandatory. Gearing up for another low-IQ score, I am certain the district's program specialist is rooting for Peyton to fail so they can finally remove her from their program. Peyton has been home without school for two months by the time district psychologist Janice Chang calls to schedule a visit and begin her assessment.

Pat had turned our large basement into a classroom several years earlier, and that is where Peyton and Ms. Chang meet to begin testing. She asks to work with Peyton alone first, but I can hear nervous giggling rise in Peyton as I climb the steps to the kitchen and then see Peyton handing Chang box after box of activities from the bookshelf. Chang, trying to balance the offerings on her lap, thanks Peyton, who is unable to stop piling them on. I halt at the top of the stairs and listen, my silent anxiety matching what I hear in my daughter. Peyton's unease is high and rising, just as it was last year when the EEG technicians at Children's Hospital dismissed Pat and me to hook up electrodes on Peyton for a forty-five-minute EEG. Pat had suggested he stay, that it might help, but they were quick to say it was easier without parents. After five long minutes of our listening to Peyton's anxiety climb, the technician came out to solicit Pat's help, and the EEG proceeded smoothly. This earned Pat a lifetime invitation to all of Peyton's medical tests from that day forth.

Today, it is a long ten minutes before Ms. Chang requests that I come down to help. I guide Peyton to return the boxes to the shelf and then offer her two activities to choose from. With the desktop cleared, Peyton begins sorting pictures into the four seasons they are associated with, offering spontaneous words and answering questions stimulated by the colorful drawings. Peyton reaches out invitingly to bring Ms. Chang's hand over to participate, smiling at her when she joins in, and Peyton's success silences the giggling. She assesses Peyton for over an hour at home, and then two other times in district testing environments. Her report comes as a shock to the district: Peyton will remain in their communicatively handicapped programs for three more years. She will have a teacher, Bonnie Thomason, who teaches from the heart for an entire year, and a part-time aide will support Peyton's success in the classroom. Her lucky age-seven year.

JANICE CHANG: 3-YEAR REVIEW, DECEMBER 1981

Reason for Referral: Required three-year evaluation.

FINDINGS:
Peyton is a seven-year-old Caucasian little girl who lives with both of her natural parents and eleven-year-old brother. Since the 1978–'79 school year, she has been enrolled in a special day class in the San Diego City Schools program, for the severely language-delayed, and this placement is now undergoing reevaluation.

Peyton was appropriately socially responsive to the examiner, wanting to interact and communicate and giving the impression of a child of normal intelligence. She engaged in verbal interchanges with the examiner in a very soft voice, using fairly simple phrases. The following samples of her language were noted:

"He go to work" (in response to *Where is Daddy?*)
"We'll play this one, OK?"
"He got a cold."
"Girl tie shoes."
"Read that book, OK."
"He cooking, that OK."
"Door, lock house."

In her home, Peyton was observed working with her mother on educational tasks for a period of approximately one hour. Peyton was fully cooperative, responsive and attentive when working with her mother, who is skilled in managing any distracting variables and was able to keep Peyton "on task." Peyton demonstrated ability to identify single words out of a pack of a hundred words and to read single words out of this group. She was able to sort pictures into categories and complete kindergarten-type worksheets. A forty-four-piece jigsaw puzzle was also completed by Peyton, but with much urging and patience on the part of her mother.

SUMMARY:
Columbia Test Score: 96

Peyton, at age seven, is a child who demonstrates extreme distractibility and a very poor ability to organize and focus her attention consistently upon a task, making it very difficult for her to function successfully in an educational setting and in standardized testing. However, when her attention is properly focused, she demonstrates age-level abstract reasoning ability and near age-level adaptive behavior. Peyton's primary educational need at this time appears to be individualized instruction in a setting which can meet her communication and sensory motor integration needs.

Like many Californians, we have a love affair with Hawaii, so for several years, during spring break at Patrick's school, we pack up and leave one paradise for another. We discovered our destination—a hideaway called Kona Village, along the Big Island's Kohala Coast—fortuitously one year after spotting a simple sign, hand-chiseled in wood like that of a Wyoming ranch, on the side of the road. It intrigued us so much that we booked our vacation there (without benefit of pictures on the Internet) the following year, and for two more consecutive years.

No one we know from San Diego is ever there, though at Lindbergh Field we do run into families from Patrick's school, leaving for their own getaway. This year, 1982, we see my friend Lee curbside, carrying skis and parkas with her family. "Where are you all off to?" she asks cheerily.

"A private paradise, Kona Village," I reply, with excitement I cannot contain. "It's our aloha haven for the week, thatched hut right on the beach. We all look forward to it so much," I say as Pat piles the luggage onto the curb.

"Sounds heavenly," replies Lee. "Maybe we should go with you next year." This remark, to my surprise, squelches my joy for a moment, leaving me stumped at how to respond.

Perhaps sensing my discomfort, Lee places her hand on my shoulder and half whispers, "Maybe part of its specialness for you is not knowing anyone there." And I realize she is absolutely right. For one precious week of the year, we all escape the stares of pity.

In pity there can be heard no joy.
You thesis that hopeless persons can effect joy in a present of
thoughtful purchase, or in vases of flowing pussy willows.
But weeds of pity wap. Sad it feeds. Persons devalued heat red.
There they fry.

From the moment we step out of the taxi from the airport on Sunday, we are never in a car again till our departure the following Sunday. (Patrick Jr. once heard Pat say that our vacation was expensive, and asked why it would cost so much to stay in a place without phones or televisions.) The pace is slow here, and we begin to notice some of the same families each year, many with little girls who share their Barbies with Peyton and boys that Patrick meets up with. Swimming is so natural for Peyton; we call her part mermaid as she splashes in the surf, goes boogie-boarding, and rides the waves with Dad on one of the surfboards offered by the resort's beach shack. She spends endless hours building castles in the peppered-white sand and looking for precious shells to fill the crystal bowl handed down from Marguerite Peyton, Peyton's great-grandmother, which sits in the center of our dining-room table at home. We feast on the most delicious food, and Pat and I try each day to exercise off our overindulgences in early-morning runs. But we always weigh four pounds more on the flight home than we had a week before.

I love having Pat all to ourselves, and every minute together is a joy. At a small resort, people study families. Given a week observing our family, inquisitive stares have time to turn to understanding, sometimes even envy. "You seem so comfortable with each other," one mother tells me as we are sitting on the beach, watching Peyton play Barbies with her daughter. To me, it seems that no other family is having as much fun as we are. Maybe we hunger for it more. Like a Pied Piper of the beach, Pat's appetite for adventure often attracts other kids as they take turns boogie-boarding or putt-putting around the bay in a glass-bottomed boat, Peyton's place in the activity subtly secured by Dad. Pat becomes best friends with the employees, joining chef Marty in the final running phase of the Ironman Triathlon, and becoming a friendly right-hand man to Keoni and his cousin Jimmy, who man the beach equipment and have lively stories for the children about Big Island volcanoes, whales, and Hawaiian lore.

A week before our trip in 1983, I find Pat and Peyton in the garage, packing the mast for the Mistral windsurfer in a long tube to be shipped over to his friend Keoni. Kona Village has small sailboats and beach equipment like boogie boards, but no windsurfers. "Why are you taking this?" I ask.

"I have a week off and I want to make sure we're able to windsurf," he says matter-of-factly. "It won't cost much to ship the mast."

I shake my head incredulously. "But how are you getting the board over there? It's monstrous."

"Don't worry—I've got it all figured out" is his confident reply.

I have learned not to challenge what I consider Pat's hare-brained schemes because I have realized over the years that, if I wait, they sometimes just fizzle out. Having married five months to the day after our first date, the give-and-take of our relationship happened after our vows. In our early years together my cautiousness and predictability met his wild ideas with an immediate, "No, you can't do that . . . People don't do that . . . Bad idea!" Peyton usually hears these debates (which do sound like typical Bert-and-Ernie skits) when Pat and I are negotiating adventures he has planned for his time together with her, the exciting opportunities that Ernie suggests nixed as unsafe by Bert.

Yet at 6:00 a.m. on the day of our departure, I find Pat in the garage, wrapping the immense boom and board in Peyton and Patrick's Snoopy sleeping bags, securing it with duct tape all around (his favorite fix-all), and loading it into the station wagon to check in at the airport. Though surfboards go free of charge on flights to the islands, this board is much too large to pass as a surfboard, and he will learn his lesson at check-in, I think to myself.

"Wow, this is the longest board we've ever seen," says the ticketing agent, eyes wide in surprise.

"Well, it's actually similar in size to the Duke's original sixteen-foot koa surfboard," replies never-say-die Pat, along with a few other friendly, convincing statements. To my amazement, the biggest surfboard ever to travel free is loaded on our flight, and the next day he is windsurfing not twenty feet from a migrating whale covered with barnacles, dancing with it through the water in a ballet, and the entire beach audience is standing there, watching.

Having been married to Pat now for more than fifteen years, I stand on the beach, finally less fearful of his feats, even cheering on his playful encounter with his fellow mammal as they leap across the stage to a standing ovation. Then Pat leaves the open ocean and sails back to shore to pick up Peyton, who stands holding onto his legs as they reach back and forth across the bay. That our family loves each other and loves life escapes no one, whether they think us wise or fools.

There queer in me is not pitied because my dad was to treasure me.
He aquaed my sweet searching sea of tepid tears.
He was happy with me. I'm not pitied in pert pouted stares.
I'm queer not.
I'm very beautifreed by him, loudly my glitter heard here.
Fresh winds blew through feelings that I'm real.

True, we cannot partake of the nightlife here. True, Peyton needs one of us with her every moment, and cannot attend the children's camp that frees other parents to share private moments. True, Pat must give up the wind and surf sounds he hungers for and sleep with the sliding doors of our oceanside Tonga shut, bolted, and barricaded with a chair so I can sleep knowing Peyton will not wander out. True, we split tacks often in the day so father and son can try scuba-diving while Peyton and I build drip sand castles and search for seashells to fill her pink, plastic bucket. Yet we cling to this escape and find it hard to let go.

If we ever missed a flight, all would guess that Pat had caused it—certainly never me. However, on this our final trip—something we do not know at the time—I insist on taking Peyton to the beach for one last swim, just the two of us, on the morning of our departure. I know we are in a bit of a time crunch when we arrive at the Tonga and Pat is shaking his head in amazement that I have dared do this.

We scurry to the taxi and drive out the gates, realizing we may not make the flight back to the mainland for work and school the next day.

"Please hurry—we're late!" I urge the taxi driver.

"No worries," he replies, smiling at me in the rearview mirror. "All things are on island time here."

Unfortunately, we do end up missing our flight, but Pat points no fingers as we find a hotel in town and arrange for a flight the next day. He might have smirked a bit to himself that careful Dianne was not vigilant, but perhaps he, better than most, would know my excuse: Paradise is hard to leave.

❧

September of 1983 solidifies my dread of back-to-school. Eight-year-old Peyton has a new school and a new teacher. As we drive to Rochester Elementary to locate Dolores Waters's class, I try to counter Peyton's nervous giggling by asking her questions.

"I like the outfit you chose for today, Pey," I begin, grateful that she has dressed herself and gone to the bathroom with only a few verbal reminders. Peyton wears a new, red plaid dress, yellow socks slipped into new loafers, and a yellow cotton vest to match, and she holds her Smurf lunchbox on her lap, all of which offer lots of topics for conversing.

"What do you like about it?"

"It's new."

"Where did you buy it?" I continue.

"Broadway," she says, looking nervously out the window.

"Who treated you to that snazzy vest?" I ask cheerfully.

"Gam."

"And what else matches the vest?" I continue.

"My yellow socks."

"You're right. Hey, how do those new loafers feel?" I ask.

"Fine."

"Watch out today, 'cause they're still new and the soles are slippery," I add, glancing at Peyton's sun-streaked hair pulled to either side with rainbow-beaded barrettes. Peyton is smiling through her new big, white teeth, a smile we cherish, not knowing it will soon vanish. I say a silent prayer that Peyton will be welcomed by a teacher's warm smile as we park the car and make our way through the crowd to meet Ms. Waters. The hallway feels like a slippery slope as we approach Peyton's classroom. Ms. Waters, an older woman with a blunt haircut and thick quarterback arms, is calling out directions like a drill sergeant as the students enter.

Sure enough, shortly after lunch I get a call to pick Peyton up.

Rochester Elementary is a thirty-minute drive from our house, so later that week, when Ms. Waters asks me to come in and "help" by staying at the school (sitting on a small, wooden chair hidden behind the cubbies at the back of the classroom), I soon realize it's only to help her get rid of Peyton thirty minutes quicker.

Many teachers either don't recognize students' learning differences,
or they are impervious to try to accommodate people
who mull data differently.
Students hurdle millions of hills and teachers are their greatest
mentors, but teachers are also their greatest hurdles if never
willing to look deep and find what is golden inside.

Once again, I am forced to watch Peyton's daily activities—not participate in or support them. I sit, stiff and wooden. Peyton knows I am there, but she must be stiff and wooden, too, never allowed to go back to talk to me or ask for help. Ms. Waters is stiff and wooden in her approach to teaching, as well; Peyton must be the one to conform—without support—to Ms. Waters's mold. When she does not, I am asked to escort her home. Every "inappropri-ate" move brings us one step closer to the exit. Peyton attempts the writing tasks but eventually tears her papers up after repeated erasing bores the tiniest of holes next to one of the answers. Frus-trated, she then wanders about the room, appearing unable to follow directions, touching other children in ill-fated attempts to communicate. It takes me a week of watching before I see that failure is the only option this teacher offers Peyton.

Years later at a conference, I will listen to a father describe how he and his wife sat watching through a two-way mirror as their son was slapped in the name of treatment each time he did not respond correctly to directives given to him. The father's words will strike me like a bolt of thunderous revelation. Why hadn't I seen that Peyton was also being slapped? Slaps of non-support. Slaps of pity. Slaps of fear and control. Slaps without onlookers lifting a finger to stop it. Like this father behind the two-way mirror, I watch as Ms. Waters "slaps" Peyton for five days.

Each destiny-errored, differently-wired but "cares-to-learn" child
needs assurance they are not weeds but fragrant flowers to be
greeted as valuable.
There in either the tested room or the classroom,
best tell each cherub that they can lead.
Say that they are the guiders to test the best ways to heat their
versed, vested, vastly valuable, vellum varied, esteemed equated
equal, red news never viewed, volumed voices.

Left alone at her desk to do a task with no support means guaranteed failure for Peyton. Each of these tasks is like a test, and Ms. Waters has deemed that Peyton does not even merit help get-ting started. Peyton has to adhere to the rules, and in the name of equality, the rules must be the same for everyone. But as Peyton will proclaim years later, *equal* doesn't mean that everyone should get the same treatment; it means that everyone should get what they *need*.

After a week of this, it is no longer possible for me to entrust Peyton to Ms. Waters's care. Peyton remains out of school while the program specialist searches for another teacher. Peyton and I continue our lessons at home, and Dr. Hagen arranges for neurologist Robert Sedgwick, a respected authority on aphasia, to see Peyton. Can medicine help with Peyton's increasing anxiety and distractibility?

———

November 21, 1983
Los Angeles

It is my opinion, as a result of my examination and review of the file, that no specific etiological diagnosis is apparent in this patient. I am in agreement with all prior examiners that primary difficulties here are in the area of speech and language. In addition, she has some motor problems as outlined by Ms. Hart. She certainly does not impress me as frankly retarded. Likewise, there is no evidence of any pervasive personality disorder inasmuch as, despite her communicative difficulties, she remains a most charming and personable little girl.

I had no further tests to suggest. She certainly has been worked up from A to Z. Likewise, I did not feel that any medication would be of value. Her present therapeutic program certainly seems optimal, and I had no changes or additions to suggest in this regard.

I am sorry not to be of more help.

Sincerely,
Robert P. Sedgwick, MD

Despite Peyton's movement challenges, Pat is anxious to teach his athletic daughter to ski, and an invitation to Deer Valley, Utah, for Christmas and Peyton's birthday in 1983 presents an opportunity. Visiting Chart Houses established in other mountain locations like Sun Valley, Lake Tahoe, and Aspen, the rest of the family has gained reasonable competence when it comes to skiing, although heaven help me if I ever end up on a black-diamond run.

Pat and Pey have enjoyed a strong success rate with other sports, like the Saturday I was scheduled to be gone all day and he decided it was time to take the training wheels off her bike.

After removing the training wheels from Pey's two-wheeler, Pat duct-taped Patrick's rollerblading knee pads over her jeans, his elbow pads over her sweatshirt, and his soccer shin guards to her pant legs. He crowned her head with Patrick's crash helmet and walked the bike and his princess mummy two blocks away to the large, empty Naval Electronics Lab parking lot. Helping her mount her bike, no time to wobble, he yelled, "Pedal, pedal, pedal . . ." Then, running alongside, he touched her bike seat only to stop a fall in motion. She teetered, she tottered, and then, in about an hour, she figured it out, reported Pat as I arrived home from a day working at the Thursday Club Rummage Sale. The next day, I witnessed her pedaling all over the parking lot, turning toward me with a smile of delight filling her face, free as I have seen her only in swimming. In awe of their accomplishment, I faced fleeting fits of fear for years, knowing that if I had been home I would have fought to stifle their daring, dangerous experiment.

Here in Deer Valley, Peyton's wide grin indicates she is willing to forge ahead to yet another summit. I have come to respect the miracle of their "dynamic duoism," so I bundle my dear Peyton in her red snowsuit, boots, and gloves and think to myself, *If they can pull this one off, they are indeed a force to be reckoned with.*

We board the lower chairlift, which doesn't go very far up the hill, and Pat lifts Peyton off for their first trip down the gentle slope—slipping, sliding, crumbling, and finally walking to the chairlift for another ride back up. He starts the lesson with short skis and no poles. At least, he says, this will minimize entanglements and leave Peyton's hands free to ease a fall. By the time we are once again at the top, Pat decides that for the next few days he will ski backwards in front of Peyton, down the hill.

Bending over, he holds the tips of her skis together between his in the snowplow position to help her glide slowly. Over and over they repeat the drill, she falling like a person made of straw and he lifting her up and setting her pie-shaped skis back inside his. Perfection by perseverance. By the end of the second day Peyton is skiing independently on the bunny slopes, with Pat encouraging her to ski where she likes, since changing direction means more experience in turning. The snow is not icy, and she has good success lowering her right or left shoulder and putting more weight on the equivalent ski. By now Peyton knows how to parallel her skis when she wants to go faster and then check her speed with a snowplow.

At one point, Peyton starts down the hill and heads straight toward a line of people in the beginning ski class. Before Pat can intercept her trajectory, she slices through the top of the line. Skiers go down like bowling pins, and an angry ski instructor calls after her. On the third day, Peyton and Pat arrange to meet me and Patrick Jr. at the second chairlift, about a ten-minute ride with gorgeous views of the evergreens and rolling white hills below. Patrick Jr. and I are anxious to see how Peyton does, and, to our amazement, Peyton skis out of her chair to our waiting applause. A radar gun would surely clock her speed somewhere below five miles per hour, but my heart soars, watching her in slow motion as she becomes one with the pure, white snow, the trees, the crisp blue sky.

Most important, Peyton's heightened confidence is just what the doctor ordered—or rather, it's what Peyton needs but *not* what the doctor ordered. Her bike riding, boat steering, swimming, and skiing will be labeled "splinter skills" by professionals, since simpler motor tasks elude her. But so much depends on the teacher, I realize. Pat's own confidence is bolstered the next day when, while eating lunch at the lodge, the lead ski instructor approaches, saying, "I have to ask—would you consider teaching us your techniques at the ski school?"

When children know their differences will be supported by you
saying you will never stop trying ways to help them find their very
best voice, their fears rest.
There, they are not awed by pity. There, esteem is greeted.
I'm in peace because someone saw all people are real and deserve
being supported to communicate their truths.

Two days later, as we are all getting in the chairlift line, several skiers fall over in a tangle, and both Pat and Peyton are knocked into the jumble of skis and poles and bodies. To rid the loading area of the chaos, the lift operators are aggressively picking people up and loading them onto the chairlift. Before Pat can yell *Stop!* Peyton gets scooped up and plunked down all by herself on a chair heading up the mountain. With no restraints, her chair clears the loading area and heads higher and higher up the hill, easily a twenty-foot drop onto the hard-packed surface below, and there is no way to get her down.

Pat and I manage to get on the chair behind her, but we don't dare call to her for fear she will turn around and plummet to the ground. Helplessly, we hold our breath and pray she gets to the top safely. Once at the offload area, Pat yells at the lift operator to help Peyton off. Skiing toward Peyton, he makes light of the mishap so as not to frighten her.

"Well, how did my big girl like taking that ride all alone?" he says, smiling as he kneels down and pulls her close in a bear hug. I can feel Pat trembling as I join in the embrace, and it will be many minutes before my own heart stops pounding.

During the next two school years, two more district teachers will be found who see Peyton as charming and personable, needing and deserving support to be successful, and Peyton will continue to progress, despite challenges . . . until the great mystery descends on our family and even fleeting trips to paradise are lost.

I'm heard zero. I'm gyred up, gyred down, whipped into sweared
want death, my meal opted over.
Queer modes of my actions festered. In dazzling sting of never
being in unity with creation, I was upped insaned.
There pouts melted me.

Over the next few months, troubling behaviors begin to brew in Peyton: spiraling anxiety, increasing distractibility, and gait changes. Dr. Ebner offers medical tests and two short-lived Ritalin trials for the puzzling neurological changes, but no answers are found. I will pursue my quest to solve the increasingly complex mystery of all these startling changes for a quarter century. The possibility that our daughter, so carefully cared for in this loving family, is being abused never crosses our minds.

Chapter 4

SILENCED

Pity weeds will nil rest until I tell.

———

11/5/84
Peyton wet her pants today. It was right after lunch, immediately after returning from the restroom. We tried to call you but there was no answer. We had no pants her size to change.

11/7/84
I'm not sure what's going on with Peyton. The class was walking back to class after lunch, and Peyton hit a couple of children. I separated her from the group. She squatted down and urinated. I had her change her clothes. We talked about what you should do when you have to go to the bathroom. I'm not sure if she thought she would get to go home because of it.

11/28/84
Peyton had a difficult time in the calendar circle this morning. She hit some children and had to leave. After the circle, the day was fine. We made Christmas ornaments (flour, salt, water) so she was really involved with that.

12/4/84
Sorry, not a wow day.

12/12/84
Poor behavior all day. Sorry. We'll try again tomorrow.

—Sonja Rodriguez, classroom teacher

For Thanksgiving 1984, we invite Aunt Bette, Uncle Gus, and their children, Duane and Connie. Walking by Peyton's room before dinner, I see Peyton sitting on her bed reading, with Bette and twenty-two-year-old Duane on the bed next to her.

Duane stares distantly toward Peyton, his face thin and pale, his stringy, black hair in disarray. His jeans, stained and full of holes, and his faded T-shirt are not appropriate for the occasion, I think as I join them. And do I detect the smell of alcohol?

"Why don't you come into the living room and talk to Pops for a while?" I say to Duane, as I lead him by the arm into the living room.

Back in the kitchen, I tell Gam, "I did not like the feeling I got, seeing Duane sitting on Peyton's bed. Please go back in there to keep an eye on her."

Just then, Bette strolls in. "You know how much Duane loves Peyton. We were having such a nice visit."

Our ten family members gather around the abundant Thanksgiving table, enlarged to an oval with two golden-oak leaves. Peyton sits between me and Gam as Duane jokes with Patrick, eight years his junior. (*Is there a tinge of bullying in his teasing? I wonder.*) Next to Duane is Aunt Bette (sour-faced in contrast to Gam, her always-smiling sister). Husbands begin hovering over the passing platters as Connie climbs meekly into the last open seat next to Pops.

"The California contingent of a loving Virginia family," Pat says as he begins the blessing, "gives thanks to God from whom all our blessings flow." Chattering and chewing commence. Connie speaks only when spoken to, and never to Duane, I notice.

The thought that she might be afraid of him flickers through my mind. Poor Connie.

A strange feeling persists in me, echoed by Gam, and we vow never to let Peyton or Patrick Jr. be around Duane again. Luckily, our concern is soon resolved, as Bette herself begins to exclude Duane from family gatherings, announcing she is the only one who loves him. We shake our heads at Bette's obsessive devotion to her son and dislike of her daughter, especially as we learn years later about Duane's troubles with the law: his arrest for DUI, and news that he was shot in the arm during a drug deal on Fiesta Island. Though we know this family is wealthy, we are more than baffled to hear Uncle Gus announce that they are selling their family home and moving to a small apartment across town. We finally deduce that all their money must be going to keep Duane out of jail.

꩜

In 1985, the San Diego Yacht Club is a century old and entering its glory days, and somehow we are at the center of it all, with Pat serving for the fourth year on its board of directors. A little over a year ago, San Diego yachtsman Dennis Conner, defending for the New York Yacht Club off the shores of Newport, Rhode Island, lost to Aussie John Bertrand, ending 132 years of US possession of the America's Cup. Sleepy San Diego has given birth to more than its share of world-class sailors, and Dennis, together with Malin Burnham, is mounting a challenge to the Royal Perth Yacht Club to win back the Cup. They will lead the challenge under the San Diego Yacht Club burgee they had both grown up sailing for.

This is the first time the America's Cup defense will be based outside of New York, and the oldest sporting trophy in the world is no longer controlled by East Coast sailing aristocracy. The three-year effort will culminate in Team Stars and Stripes going down under to race in the whipping whitecaps of the Indian Ocean and, thanks to Dennis, ESPN will install cameras on the boats, inviting the entire world aboard the formerly exclusive sailing event.

Pat's involvement in all this excitement means more demands on our social life—more meetings, more parties. Previously, we had few required social engagements, other than annual executive gatherings for Chart House, but for eight years we will walk the political and social tightropes, deciding when Pat will attend alone and when I will join him.

❧

When my mother Gam cannot fill my shoes on the home front, we continue to call on my cousin Connie. She is twenty-six now and in between jobs, having just been fired for stealing twenty dollars from the till as she closed down her cash register at Brady's Department Store. Gam had gotten her the job by asking their personnel director to hire her. Just a few weeks later, however, the director called Gam to say they had proof, plus a confession of theft, and were going to let her go without pressing charges. Her mother Bette's only comment was, "I don't know why she does things like that, embarrassing our family." Once again, we simply shook our heads and wondered what Connie was thinking.

Sadly, her brother Duane is increasingly getting into one sort of trouble or another. Gam hears whispers of it from Bette in unsolicited declarations that are scant on details but heavy on defensiveness.

❧

In June, Patrick Jr. will graduate from the Middle School of Francis Parker and tonight is the April Spring Sing dinner honoring the soon-to-be graduates. Since it is payroll time for Gam at work, she will need to stay late. I hear Connie's 1965 Volkswagen Bug sputter into the driveway. I am scurrying to brush Peyton's teeth as Connie comes in with her backpack slung over her shoulder. Peyton has already eaten and is in her pajamas, since I like to leave Connie with as few "duties" as possible, and plenty of time for books and puzzles, an enjoyable evening for the girls.

"Have fun, you two!" I call out as we leave.

Decades later, I will learn the unthinkable truth of what happened whenever Connie came to babysit.

Rips are in me that years I'm hearted hell. Grief each time she came. The terror, brothelling, bumpered tortures.

Connie's quiet demeanor lasts only until the car pulls out of the driveway. Then she begins. Tonight she starts by grabbing a puzzle box and whacking Peyton on the side of the head. "Get out of my sight, you worthless piece of shit." *Whop. Whop.* "And don't start wailing, you retard," she snickers, smacking Peyton's head with the back of her hand.

Greedy she is to hurt me. Am I the trash she is calling me? I am very pitier of I.

"Jesus Christ. Look at this fucking house. You have a yacht, retard. How is that fucking fair? Did your perfect mother buy you all those dolls? Well, you are not perfect. You are no treasure. Your own mother doesn't really love you because you are a hopeless retard. She wants to be rid of you. That's why she leaves you with me."

Her fiendish diatribe continues as Peyton tries to get away, but Connie pursues relentlessly with sweeping blows to her head.

Connie, poured easily by hate, hit me in the head trying to get me festered in fears to insanity.
There I'm brain pounded as jungles of electricity gyre me.
Red frying rung guns re-popped in me as her harsh hands hit my popping, pouting, peppered brains as she utters
I'm treasured never.

Peyton runs into her room, trying not to cry since tears only bring more slaps.

I'm rester in my bed crying tears, pillows drenched by pity.

A few minutes pass, and then Connie bursts wildly into Peyton's room, holding a hot water bottle and squealing continuously, as if on replay, "You whore! You're filled with trash!" Connie pulls Peyton's pajama bottoms off, slapping her on the ear to halt her cries.

"You're pitiful," she says, pulling her by the hair to keep her head down. "I need to wash this trash out of you." Connie inserts a douche hose into Peyton, who freezes; then Connie holds Peyton by the neck with one hand while the other squeezes hot water into Peyton's vagina.

"No, no, no!" howls Peyton, whose pleas are answered by devilish laughter and more slaps to the skull.

Retortured I was each time Connie entered I. I saw her murder me.
Connie raped me seared by hot and cold watered.

A well of tears gels in Peyton as she imagines herself witnessing these cruelties inflicted on some other girl, watching some other child suffer these tortures.

*Each time Connie fries me, I feel dead. I'm not reality real. I'm
nothing in me. I'm not able to feel.
I'm only a watcher each time I'm raped. I became a jeered jelly
pierced person, a gummy girl wedded to pity.
I'm walled in. I'm puny, pitifully unteared, unfeeling.
I nothing can do because Connie killed I.
I'm red, ired by tortures happening to the mired me who spelled
reality me from the raw, rasty rapes and tortured fears.
Tortured red by my inability to weep for me,
it was the other girl I pitied.
Tortures hit her not I, yet I beast became.*

Looking at the clock, Connie begins cleaning up.

"Keep crying and I'll bring Duane to teach you a lesson next time, you little piece of trash."

❦

Once I see the big, brass antique bed in the Ocean Beach Antique shop, I know I have to buy it for Peyton. The bed has been restored to its magnificent Victorian sheen by Chester, the man who has refinished all the brass decor in the dozens of historical buildings—former rowing clubs, brush mills, taverns—that have become Chart House restaurants. This kind of obsession comes over me rarely, but when it does, it engulfs me totally. I know the brass bed is important for Peyton, just as I was sure all those Madame Alexander dolls were. The sturdy vertical bars on the headboard and footboard have the graceful appeal of an antique heirloom made to last another hundred years; large, round bulbs adorn the four posts. Peyton's old bed is too small for me to snuggle in with her at night and read flash cards or peruse one of the scads of albums filled already with hundreds of pictures of our family adventures. I can picture the bed piled with ruffled pillows and a peach-flowered quilt. And I even dream of a perfect future that includes this bed: Peyton lying in it, with the love of her life.

Pat is easily sold, and the bed is purchased, brought home, and set up.

⁂

May 18, 1985. Tonight is the Centennial Ball at the San Diego Yacht Club. I, in my perfect lavender taffeta gown, and Pat, in his striped coattails, will join our closest friends for an evening of refined glory. I am Miss Congeniality on my handsome Rhett's arm as we smile and circulate through the giant, white tent strung with ten thousand lights. The shades of regret I felt in leaving Peyton are all but forgotten on this once-in-a-lifetime night.

I do not know how to tell you about the terror.

Duane slips into Peyton's bedroom, his greasy hair smelling of Miller and marijuana.

Duane says I'm a meal he will eat.

Duane leaps on Peyton, throws off her flowered comforter, yanks down her pink pajama bottoms.

Wedded with tears, I see his gun.

The Centennial Ball begins in the early evening, my favorite time of the day on San Diego Bay, because as the sun sets over the peninsula, the sky fills with the most incredible purples and pinks, as if painted by a master artist. On the front deck for cocktails, we float like classic yachts through the hundreds of fellow revelers, tacking and jockeying for position to share in the social banter. I flirt with feelings of joy, and allow myself to taste a rare, don't-worry-be-happy confidence.

I try to eke out "Help me" by trepidly calling my dad.

"Oh, you want your daddy?" Duane slurs, now unbuckling his belt. "I'll give you Daddy, you little moron."

⤚⤙

As night falls, all join in the Grand March to the huge, white tent that fills the parking lot of the Yacht Club. Inside, a sea of tables with starched white tablecloths hold centerpieces of white tea roses, baby's breath, and frothy lace fans for each lady. Support posts soar skyward wrapped in billowing snow-white toile and twisting vines of ivy. Pots of gardenias overflow onto the orchestra's gazebo steps, filling the air with sweetness. Board members and wives promenade in, each announced to a trumpet call. Pat and I join our dearest friends, along with Gam and Pops, at our table. I whisper clever witticisms to the men on my right and left and share stories and laughter with their wives as we dine on lobster and steak and sip Chablis and vintage Cabernet.

Duane urges me under sheets to trespass sweet,
joyous Peyton with his penis leaping me open.

Pressing down on her wrists. Jab. Jab. Jab. Peyton gagging, choking on drool and tears.

I hear Connie yell with ogred dread that I might get pregnant.

Jab. Jab. Jab. The brass bed rings and clangs as it beats against the wall.

He is in me tunneling. Sap pours. It waters my quiet, virgin vagina.
Waters that wash fast from my vagina tease red.

When the sweet sounds of Les Brown and His Band of Renown begin to fill the tent, Pat and I dance the first waltz. I boogie, twist, fox-trot, and jitterbug with the many other revelers. The night is full, and I am full of the night.

Duane puts the gun in my mouth.

"You tell your daddy and I'll blow your fucking brains out."

I poop. This pisses Duane.

"Awwww, *shit!* Goddammit, you little fuck!" Duane leaps off the bed, now stained with feces, semen, and blood, pulls on his jeans, and stomps out of the room.

Connie bursts in. "For God's sake, Duane! Did you have to make such a fucking mess? Now I have to call Mom, you asshole," she yells down the hall as he leaves.

There in the point of no return to sweet, he troughed my real.
The heartbreak eats me up.
I'm numb.
I'm POW.
I'm trash.

Like Cinderella, my carefree moments are counting down. Champagne glasses are raised. Commodore Knoth's toast salutes our close-knit yachting community: "To those who came before us, creating the proud legacy that allows our children to sail onward to destinations unlimited . . ."

⤜

Cold fingers with chipped burgundy nail polish work quickly, efficiently, plunging Peyton into a tub of tepid water, scrubbing her vigorously with a washcloth.

"If you tell, it will just kill your grandmother, you see? She's frail. She'll have a heart attack on the spot." Aunt Bette splashes water between Peyton's legs.

"We can't have you getting pregnant, now. Not with all your problems. Lordy."

Bette's dirty blonde hair, normally pinned tightly into an immovable mound on top of her head, is now falling in her face as she yanks Peyton out of the tub and buffs her dry with the towel. "People like you can't have children of their own."

⤜

It's after midnight—later than we had told Connie—and I move quickly from the garage to the kitchen door. I am surprised when I unlock the door to find Aunt Bette there and Peyton still awake, though looking very tired, slumped on the armchair in the living room.

"Peyton pooped in her pants—quite a mess—and Connie, she just couldn't handle it alone," says Bette matter-of-factly. "I came over to do the cleanup and sent Connie home."

I see Peyton's pajamas and sheets washed, dried, and folded on the bed.

"I just couldn't get Peyton to go back to sleep, the poor dear, so I let her stay up and wait for her mom," she says, grabbing her pocketbook and keys.

Bathrooming accidents do occur, but only rarely. Pat, Gam, and I are all able to understand Peyton's verbal and nonverbal cues, so I am shocked, but not totally. Connie might have been distracted, and she is not around Peyton enough to understand her like we do. I dismiss it, feeling grateful that my trusty aunt was there to step in. As Bette leaves hastily, I call out, "Thanks for your help. Sorry for all the trouble!"

I hurry to put on my pajamas, skip face washing and teeth brushing, and just climb with Peyton into her brass bed. Peyton tosses a while, repeating a fretful moan. I reassure her softly, saying, "Not to worry, accidents happen." Peyton finally falls asleep with my arms wrapped securely around her.

Each time I'm killed by Connie and Duane.
I'm more unreal than real. I'm a lawyer . . . judging pimpers . . .
I prosecute them for killing Peyton.

❧

Late spring means Peyton and I are shopping at Lord & Taylor for a new swimsuit for our annual fourth of July rafting in Coronado.

Peyton tells me she has to tinkle. In the second-floor ladies' room, Peyton waits while I carefully place paper on the toilet seat and then help her pull down her underpants. There is a spot of blood on them. I wipe Peyton with toilet paper after she urinates and see a red streak. *Could it be early puberty?* Dr. Lennie, our pediatric endocrinologist, has, in fact, been measuring hormones in Peyton's blood to see if that could be a possible reason for the recent changes in her behavior.

Using the pay phone right outside the bathroom door, I get an appointment with Dr. Lennie for later that day. During the examination, the doctor and I spot an inch-long scratch on one side of Peyton's vaginal opening.

"Could she have scratched herself?" asks Dr. Lennie.

"I suppose," I reply. "But I haven't seen her do this sort of thing. We were at the beach this morning, digging in the sand."

"Yes, I suppose it could be a scratch from playing in the sand," he says. "It's superficial, so it should heal in a day or two. Nothing to worry about."

My mouth freezes as returning pimps try to keep me silent.
I'm read as retarded, but I hurt just like a real child.

Chapter 5

INSTITUTIONS

Each day is an eternity to survive.
Waste is quietly, barely tolerable.
Plotting one's death is fearless.
I take joy each day in hoping waste will end.

Date of Report: 2-17-85
Both hands and shirt collar are almost constantly in her mouth.
On most tasks Peyton shows poor control, with the task being
done fast and messy. Frustration happens quickly and papers are
torn up. She perseverates on an incorrect response. Equipment
used briefly and then she wants to stop. Difficulty in staying with
any task for long.

—Lauren Hart, MHS, OTR

Date of Report: 3-31-85
This year Peyton was expected to work more independently than
ever before. Due to the nature of Peyton's disabilities, she continues
to NEED additional instructions and prompts to initiate, continue,
or complete activities. When expected to work independently, Peyton becomes disruptive due to perseverative behavior, seeking help
and attention, and refusing to try work papers. Peyton knows the
other children are working quietly as assigned and becomes even
more stressed that her performance does not match theirs.

—Lauren Hart, MHS, OTR

Date of Report: 7-31-85
Of definite disadvantage to Peyton is her tendency to show emotional responses that don't seem appropriate to a situation or event. Unfortunately, Peyton's stress reactions of giggling, smiling, and laughing often look more like misbehavior. If Peyton cried instead of giggling, adults would be quicker to check situations and adjust them to relieve her anxiety and stress. At this time, Peyton's internal system does not organize her to respond by crying at stress.

—Lauren Hart, MHS, OTR

Peyton is ten and in the past year, changes in her behavior have appeared out of nowhere—wetting herself, hitting, sleep disturbances, hysterical giggling bordering on tears, purposeless motor movements. Even more alarming is her fading voice as she slowly decrescendoes into silence after nearly a decade of speech therapy. I can no longer fight the battle of mismeasured intellectual competence since I feel myself increasingly swept into a category-four hurricane, daily less and less able to figure out what is going on.

My aunt asked me to not ever tell that her beloved son molested me.
Oppose her I did not. Instead I chose to never talk again in my life.
Up in heaven joyously I envisioned I would talk, mute no longer.
Looking to that day, I longed to plot my opportunity to die.
There can be millions of causes, none justifiable, that an adult
asks a child to mute be, but the most villainous effects result in
thoughts of suicide and moments spent plotting how to live
with this insanity.

In June 1985 Peyton is referred to the Central IEP Team for placement review because her behavior in the public school classroom has become "unmanageable." Since March I have been going to the class for several hours each day to do reading and math with Peyton upon the invitation of her teacher, Sonja Rodriguez, who has been carefully observing the changes in Peyton. Sonja tells us she thinks Peyton can stay if the district gives her an aide for support, as they have done for Peyton in previous years, but the answer comes back that the district no longer provides aides for individual students.

This surprises me, since the law guarantees "supports and services in the least restrictive environment." I will do anything to avoid this oncoming fate of private placement, which has hovered above Peyton's and my head like a dark storm cloud since Peyton's first district teacher declared, "You know, with Peyton's multiple challenges requiring speech and OT, private placement might be best." For whom, I wondered? A decade later, watching *Forrest Gump* in a theater, I seem to be the only one not laughing at the scene where Forrest's mother offers her body for sexual favors to the school administrator in exchange for Forrest being included in the public school classroom.

Immediately following the referral, Dr. Ted Woodward, owner and headmaster of a private developmental treatment facility called the Marshall Institute, comes to Sonja Rodriguez's class to assess Peyton for his program. He watches Peyton working with me on academics and in a group classroom activity. After a few minutes, he draws his conclusion: "I've seen enough. I have other students with many more concerns than Peyton," he assures me. Somehow I am not comforted at his quick dismissal, which sounds like "Peyton will have no problem in my program."

When Peyton's speech pathologist and occupational therapist join me on a visit to Marshall Institute, all three of us agree that Peyton will indeed have a problem there. As a teacher, I did some substitute teaching there in the late seventies. But now it is under new ownership, and the program strikes me as detached and mechanical. Children sit in chairs across from adults who give short, two- to three-word commands, wait for a response, make a mark on a graph, and then repeat the command: *Stay in chair . . . Quiet hands . . . Pick up pencil.* Adults robotically repeat commands if the task is not robotically accomplished. Zero marked on graph = *Failed.* Check marked on graph = *Good job.* Give child a Cheerio (still no emotion).

Peyton's therapists and I know this approach will be frustrating for her, especially now with her rising anxiety and perplexing behaviors. To me, school should be an interaction between student and teacher, a teacher who expresses the attitude of "I know you can learn, and I can teach you." Here, I don't hear, see, feel, smell, or taste anything but behavioral control, and my mind flashes to the sea lion show at the San Diego Zoo. Even the ever-changing, one-on-one aides seem to work with the children on rote, repetitive tasks only to accumulate data, and to swiftly punish failure. I feel like I'm on a planet in a distant galaxy. Yet, I am told, spots at Marshall Institute are in demand and—lucky for Peyton—there is one opening for the summer program, which will guarantee her a slot for the fall.

There are no more forks in the road as the San Diego Unified School District ejects Peyton from its programs. Years too late, I will learn that in 1985 the district did indeed hire aides to support some children. Years too late, I will realize that these private "schools" are actually institutions—big boxes that for seven hours a day lock children in and parents out.

I daily went not to school, but to various institutions, defined by me as any place that all people are not included and therefore denied living the wonders of God.

I never joy thinking that separate could ever be equal.
Never interpret equal as the same gets everyone,
but that everyone gets what they need.
God each time wanted that in the very making each person
different. Emancipate the culture by freeing all people to the joys
of knowing and supporting each other and learning together from
and with each other the great lessons of life.
Do radical things to change education because each
day you and I dillydally, kids suffer and the world fills
without love and looks angry.

When Peyton enters Marshall Institute for summer school, Dr. Woodward assigns her to the highest functioning of four groups. I insist that a district speech pathologist be allowed in the classroom weekly for the first few months to aid in her transition and to supply them with methods and materials that have been successful for Peyton in the past. But after two months, the therapist reports that teachers at Marshall do not want her advice, refusing it as if they do not understand her purpose there. Peyton's longtime occupational therapist, Lauren Hart, is not even allowed inside to work with Peyton or to consult with their OTs; they have their own techniques, she is told. At the end of just six weeks at Marshall, Peyton is moved to the second-lowest-functioning group.

October 22, 1985

Dear Dr. Lennie:

I have worked with Peyton Goddard in occupational therapy sessions since October 1982. I have watched her grow and change, learn and refine many skills.

When working this week with Peyton, I noted many large and rapid mood swings within a very short time: agitation, rapid speech perseverating on a few sentences, giggling alternating with real tears and real sorrow, key phrases of discipline repeated to herself as if to pull herself together, increase in extraneous movements of tapping feet, hands, etc. Not any of these behaviors is new to Peyton. The intensity of the emotional/behavioral responses is what is different.

On November 6th there will be a meeting of the staff who work with Peyton and administrators who direct their programs. The purpose of the meeting will be to set goals for Peyton's educational program. The present staff are not yet familiar with Peyton's language and abilities, and her mood swings are interpreted as simple misbehavior.

If there is some biomedical basis for her behaviors, it would be helpful for all personnel at that meeting to understand some of the possible WHY's of the behavior. The QUALITY of an adult's voice and gestures can be very different when the adult understands Peyton.

Sincerely,
Lauren Hart, MHS, OTR

Though a one-on-one aide could have facilitated Peyton's successful participation in a district classroom (as I had been doing in Sonja's class), the private institution provides aides who often stand in for certified teachers. Peyton and other children spend most of their days with various, varying aides who work with them on behavior modification, not successful participation in group activities, since there are very few of these. Usually, these aides are the ones who deliver the program to Peyton, not the "teacher," who is most often working on a temporary credential, allowing aides to teach while completing their studies. Most of them will move on to district jobs where the pay is higher once they have finished their credentialing.

When I question the school about Peyton's group having a certified teacher, they tell me that on paper, they have assigned the headmaster to lead that group, though he spends perhaps only fifteen minutes with Peyton per day. I am gradually filling up with hopelessness; however, I do not recognize that if I am despairing, Peyton certainly is too.

My freedoms were torn hurtfully great from me and suddenly ill I became in the multiple confines that the educators put me into.
For me, the confines involved emotional, physical,
and intellectual enslavement.
I did not have an adequate system of communication, and there was no accommodation of my unique learning styles.
Support combined a roller-coaster ride and a guessing game, without success. In my silence, ongoing and intensifying trauma paralyzed me and fear constantly plagued me.
Ultimately, I lived in insanity.

It is October 1985, and Pat has borrowed a video camera to film Peyton doing "homework," sharing a learning activity with me and then with him. The antique double-seat school desk I found in an Adams Avenue collectibles shop is perfect for our learning sessions. Today, like most days after dinner, while Patrick is working on his high school homework, Peyton and I slide into the sturdy desk and settle into our favorite time of day. The chores are over, including the twenty-minute commute to and from Peyton's school in Parkview, an after-school stop for speech therapy at Children's Hospital, and then an appointment with pediatric endocrinologist Dr. Lennie, to check on the results of last week's blood work.

Already in her flannel nightie, Peyton has asked several times, "Can we do homework now?" Pat has set up the borrowed video camera to film tonight's homework session because the same ten-year-old that runs enthusiastically to get the Edmark Reading Program box (or another of the hundred educational games that showcase her amazing visual strength) is called noncompliant by her various aides and "teachers" at Marshall.

Peyton works for forty minutes with paper strips of phrases and sentences that she excitedly matches with pictures, and sight words she points to and reads out loud. She is in charge, though I support her by asking, "What's next?" or "Take just one card at a time, please." She never leaves the desk, but when necessary I refocus her gently on the task so that her hands, which Peyton cannot seem to inhibit, do not interrupt the rhythm of the action. Here, in the dance, she is full of life with the beautiful interchange of volleying, rhythmic speech sweetly shared between mother and daughter. These great connections flow over into our non-desk time, like when we shop for outfits with Gam at the Broadway Department Store, or when she sits in the chair at Tami's Hair Salon (with lots of support and encouragement) for a perm that highlights her pretty princess face.

Yes, there are challenges I cannot deny, like when Peyton gets stuck repeating phrases or picks up the whole stack of cards instead of just one: "Where's the horse? Where's the horse? Where's the horse? Here's the horse. Here's the big one. I find the girl. This one's the girl," she says spreading the cards helter-skelter all over the slanted pine desk.

I refocus her, saying softly: "I know you're looking for a particular one in the pile. I think it's better if you just draw one," and Peyton puts the cards back and takes the top one.

"Let me see . . . This one goes here. Yes, the big yellow airplane goes here," says Peyton as she turns to receive my confirmation, though she knows she is correct.

"Why didn't you put that one over here?" I ask.

Peyton looks at me with engaging affect, shrugging her shoulders as she raises her palms and says charmingly, "Because . . . it doesn't go there."

"It doesn't go there? Why? What kind of horse is this?" I continue, smiling.

Peyton replies immediately, "A little horse."

I realize that Peyton's speech is intelligible only to her family and a few professionals who are familiar with her. And yes, I sometimes repeat Peyton's words to cue her to move to the next phrase:

Peyton: A girl.

Dianne: A girl . . . what's the verb? A girl . . .

Peyton: . . . is with . . .

Dianne: . . . is with . . .

Peyton: . . . a boy.

Dianne: A boy . . . what's the preposition?

Peyton: In.

Dianne: In what?

Peyton: . . . yellow.

Dianne: Yellow. Let's start again on this phrase, from the beginning.

Peyton: A girl . . . is with a boy . . . in yellow.

Dianne: Wow, that was a long sentence!

Yes, she is about to turn eleven, and her reading was last assessed at a beginning-second-grade level, but her verbal inflections are as delightful as the way she raises her eyebrows when she smiles and laughs with a joy I feel comes from her mind working productively.

Tomorrow I will take the video to show Dr. Woodward how much Peyton loves to learn—how well she does with support and encouragement. After several months of hearing "Peyton continues to be noncompliant," I will furnish them with a complete set of the Edmark Reading Program, the one Peyton was successful with in the district programs. I will take these and many other learning tools to help them help Peyton, praying they might explore alternatives to their one, inflexible approach, stern and rigid in its demands to sit still, with quiet hands, before they offer a girl who is hungry to be taught, hungry to please, the opportunity to learn. I'm beginning to think that they are the noncompliant ones.

⤬

The only saving grace in her first months at Marshall is her speech therapist, Sharon Singh, who in her first assessment of Peyton noted, "I never saw a child who could sense how another person felt about her as quickly and correctly as Peyton." Sharon tells me about a session she witnessed in spring of 1986, with Dr. Woodward "teaching" Peyton. He has been working with her using his strict behavioral approach and having no success.

"Her noncompliance is exasperating," Dr. Woodward tells Sharon as they bring Peyton into a room with a table and two chairs sitting across from each other, like an interrogation room. Dr. Woodward sits Peyton down, places a pencil on the table, and then commands her, "Pick up the pencil."

Peyton sits frozen.

"Pick up the pencil. Pick up the pencil. Pick. Up. The. Pencil."

No response. Recording the number of failed responses on a clipboard, he looks up at Sharon. "You see what I mean?"

Sharon sits down across from Peyton and takes a notepad out of her bag. Placing it on the table, she asks Peyton gently, "Please pick up the pencil, Peyton, and add something you think I need on this paper." Peyton picks up the pencil and begins doodling. Sharon turns to a speechless Dr. Woodward and inquires, "Which way would you prefer to be asked?"

SPEECH AND LANGUAGE REPORT
SCHOOL YEAR 1985–1986
JULY 31, 1986
MARSHALL INSTITUTE

Careful planning in academic assignments and speech and language tasks is necessary to prevent a cycle of reluctance. Often a goal must be slightly adjusted or a request rephrased in order for Peyton to comply. If the instructor is insistent, the result can be greatly out of proportion to the issue. To further complicate the problem, Peyton appears to anticipate the same power struggle for days afterward. She does not appear to be the type of student who chooses to be disruptive, but rather does not have the mechanism which allows her to learn alternatives.

—Sharon Singh, Speech Therapist

Ignoring advice and evidence from me and Sharon, the school's response is as inflexible as its methodology: Do it our way, Peyton, regardless of our not supporting your movement challenges (which we don't even care to understand), or it's the time-out room. And when you can't do it our way, we will not wonder if the video we haven't watched might hold a better approach. We will break you in order to control you. We measure only what we think is important here. We measure deficits. We chart each time you are asked to sit down and you do not. But we do not measure your sitting down when we facilitate your wandering body to come to a desk that holds things of interest to you because, bottom line, we do not believe you can learn. After all, this is only an "institute." We don't even dare to call this a school.

The never successful strategy of control is why these behavioral control placements failed to support me.

If the necessary accommodation for the success of my purposeful
movement is not supplied, then the hulk of my life is insanity
because you, the educator, and
I, the student, cannot coexist in peace.
You become the care-less oppressor daring to try constantly the
ploy of controlling my behavior.
I become the oppressed, even though I am neurologically unable to
dependably move in complying ways to your exploiting directives.
Ill we both become because you become oppressed also by the
never successful strategy of control.
Looking at climbing this hill we should not be.
Your being able to hear what I say is what eventually frees the
fullness of a life I gut-wrenchingly desire.

I am finally forced to give in to the school's verdict about Peyton when I am matter-of-factly informed by the district psychologist for private placement of a startling discovery: Janice Chang made an error in scoring the Columbia IQ test administered to Peyton five years earlier, and therefore her IQ score has been lowered from 96 to 59:

An error was made in computation . . . Mental retardation is in the
moderate to severe range, with deficits in adapting to the demands
and explorations of society evidenced by severe difficulty learning,
problem solving, adapting to new situations and abstract thinking,
with unknown etiology. Peyton is capable of developing self-help skills
but will always require complete supervision.

In a sloppily scribbled note on the bottom of her handwritten report—an edict allowing no debate—almost 40 precious IQ points are abruptly swept away. I am stunned by the message, and the unprofessionalism of the messenger.

I call for an appointment with her supervisor, Robert Plath.

"How can this be? How can one lose forty IQ points?" I demand of him, quoting Chang's evaluation summary ("She demonstrates age-level abstract reasoning ability . . ."). "Chang was a seasoned psychologist, not a neophyte easily fooled by a seven-year-old!"

"I stand behind the rescoring," he declares.

The unequivocal declaration that my daughter is severely mentally retarded stops me in my tracks. This news, coupled with the bonfire of baffling behaviors exploding like a nonstop fireworks production and the impenetrable inflexibility of the institution, brings me to my knees. I give up by giving in, and begin to accept that the brightness I once saw in Peyton has since burned out.

Years I'm tested, therapied, dataed in IEPs, evaluations educators
and doctors millions, determinators depth dares pity.
Labels layer on.
I'm nothing jolly. I taste the ugly news I'm x, I'm y, I'm z.

I cannot hide my agonizing grief from my mother. I know she shares it. She knows what our lives are like because she comes to help every moment she can. My mother worries about the disintegration of Peyton and of me. She loves us in ways she reserves only for us. And I love her right back. I do not allow myself to break down often, and, then, only in front of my mother.

On the day that I learn of the miscalculated IQ, I pick up Peyton from school, give her a bath, and lay her on the bed, chewing on a washcloth. I hear my mother come in, and as she walks toward me, the floodgates open. We stand in the middle of the room, holding each other up as I tell her. I accept the verdict imposed—that Peyton is severely retarded. I can battle it no longer.

"Cry—it will be good for you," says Gam in her soft, Southern tone, and I do, till the well of tears finally dries up. My mother looks at me, and, to comfort me, says, "They say retarded people don't suffer as much because they don't know."

Peyton lies just one room away.

Bitten by the beast of separation, resolved I became
to never being included in the real world.
My yells for a just peace wallowed.
Segregation denied me reaping a potent education.
Accommodations and true support were absent.
Segregation denied me desired friendships.
Each day I typically wished a death to the relegated existence in
which a culture fearing differences re-proposed day by
verified day to tepidly control me.
Joy was a word lost. Hope I filed as a barren cause.
Wisps of doubt things would ever change
were quoted in my teasing life.

Peyton remains in the second-lowest group at Marshall for four years, with children increasingly younger than herself (while others move on) and nearly fifteen changes in teachers (most without valid certification). As she disintegrates until she is barely recognizable to anyone who knew her before the age of ten, we continue to ask *Why? Why?* of every professional we meet. The more restrictive special education becomes, the more "special" restricted Peyton becomes.

I know intelligence in my somewhat differently operating brain; you
presently are verifying by the daffy ways I move that I am an idiot.
Therefore, opportunities for learning and living
I am not allowed, and wasting I am.

*Please kill my movement insanity with the quest of your touch,
allowing the tilting of my brain compartment so that my moments
turn jolly as I mull plotting golden dependable movement mopping
my brain, and mull never the insanity of motor madness again.
It's your move.*

Compounding Peyton's growing medical and emotional challenges, increasingly unbearable bouts of insomnia begin to assault Peyton, which take their toll on the entire family, especially me. Pat is out of town during the week at least half of each month, and needs sleep to stay strong at the office when he is in town. So Peyton and I become roommates during these episodes, and in between flare-ups I sleep in our room next door, separated only by a bathroom. The three rooms are cordoned off from the rest of the house by a door we installed with a keyed dead-bolt lock to assure that when each new episode announces itself in the middle of the night, Peyton will eventually make her way to our room. A number of times, I awaken to find Peyton in various startling conditions that I cannot bring myself to speak about with the doctors, even our lead physician, Dr. Tabler, a pediatric neurologist at Children's Hospital who oversees Peyton's care. How we are sleeping is always his first question at appointments, since he knows how crucial it is in order for families to cope.

We first seek his help to address the changes in Peyton—attention shifts and regressions in functioning (especially incontinence), speech concerns, nervous anxiety, and this sleep disorder. He starts her on a trial with Ritalin to help with her hyperactivity (or is it hysteria?), but this only brings an increase in driven, repetitive verbalizations as well as increased insomnia.

One Monday in June of 1987, following a weekend of two evening galas during which Connie cared for Peyton, the situation suddenly becomes dire. When I try to move Peyton through her morning routine, I notice her stumbling down the hall, bumping into the walls. I catch her and move her to the bed. "I think something is wrong with Peyton," I tell Pat, who is preparing to leave.

Perhaps I have said this too often because Pat, kissing us both, simply replies, "Let me know," and leaves for the office, thirty minutes away.

I sit with Peyton on the bed, trying to get her to respond. Could it be the Ritalin? She opens her eyes. "What is your name?" I shout in a panic.

"Peyton," she replies lightly. I throw on my clothes from yesterday, ask Peyton her name again, pick up the phone, and leave a message at the Chart House office for Pat to meet us at Children's Hospital.

Supporting Peyton from behind, I slowly transport her to the backseat of the car, lay her down, and begin the equivalent of Mr. Toad's wild ride in our white Volvo wagon. I get to the last stoplight before reaching the freeway, trying to rouse Peyton with questions, listening to hear if she can answer. I have a choice here: turn right and go to Cabrillo Hospital a mile away, or get onto the freeway and make the ten-minute drive to Dr. Tabler at Children's Hospital.

Peyton's responses become fewer. Seeing a police car in the rearview mirror, I wave both arms frantically out the window to get his attention. I fumble to switch on my hazard lights, blow my horn repeatedly, and turn left to pull off the busy road. Fortunately, the police car follows and the officer calls firefighters and an ambulance. The firefighters check Peyton's vital signs and tell me to follow them in my car.

Pat is at the hospital when we arrive, along with Dr. Tabler, who orders Peyton to be hooked up to an EEG. I lean forward to try and catch a phrase Peyton is mumbling. But within a minute of the last electrode being secured, Peyton's right hand begins twitching, progressing to her right arm jerking, right cheek twitching, and right eye deviating. Then her right leg begins jerking as if struck by lightning. Dr. Tabler orders the IV inserted in her left arm for Lorazepam to begin as the lightning strikes the left leg, moving up her body. A full generalized seizure electrifies Peyton—her body in full gyration—each convulsion convulsing Pat and me as well.

The Lorazepam leaks into her; they give more, and it begins to quiet the electric storm in Peyton as they work frantically. From the EEG, they know the seizure originated in the speech and language part of her brain.

"Will she be okay?" I sob as they confirm that she has been stabilized. *What will* okay *look like,* I wonder.

Peyton is in the hospital for a week with Pat or me at her side every moment. Medication becomes a permanent part of Peyton's cellular being from that day forward, that memorable day when we were all seized by Mr. Toad to ride endlessly, wildly, through this life, leaving no one ever the same.

We actually welcome Dr. Tabler's diagnosis of epileptic aphasia since it is treatable. His report also states that Peyton exhibits "autistic-like behavior," rather than describing her as *trainable mentally retarded,* which is the label the district had given her. Peyton was far too friendly and visually engaging in her earlier years to be thought of as autistic, and it was thought that a child could not "get" autism at age twelve.

We begin the regimen of various antiseizure, mood-stabilizing, and antianxiety drugs, but they don't work. Tests are ordered: MRIs, EEGs, CAT and PET scans, tests for regressive genetic disorders, and numerous blood tests to help determine the next step, especially during the growing onslaught of insomnia (weeks at a time of barely any sleep), followed by several months of an almost catatonic state, with Peyton sleeping seventeen hours a day.

⟨≈⟩

It's December 26, 1987. With Peyton's one friend Hollyn out of town skiing, it is Gam and Pops, Patrick Jr., and Aunt Bette who join me, Peyton, and Pat for cake to celebrate Peyton's thirteenth birthday. I wonder if Peyton even knows what day it is. I remember her as a small child loving Christmas and her birthday, smiling, opening presents, stuffing cake in her mouth, frosting everywhere. Today, she lies on the couch as she did yesterday and will tomorrow, chewing on a rag. I say again and again, "Peyton is not herself." Her only motion is twisting the rag, sopping wet, in her mouth until she darts up and wanders about in a driven fashion, picking up any object (there are few left out by this point), tearing it, biting it, sometimes throwing it.

She moves from lethargy to jumping jacks, arms flailing with no regard to anything in the way of her frenzied limbs. She is no longer interested in things she used to enjoy. Puzzles are now just pieces to chew on and books are only pages to tear. No more homeworking together; no more sharing sweet moments—and how I *miss* them. These days, I do things *to* her, no longer *with* her. I feed her, bathroom her, clean her, medicate her, move her, clear impending dangers away from her. Soon I make another appointment, this time with a psychologist. Three days later, Dr. Slayter calls it *neurological depression.*

I inform Dr. Tabler of every new, challenging, bizarre behavior, which I log diligently in notebooks, including:

March 1988:

- teeth grinding loud enough to be heard two rooms away;
- fingers/hand in mouth constantly;
- eating non-food items she seems to search out on floors;
- alarming loss of bladder and bowel control, and seeming unawareness of the mess to be cleaned up, night and day;
- pushing and hitting that steadily increases in aggressive-ness as her size and strength grow; and
- her curious drinking of swimming-pool water.

{PERSONAL JOURNAL: JULY 1988}

Sleepy, lethargic, begs to go to bed, no stamina, spacey, out of it, headache, stomachache, no appetite, can't stay in school all day, no written work, squints, turns away, drinking few liquids (I squirt cartons of juice in her mouth), wetting and unaware of it, giggling intermittently—sleeping fifteen to seventeen hours a day, hard to awaken—staring, especially at reflections, startles easily.

When awake, cannot occupy her own time, wanders from room to room, but used to entertain herself with games, toys, dolls, puzzles. Home used to be haven, comfortable here. NO TALKING. Destructive, folding puzzle pieces, tearing out book pages, hurting self, like pulling bracelet off, drinking water out of flower vase. Aggression, touching to communicate, sometimes hurting others. Sleeping has more body jerks. Rises only to occasional activities with friends like dinner, swimming.

Is this depression? What about medicine, dosage-related? Is this antisocial personality disorder, schizophrenic, psychiatric disorder? Is this transient or mood-related psychiatric illness? What about lithium?

When life clips your hopes another, another, another, and another yet time, you despair and depression pollutes your never hoping mind, searching for glimmers of data that journey polluted will change. Daggers of torn hopes list long.

Outings for Peyton and me are next to impossible; only Pat, graced with a bravery I can no longer muster, is able to share constructive time with Peyton, and this is getting increasingly difficult. I marvel at him as he suits her up for an occasional four-mile bike ride around Shelter Island. Riding by her side, his right hand on her shoulder, he has to keep up and keep her safe as she takes off like a bat out of hell. Long after they turn the corner away from my view, I can hear her hollow, psychotic giggling, and for the next forty minutes I am frozen in prayer. If I hear a siren or if they are gone longer than fifty minutes, I jump in the car and search for them, trying to stay out of their sight.

Sometimes when Peyton has tired, she will abruptly dismount from her bike and abandon it in the street. I will find two bikes lying riderless, and Pat and Peyton lying nearby on the grass, looking up at the sky; or sometimes, Peyton, facedown, eating blades of grass she is pulling out of the ground cover. Then we load the bikes into the station wagon, Peyton into the car, and drive home. One time Pat reports that they were signaled by a police car to pull over, the screech of the siren causing Peyton to go ballistic. The policeman chastised them for riding side by side in the bike lane, treating Pat initially as a dirty old man with a much younger woman. He then proclaimed in front of a panicked Peyton, "If I ever see you riding this way again, I'm going to write you a ticket."

Pat continues to take her riding anyway. Strangely, I do not challenge Pat on the worth (or safety) of these dicey outings for Peyton. And I cannot deny pangs of jealousy when neighbors comment to me about how happy they are to see these rare glimpses of Peyton biking, laughing, and appearing joyous. I nod and say thanks.

Sorrow envelops me, yet my mind continues to work in overdrive. I am not able to turn it off and go to a peaceful place, let alone abandon myself to passion. In bed beside Pat, I embrace him and breathe deeply, attempting to be only in the moment. Trying to shift gears to ideas of intimacy, I recall earlier infinite hungers for union with this man I love immensely, with every part of me. But I feel myself losing my ultimate connection with Pat too, and romantic flights of fantasy do not entice me. I consult my gynecologist, who labels it as decreased libido. He prescribes testosterone injections, which I begin receiving, believing only a powerful chemical explosion will return sexual desire to my mind, which is crowded with concerns. I'm willing to live with the resulting hair loss, even though I consider my thick, brown hair my best physical attribute. But after six months, it is falling out in clumps, and I call the chemical experiment a failure. Fortunately the chemistry of Pat's hunger for me is at times enough to idle my burdensome brain, fueling the intimacy I used to love but have now forgotten how to remember.

⤶

During these years, I abandon my efforts to fix Peyton's differences, instead focusing simply on keeping her alive long enough to solve the mystery and reverse the free fall. Yet as I race to find a cure to save Peyton's life, I never consider what living is really like for my daughter. Because of behavior labeled as noncompliant, I am told that Peyton must be pulled out of her classroom at Marshall, to "work" in a tiny kitchenette. However, this is not very successful, they say, because Peyton will not comply by doing the worksheet with an aide but just sits, stuck to the floor, and does not get up.

I later learn that Peyton spends hours each day in this "time-out room," eating bits of trash she finds on the floor or exploding in wild bursts of movement—clapping, jumping, arms flying, and striking anyone who approaches in a threatening manner. With no activity to challenge her brain, she is left to simply listen to the activity outside her small, secluded area.

I do not fully comprehend the torment she suffers here until a year later in another movie theater, while watching *Awakenings.* In the film, Robin Williams, playing a neurologist, compares his catatonic patients to the caged panther in a poem by Rilke:

> *His vision, from the constantly passing bars,*
> *has grown so weary that it cannot hold*
> *anything else. It seems to him there are*
> *a thousand bars; and behind the bars, no world.*

The realization horrifies me, and I hear myself cry out, "Peyton!" in the silent theater, surprising even myself.

Concerned on many counts, I call a toxicologist in spring of 1989 to test the chemicals in the flooring at Marshall, thinking they might be responsible for my daughter's disintegration. With stealth, I assist Dr. Moreno of Environmental Consulting, Inc., to penetrate the guarded, prison-like school in an old house on F Street, which never allows unannounced visits from parents or private occupational therapists such as Lauren Hart. Though I have left a message that we will be coming one afternoon to visit, an aide is clearly surprised when we enter through a side door near the end of the school day. I inform her that we are expected, and the aide complies by leading us through another door to the hovel-like room where Peyton has been placed for several weeks.

Dr. Moreno collects samples and takes photos, while I witness my daughter sitting on the shattered, ancient linoleum, picking up dirt and broken bits of flooring, putting them into her drooling mouth and eating them. All Peyton's attention is focused on finding the next piece. She is a prisoner in solitary confinement.

Code Red! flashes through me as I reach out to take hold of Peyton's hands and lift her now-skinny, almost anorexic body up, scooping a piece of flooring out of her mouth with my own finger.

My behaviors are incomprehensible to a true person.
But torture makes true persons into pitiers pointed to wasted lives.
Pitied persons understand it is feeling like shit guttered that
makes you nothing care to averaged be.
It makes you want to die.

Another concerned aide opens the door to see what we are doing, and I chat with her, hoping Dr. Moreno can finish his work as I slowly pack Peyton up to leave the premises. Clearly, Dr. Woodward did not get the message about my intended visit. He will tomorrow when I remove Peyton permanently from their grip. Dr. Moreno's report reveals asbestos in the flooring. Once informed of this, the school quickly commissions its own study, which finds "No asbestos present in the material" using a method of analysis "acceptable to the EPA." To me, it doesn't matter what the report says. After coming face-to-face with my daughter's life at that place, I know Peyton must never return.

Each radically, righteously, eagerly lost day touches opposition,
towing your soul pleasurably toward plotting death.
It becomes the only joy easily tugging on your liking-not life.
Then, when I looked around and found no one there to help tilt me
away from suicide or help me commit the meant act, I feared I was
forever doomed to pain and suffering.

Pat and I know the only option for Peyton will be Hudson Academy, the district's most restrictive environment before residential placement. We do not pretend it will be better, only different.

Since a pool seems to be the only place where Peyton smiles and giggles, we have one built in our backyard because Peyton cannot manage herself among other children these days, approaching, bothering, pushing them in what seem like attempts to interact. And her loss of bowel control banishes her from pools other than our own.

Yet in the hours following what appears to be enjoyable pool play, Peyton's bladder empties like an erratic faucet. Timed trips to the bathroom do not work because, once there, Peyton cannot initiate emptying her bladder, so within minutes of leaving a long, fruitless stay on the toilet (insisted on by me), she releases a flood forced by drinking what we calculate as several gallons of pool water each time she swims. We spend up to three hours a day in the bathroom, hoping to avoid the ever-increasing bowel and bladder accidents as laundry piles up.

The big brass bed, with its frilly pillows, fluffy comforter, sheets, and absorbent mattress pad, becomes a source of continuous loads of laundry—never-ending, never over, until its floral pattern fades and it appears to me a white elephant we will never be able to keep clean and dry. I come to dread the sight of what had once brought me such hope and delight. It is more than just the dread of laundry and insomnia it has come to represent. I do not know what it is, exactly, but it has to go, replaced swiftly by two barren twin beds.

⊱

This year, 1989, marks Pat's tenure as commodore of the San Diego Yacht Club at a critical period in the club's history. Though yachtsman Dennis Conner and the San Diego Yacht Club had just reclaimed the America's Cup from Australia in 1987, New Zealand announced a surprise challenge, trumping San Diego's opportunity to set the terms for the next race and forcing them to race again in 1988. New Zealand's rogue challenge, using an enormous 133-foot sloop they had already started building, gave San Diego little time to create and compete with a similar yacht.

In an innovative response, Dennis and the San Diego Yacht Club chose to defend with a catamaran. Dennis won, but New Zealand yachtsman Michael Fay took San Diego Yacht Club to court, claiming that the catamaran was an illegal vessel, and the Cup was placed in a vault in New York pending the outcome. San Diego had defended the Cup on the water; now it must defend it in the courts, in what has become the most contentious Cup match ever. It is estimated that millions of dollars in expected revenue are at risk for San Diego businesses if they are stripped of the right to host the next Cup races. But even more important is the integrity of the club. These are the challenges Pat has inherited as the new commodore.

After two initial court rulings validating the legality of the catamaran, Justice Carmen Ciparick of the New York State Supreme Court rules in favor of New Zealand in March 1989, declaring that the Cup must be forfeited. America's Cup news makes international headlines, putting Pat on nightly news channels throughout the world. "We strongly feel that the court should not have the right to overturn the results of a sporting event seven months after it is over," he announces at a press conference. "It is incomprehensible to us that a court would order the America's Cup be sent to a yacht club that has never won an America's Cup match. We believe that yacht races should be decided on the water." As San Diego appeals the decision and continues the legal battle for the Cup, Pat guides his proud membership through rough waters.

I join in when I can, and must, often throwing on an outfit, donning lipstick and headband en route as I sprint last-minute down the bayside path past the thirteen homes that lie between ours and the club to join him in a commitment. I realize one day how close to the edge I am, as I say good-bye to the ambassador from New Zealand with whom Pat and I have just had lunch. The ambassador and I chat alone in the historic hallway, lined with teak and glass cabinets that contain hundreds of sterling-silver trophies. We shake hands, and he turns to exit for his flight.

At that very moment, my floral wraparound skirt slides off me, landing in a puddle at my feet. My hastily tied knot must not have been nautically secured. I hoist it up, loop a definite square knot, and pray there were no witnesses—only the catering manager, thank goodness, a woman who flashes me an understanding smile. I tell myself I must make more time for this important year, but I don't know how, as I scurry to our home at the water's edge, to Peyton and Gam, watching our cove from our bright bay window. I admire Pat's mastery of both worlds as he leads wisely, staying in that world only the amount of time necessary, then returning home as fast as he can to help.

Our son Patrick graduates in June (yet another family event Peyton is unable to attend), and he'll be off to Boston College in August, on his own journey. I will miss him, and guess that Peyton will too. He lovingly wrote about her in his college application essay:

She is a prisoner, locked in her lonely world. Only those of us who know her can see beyond her disorders and definitions to see a being void of maliciousness, a being untouched by Pandora's evils, a being capable of trust and love only in the purest sense.

I cry at Patrick's good-bye, but not as many tears as I would if he were not moving on. Perhaps leaving home will be a relief for him, though this is an openhearted conversation I seem incapable of initiating. I am thankful Pat can.

⤴

In January 1990, several months after Peyton began at Hudson, I am called to pick her up early. I arrive at the school to find my daughter puffy-faced, sitting on a chair in the office. It seems that on a rare field trip to the local 7-Eleven, Peyton was placed in a car beside a boy known to be aggressive while the two aides sat up front. He hit Peyton several times in the face before the driver could pull over and ply him off.

"Why were the two adults sitting up front?" I ask incredulously, wondering if Peyton's nose is broken. I take Peyton home and write my strongest possible "Please do not allow this to happen again" letter to the school administrators, but sadly, I lack the courage to say what I really want to: "One more incompetency on your part, and we're out of here."

Or perhaps I dislike their predictable response, "Okay, goodbye . . . good luck . . . and, by the way, if you didn't like it here, you'll really dislike the next stop."

> *Coolly either I would learn joy of heaven or plot life of hell.*
> *Killing oneself is to plot killing those who love one in life.*
> *I did not decide to give up all hope for joy till I was again molested,*
> *this time by a school staff person who told me that*
> *he would kill my family if I told the truth.*
> *Oppose I the killing of my family, care I so much for them that I*
> *again decided not to look for death.*

After seven months at Hudson Academy, Peyton's fragmentation is nearly complete. Her five-foot-eight-inch frame is down to ninety-three pounds, and she has no appetite. Daily our thirty-minute drive east to Hudson Academy feels to me like the four-and-a-half-hour drive to Lompoc Federal Prison. I pull up behind the buses and wait outside the fully fenced property until a monitor opens Peyton's car door and pulls her out. Tightly entwining the fingers of her right hand with Peyton's and encircling her left arm around Peyton's waist, the monitor moves Peyton through the gate.

I watch Peyton disappear behind the chain-link fence and turn away; it is too painful to visit her there. Here, like Lompoc, there is no open-door policy. But increasingly, I understand why institutions, nursing homes, and "special schools" like this have few visitors. You drop off your loved one and pretend it's better for them there. I have finally resigned myself to what had been unthinkable before. I see myself in disturbing dreams lifting Peyton's limp body and handing her off to the institutional developmental center, knowing they have control over her. The only way I can continue is to turn away. I handle what is left of Peyton's physical presence when I pick her up after school, but I have lost sight of Peyton's struggling spirit. As Peyton appears to lose physical functioning, I try to reassure myself that she probably cannot feel emotions anymore.

I will learn only at review meetings that after Peyton fades from my view through the guard gate at school, the monitor tries to keep her body moving across the blacktop toward her portable classroom, but midway Peyton drops to the ground—a "sit-out," they call it. Rather than help her up, the monitor simply repeats, "Stand up. Stand up. Stand up . . . ," and records the amount of time Peyton sits. Daily counts are reported to be up to forty-six minutes until urine puddles under her saturated Depends necessitate that they *cease* their commands and *desist* their timings and *assist* her to get her up and move on . . . but, to what? More of that wasteful nothingness that enlightened educators aptly label "dead time," since it is devoid of teaching and learning.

Only once—when I come to pick Peyton up for an unexpected appointment—do I see her classroom, a portable bungalow all the way across the blacktop from the main building. I pass the new jungle gym just donated to the school by Thursday Club Juniors of San Diego, following my pitch to them about the school's need for one (though I long ago tendered my resignation from all organizations, including this one). It sits gleaming in its primary colors, but no students hang from its bars or fly down its wavy slide.

I open the door of the classroom, dark and smelling of bodily fluids—yet the room is empty. I search in the cubbies near the door for Peyton's lunchbox. Grabbing it, I turn to leave so I can go and find Peyton, but stop suddenly, frozen. As a teacher, I have substituted in many classrooms before, and this huge wooden box I see in front of me is not standard equipment. The box has a door, which is closed, and a peek window level with my questioning eyes. Still frozen in fear of allowing my brain to contemplate the unthinkable, I do not approach it to look inside. As my eyes move to the exit's promise of the open, blue sky, I notice the latch on the big box's door, and I rush out to locate Peyton.

On my way, I witness some personnel at the school carrying a spray bottle. Recently we have noticed how nervous Peyton acts around spray bottles of any kind, in our home or wherever she encounters them. She grabs them and squirts them furiously, giggling nervously. I struggle not to make the obvious connections in my mind as I buckle Peyton into her seat.

⮞

Intensifying my anxiety about Hudson is the fact that for nearly the entire school year, Peyton has had no certified teacher in her classroom. Her assigned teacher had major surgery in late September and never came back. We complain to the district for months about Peyton having no credentialed teacher, and even attempt to write that into Peyton's IEP; however, the district administrator for private placements, Robert Plath, tells us it cannot be written into the IEP since it is already the law. I have learned through experience that these private developmental centers operate outside of the law, a tragic fact of segregation. Those banished outside the "all" forfeit the rights of "all."

Pat and I convey our concern in a meeting with Frank Dalbo, school psychologist and second in command. Tall and thin, dressed in professorial tweed, Dr. Dalbo invites us into his office.

"Is it not the legal responsibility of Hudson Academy to have a credentialed teacher in the classroom?" says Pat, getting right to the point.

Dr. Dalbo strokes his beard and calmly replies, "We've had an ad running for months, but so far, no one who conforms to our philosophy has answered." He shifts in his chair as we press him.

"Peyton needs a strong, credentialed professional who will focus on communication—not just getting her to listen and obey, but to *talk*," insists Pat.

Dr. Dalbo straightens up, pulling off his wire-rimmed glasses.

"Look," he says, leaning forward, "if you insist on challenging us on this, you put all the children in Peyton's grouping at risk of losing their placement."

Pat, who has negotiated seventy-five leases for unique Chart Houses in his career, knows intimidation when he sees it. He leans toward Dr. Dalbo and calmly pronounces, "We are left with no choice. We will begin the legal process to release Peyton from Hudson Academy."

Six years later, we will learn that Dr. Dalbo has been incarcerated with multiple life sentences for molesting children and participating in a massive international child pornography ring, and that some of his victims were mentally impaired students.

ཨེ

To Pat and me, the unknown ahead is better than what we know of Hudson, so with Lauren Hart's help, in the spring of 1990, we draft a needs justification in the IEP to get Peyton released from Hudson Academy and transferred into a severely handicapped classroom on a public school campus. We are hopeful after hearing that the new head of Severely Handicapped Programs for the district, Dr. Eric Saunders, is supportive of inclusive education, believing that even students with significant disabilities should be supported to participate in general education classrooms with their peers. This time, we fight hard for the district's written commitment to provide a one-on-one aide to facilitate Peyton's success:

HUDSON ACADEMY
4-26-90 IEP

Peyton needs to be fully included in an age-appropriate, non-disabled educational setting (with peers who do not have disabilities) in her own neighborhood with ongoing, familiar support staff that ensures her learning, participation, and safety. She needs continuing opportunities for appropriate educational classes where she participates and learns and is able to make friendships. She needs a work setting that enables increasing familiarity with job tasks, coworkers, and physical environment, ensuring successful transition to stable, long-term employment and ongoing social relationships.

Queer is in all of us.
Fear it we do not need.
You and I are one in unity of creation.
Sadder we both are separated than togethered.
It is wepted ignorance of each other that will cheat us all.
In the awe of togethered lie golden poignant possibilities.

Another exit IEP is signed with sighs of relief in being released from Hudson, yet concerns continue to mount. Peyton has begun bolting, running away from Pat and me, sometimes out onto the busy street. We install keyed dead bolts on all exit doors and even on some internal doors, allowing us to block off areas of the house during the day and limit the aimless wandering that appears to torment her. We must now carry the keys (one for the internal doors, one for the exiting doors) with us at all times, because if any of the keys is left in a door, Peyton pulls it out and puts it in her mouth or loses it. (She does not have the motor ability to insert the key and unlock the door herself.) Our second line of defense is another dead bolt on the fence gate outside, which is particularly frustrating for Pat, who has locked few doors in his lifetime. When friends drop by, the simple act of entering the house resembles the penetration of Fort Knox.

I thought of many great cases of daggers for daring my death—
starvation, drowning, and repeated wail for eating disorder.
The sassy gut-wrenching eagerness of my sapping mother loomed
opposing my success.
One will never measure like her any other person;
she was sullen never and journeyed fearlessly
reaching to thwart my ploys.
She never rested.
My desire to die was jilted by her tirelessness at keeping me alive.

Undoubtedly, the most devastating symptom of Peyton's downfall is her steady decline to total cessation of speech, a skill hard fought for with years of therapy (two to four days a week, beginning at the age of two). Reports between 1982 and 1986 confirm that "At Peyton's highest level of functioning, she was able to verbally express her wants, needs, feelings—past and future." No longer able to communicate either verbally or nonverbally, Peyton's primary mode of expression is impulsive, self-motivated motor activity that appears to be self-stimulating. She is internally, not externally motivated. Her eyes read like gauges registering EMPTY. Is it that she *can't* or that she *won't* do things that are asked of her?

Every night, every scary, I-don't-understand-why-the-medicines-aren't-working night, I am more tired and desire less and less to go out anywhere. If Peyton sleeps, I want to sleep. I am rushing to find the answer, the cure, before I become unable to continue. Accommodations like locks and custom-made pj's (to help prevent her from smearing feces on herself at night) help us survive, but I always wonder, *What's next? How long can I keep up?*

And in the back of my mind there is always the sobering realization that what *I* do for Peyton would not be done anywhere else, and certainly not in institutions.

> *I lived, even though I eagerly cared quest of peace,*
> *coping with being told daily that I must live not die.*
> *Mulling this destiny forever was unbearable.*
> *I wanted help to die, but I only got help to live.*

Peyton is slip-sliding away, and Dr. Tabler's words ring repeatedly in my mind: "You know, I think that if this youngster were capable of doing away with her life, she would." All the years focused on finding and holding onto those elusive academic placements, trying to build bridges that caring teachers would cross to meet and welcome Peyton's progress, seem wasted. I know I'm losing Peyton. Is she dying? Does she want to go? These are questions I cannot allow myself to ponder. I cry at any sad story on TV or in print about a mother and child. Yet, so consumed am I with sustaining Peyton's life that I never allow myself to ponder, If Peyton is dying, how would she want to spend her last days?

I'm dead carried by pity readying eddies,
petty pimping pall bearers that I'm nothing to.
Errorers surround my hearse.

Chapter 6

SEEKING A SEAT AT THE TABLE

Each union utters pity. Red ants bite me.

Five years in the confines of private placements have yielded not one friendship for Peyton, and active Hollyn, also fifteen, has few moments to spare now except for a rare special event. Pat is Peyton's only companion, and, if that is how it is to be, he celebrates every minute of it, never begrudging stowing his well-used Eaton surfboard in the garage rafters. But beautiful as their friendship is, for whom is that enough? My mother's mantra to me was always "If you want a friend, be a friend," but I can't envision it working for now-mute, deeply depressed, barely functioning Peyton.

Desperately seeking a solution, I begin attending conferences on the inclusion of special-needs students in school and community life. Each conference usually contains a breakout session on the importance of friendship, based on research among non-labeled persons. I conclude that if "normal" people need friends, those who face challenges must need them even more. With no peer interaction, Peyton's sad Saturdays turn into morose Mondays amid nightmarish episodes of insomnia. Though she has essentially stopped talking, I do hear her utter one phrase repeatedly in the wee hours of the morning.

At 2:00 a.m., following totally mute days, I walk her to the dark bathroom to help her empty her bladder before I change the saturated Depends she now wears day and night. Standing in the pink glow of the nightlight, I hear Peyton ask again and again the same question: "Where are the kids? Where are the kids?" *They are gone from her waking life, but are they there in her dreams?* I wonder. And I feel the hopelessness of never knowing why my daughter says this—and only this—phrase.

You and I know that most opportunities for reaching one's potential do not occur in isolation or segregation, but through those golden opportunities for critical thinking afforded us by experiencing the reality of true life with its diverse people and circumstances.

In Peyton's bleakest years, we witness times when she rises to partake a bit in life, whenever a fleeting friendship briefly awakens her, so we begin to seek out opportunities for Peyton's inclusion in community activities.

Pat had been taking her down to the local soccer field to expend some of her fired-up, cannot-calm-my-body-down energy in hopes of helping her sleep at night. Then one night in the summer of 1990 he decides to call his friend Shannon, president of the Peninsula Soccer League, asking, "Would it be okay with the league if Peyton joins a team in a very limited fashion?" Shannon gets others' approval, and we sign Peyton up for a local soccer team, not expecting her to play, but simply to interact with the girls at practices and games.

There are a dozen girls, and only a few have played together before. We hope that these girls will provide some badly needed acceptance and friendship simply by saying "Hi, Peyton," or maybe "Good kick, Peyton," all angelic murmurings that Pat and

I long to hear. There is a trip to Sports Chalet for shoes, shin guards, and knee-high socks, and when uniforms are given out at the first practice, number eighteen is born. At the first game, she wears her uniform, watches, cheers (with Pat's encouragement), and works out with him on the sidelines. However, when none of the girls say, "Hi" or "Come sit with me" or "Let's kick the ball together," or even "Good-bye," parental discouragement sets in. *Is this just another way for Peyton to feel excluded?* we wonder. *Did we set her up for this?*

> *In me pity lowed I. Pity, sweet-never looks yell urges that ply real out of my sad breaking heart.*
> *Was I devil's child? Was I God's child with festers that important I'm not?*
> *I'm a nary-loved person with a pity heart. Aquaed by your hurts, you hurt I, but I yearn you would try not to break my heart.*
> *Pointed pity net pulls us all dauntingly down.*

The next game, scheduled for 8:00 a.m. Saturday, is preceded by several sleepless nights. As I scurry around, exhausted, trying to get Peyton ready for the pregame warm-up exercises, I can't help but mutter a few curse words before quickly catching myself.

Shame on you, Dianne, I think. *Is this really harder than doing nothing, being expected nowhere? Get a grip . . . and get your butt in gear.*

As Pat sits with Peyton on the sidelines, cheering the team, one mother asks, "Is she kind of like a mascot?" Pat dismisses the comment, but cannot dismiss the fact that the girls on the team still ignore Peyton as she and Pat continue their lone scrimmage. The girls' indifference is wearing thin, and he decides to say something about these egocentric teammates just as they all sit down to decide on the team name. Each girl has her own idea, and they argue back and forth while Peyton and Pat sit in the background, waiting for someone to break the stalemate.

After about ten minutes, one of the girls chimes in, "Hey, how about calling ourselves the Peytons? Peyton is such a special girl, and she's trying so hard to play. This could really inspire us to do our best." To our amazement, the consensus is unanimous, and each girl enthusiastically accepts the new team name. Pat is shaken by the realization of his own prejudgment—thinking these girls were apathetic rather than realizing that they simply did not know how to express their caring for Peyton. For the next two seasons, Peyton continues to participate in the Peninsula Soccer League, moving from being tolerated toward being welcomed with smiles, greetings, and opportunities to kick the ball around before the games.

Try to understand I'm destiny pity in each deck of cards you deal me.

This summer, sees Patrick Jr. getting ready for his second year at Boston College as Peyton prepares to reenter a San Diego Unified School District special day class, barely a shadow of the girl she was when she left.

And with predictable unpredictability, troublesome behaviors flare up. Calm and attentive Peyton can change in a millisecond to darting, grabbing, throwing, pushing Peyton—displaying constant movement but to nowhere in particular, and everywhere in general. Hysterical giggling (so close to crying yet absent the tears) erupts unexpectedly. And the periods of consecutive all-nighters surpass what any med student could possibly survive, I think. When San Diego Unified school psychologist Cindy Wright reviews Peyton for her IEP, she tells me, "I have rarely heard of such significant losses of functioning, especially speech, except in the case of abuse." I am shocked and, frankly, a little offended at her comment.

To prepare Peyton for her reentry into public school, we ask Lauren Hart to resume OT sessions with her, the most pressing concern being to redirect Peyton's incessant hand-to-mouth movement. Her fingers seem magnetically drawn to her mouth, and a constant stream of drool runs down her arm. Dusting off my collection of educational activities, I am pleased to find that Peyton is able to maintain focus when she is actively engaged; however, if we are interrupted or if I am distracted for just a few seconds, Peyton's hands go back in her mouth.

What can we do to eliminate this behavior in school? This is the final question in the *Jeopardy!* of reentry. I can think of no better, no other way, but to use arm splints to restrain the maddening movement. Specially designed, prescribed by Dr. Tabler, they are custom-made for Peyton by a medical device company. Plastic forms are molded to fit her arm and padded by foam cushions; these are then Velcroed around her forearm and upper arm, and a metal rod prohibits Peyton from bending her elbow more than 45 degrees. I justify this restraint by telling myself that Peyton is probably frustrated by her own hand-to-mouth movement and constantly hearing "Hands down" from me and Pat as we mop drool from the pages of her books, dry her chin, and then redirect her. I am so sure this restraint is necessary that even seeing Peyton struggling in vain to get her plastic water bottle up to her lips to quench the Lithium-driven thirst does not shake my resolve.

On the first day of school in the fall of 1990, I bring Peyton to Wingfield Middle School. Mr. Kotzer teaches the severely handicapped class, made up of ten students, in a portable classroom on the edge of the campus, which can be accessed without ever stepping on the grounds populated by the "regular" kids. I take

Peyton into the classroom where her one-on-one aide, Melissa, just hired last Friday, is waiting for her. Though Melissa has never received professional training, I believe she is made of good stuff. In an extra backpack I have brought some activities, along with the arm restraints, and explain to Melissa that the arm restraints are to be used only during interactive teaching opportunities when Peyton is engaged—but absolutely not during "dead time."

On the second day, Melissa meets me after school. "Could you please send more activities for Peyton?" she asks. This I do over the next two weeks, praying Melissa and Peyton can work together for more positive than negative minutes each day. What I come to learn is that Mr. Kotzer does not actually do any teaching activities with the students, leaving Melissa to support Peyton while the other students, when not working with an aide, spend most of the day in "dead time," sitting or roaming about the classroom. I am astonished to hear this—and even more stunned when I hear other teachers and even the school principal voice their respect for Mr. Kotzer. Then one day it all becomes clear when an admiring colleague finishes his sentence with ". . . after all, he spends the entire day with *those* children."

At the end of the second week, I ask Mr. Kotzer if he'd like a parent volunteer in the class. He seems excited about this, and each day I arrive with more of my stash of educational activities (I now own about three hundred of them). In the class, I work with Melissa and the other aides while Mr. Kotzer steps out for long periods of time, often pushing one of the students who uses a wheelchair on some errand. He seems happy that I am there, and I love spending time with the kids again after being banned from the classroom for five years. More important, I feel I must support Melissa so that Peyton does not fail simply because Mr. Kotzer is not doing his job. With positive learning occurring, I leave the restraints at home—for good. (Fifteen years later, in search of something else, I will discover them tucked high in a storage closet and, dropping to the floor, cry my eyes out.)

I sense that the district will do anything (even pay up to five times as much for private placement) rather than hire a one-on-one aide for a child to be supported at a public school. Though we fought hard for this needed support, the district will review the plan after six weeks of school to see if the aide's hours can be reduced. After several weeks of being in the classroom, I make an appointment with the resource team to tell them in advance that deleting the aide's hours will be impossible due to the lack of any planned activities in Mr. Kotzer's classroom. Surprisingly, they accept my conclusion without argument, admitting they know about Mr. Kotzer's deficits.

"But why is he allowed to keep his teaching position?" I demand incredulously.

"It is nearly impossible to get a teacher fired," is their sadly predictable response.

Relieved that there will be no challenge on the aide, back into the classroom I go, increasing to all day now. We offer Melissa a few extra dollars an hour out of our own pocket to encourage her to stay with Peyton. Melissa does not ask for this, but we are worried she might grow weary of the challenge, and we do not want Peyton going back to a restrictive private placement.

One day, she asks me, "Does Peyton understand consequences?" I know what she means because, while consequences are useful to most teachers, telling Peyton "If you do X then this punishment will occur" usually only results in Peyton doing more of X.

I think about this for a moment and reply, "I know the way Peyton acts often makes one doubtful that she understands, so I don't really have a way of proving she does. However, I feel she does understand but cannot always control herself. And sometimes I think she lives in fear of that."

Over the next few weeks, I notice administrative visits from various members of the resource team to the classroom. When Mr. Kotzer is there (generally sitting at his desk), he appears bothered and glares at me. Perhaps the fact that I hold a Lifetime California Teaching Credential prevents him from kicking me out of his classroom. However, this changes on Halloween when, dressed as a circus clown, I am greeted by two of the resource people.

"It seems that Mr. Kotzer no longer wants your help in his classroom," they say cautiously. However, it is clear to me that *they* are not asking me to leave.

"I will leave only when teaching is occurring full-time in this class," I reply.

They promise to deal with Mr. Kotzer, and I remain in the classroom. By now I am part of the team of aides that together cheerfully seek real educational opportunities for the students.

～

It's not quite *American Bandstand,* but every Friday after lunch, we turn on the music in the classroom, and all the students, aides, and peer tutors begin to dance. Any kind of dance step works—there are no judgments. The music seems to make frozen people come alive, like in the movie *Awakenings.* I can't resist moving to the rhythm and love being surrounded by other dancers who will never mock my moves. The peer tutors (student volunteers from the campus) are definitely the hippest of the bunch, but they still come excited to partner with the aides and students who call this annex (so far from the everyday life of the school) home. As usual, Mr. Kotzer is missing in action, but the party rages on without him. Peyton loves music and moves as if the rhythm fills a void in her. She has no inhibitions. Her step of choice is jumping, which she does with a rarely seen smile. We all love Friday afternoons, even the silent boy, Adam Lowe, though I have no real proof.

As always, he approaches no one, bothers no one. He watches, standing farthest away from the music in his standard pose: right arm tucked under his left elbow and left hand pointing skyward. One day in November Mr. Kotzer announces to me and the aides that Adam has a kidney disorder and his parents have chosen to forgo treatment.

That Friday afternoon, as always, the peer tutors burst in after lunch, turn on the music, and we all begin to come unglued in the best sense. I am well into my sashaying around to wiggle and giggle with all the active players. When I open my eyes after doubling over with laughter, I see Adam reaching out his arms to me. I take them and joyfully dance with him around the room. When the music ends, Adam moves back into position alongside the wall, left arm skyward.

On the last class day in December, we have a grand Christmas party, including a visit from the real Santa (Pat) and Santa's helper in magic-making (Patrick, home from his study abroad term in Oxford for the holidays). My eyes dampen as I see Patrick coax Adam from the wall to sit on Santa's lap.

Rather than waiting out the year with Mr. Kotzer, we decide to move Peyton to Balboa High School in January of 1991. By spring, we will get the news that Adam has passed away. A statue in the corner except for one blissful dance, he was allowed to die because treatment, which is standard for non-statues, was not given to him.

I ultimately have no Self except for what you think of I.
Eagerly I await your lifting of the veil.
It can only happen if you and I know wasted-not moments and
learn to understand and love each other.
Ultimately the veil will drop when you, like me, are looking through
eyes years rested on prejudice not, in God's hands equal and
fearless of the dashing hurdles that face us.

Hungry for more inclusive opportunities, we join a group recommended by a psychologist for "friendless people with significant handicaps." It meets Saturday mornings in a living-room-like office of a restored Victorian on Fourth Avenue. At a price of seventy-five dollars for each forty-five-minute session, a psychologist meets with parents for about ten minutes while two psychology students earning university credit oversee a group of six handicapped people with no ability to talk to one another (basically making sure they do not destroy the furniture).

To me, it is like a reenactment of the bar scene from *Star Wars* in its awkwardness. After the first ten minutes, we all trek outside and cross several intersections to the Balboa Park playground, much like a chain gang traverses to and from the job—together, but not interacting. The handicapped individuals then play on the playground (mostly filled by six-year-olds), appearing like giants invading Munchkinland. Walking back to the office, the parents make attempts to include their speechless child in the sparse chatter of the anything-but-gathered group. After three sessions, Pat declares enough—chance of future friendships nil here—and suggests that we create our own group.

You and I must realize there is joy in the opportunity for all kids to
greatly contribute to the necessary improvement of humanity by

participating and belonging and contributing and
having diverse friends.
This is the answer to their depression and despair and
trouble in our culture.

By this time, we know about three other teens with sad Saturdays. They too have IEPs; they too are segregated, but not in restrictive private placements; they too desire social contacts; and they are verbal. We ask our church about forming a club, and two women enthusiastically volunteer, one bringing another teen to the fun-loving group. We arrange outings, many at our home, for swimming, boat rides, or trips to SeaWorld. All of these activities are more fun for Peyton with friends, and we notice a few more smiles. Saturdays are beginning to be looked forward to. Several times Pastor Ken joins us, and I wonder what he must think, watching the smiling swimmers from his perch on our redwood deck.

With our growing understanding of inclusion, Pat and I suggest that our cheery club swap its separateness and join the real teen fellowship group at our church, with the support of the adults in our group, as a benefit to all. No, says the church leadership, and our meetings fizzle out.

Undaunted, Pat speaks with the head pastor, whom we also know socially. He consents to having Peyton join the teen fellowship group as long as we get an okay from Pastor Bill, who leads them. By now we have met with Dr. Caren Sax, a San Diego State University professor and education reformer who works with us to find inclusive opportunities for Peyton through a Department of Education–funded program called "Circle of Friends." She is the inflatable raft of wisdom into which we climb. She and her cohorts at Interwork Institute at San Diego State are like the Brookings

Institute on friendship, and they aid us in the journey toward social integration for Peyton. The ride takes the family through class-five white-water rapids, and one afternoon our inflatable raft enters the equivalent of the Grand Canyon's Lava Falls.

On an uncommonly humid August day in 1991, Pat, Caren, and I are right on time as we climb the stairs of the new two-story Brotherhood Building of our church. Pastor Bill's office is off the huge room that hops with activity every Sunday night. This is the largest youth congregation in the community, and the teen fellowship gatherings are a happening destination for many adolescents, no matter their church home, or lack of one. Pastor Bill knows us, and we introduce Caren as we fill the four chairs around the table in the center of his office. Bill is a perfect pastor—devout, well-groomed—and in a year he will be off to Yale to teach other students how to be perfect pastors. We share with him our desire for Peyton to join the teen fellowship group that will begin meeting after Labor Day, and Caren offers her unlimited support.

Then the river takes a sharp turn no one saw coming.

"It will be impossible for me to have Peyton come when fellowship starts in September," says Pastor Bill matter-of-factly. "I have only two or three Sundays to engage the regular kids and encourage their joining."

Pat and Caren continue conversing with Pastor Bill. Pat, in lease negotiations for Chart House, knows how to build bridges of diplomacy that span relationships more challenging than any Colorado rapids. He and Caren offer approaches to how Peyton could be supported in the group. Caren offers to come the first night and lead a fun and insightful activity—we're all unique, but we have many more similarities than differences. Pat will be there to support Peyton.

I do not talk as tears leak down my face, and I do not move to wipe them as I listen to the others talk. After a few minutes Pastor Bill, noticing me, reaches out his hand and lays it on my arm: "I see you are in pain. Can I help?"

You see others as valuable and Peyton as not, is what I do *not* say as I shake my head in reply to his perfectly ignorant attempt to comfort me.

After much negotiation, Pat and Peyton are allowed to attend fellowship on Sunday nights. Peyton seems to enjoy interacting with the few peers who care to try, but eventually the paid youth leaders (who never even attempt to facilitate Peyton's participation) say it will work better if Pat does not come. But he continues to attend with Peyton, staying in the far corner of the huge room till he sees Peyton left standing alone for some time, everyone avoiding her.

I go with Pat the following day to see the head pastor. Waiting outside the office and chatting with the secretary, I hear Pat say loudly, "Having Peyton be part of the church was an opportunity—for the church. And the church blew it!" I also hear Pat's exclamation mark as his hand hits the pastor's desktop, signaling our separation from the church. We learn several years later that while Pastor Bill is teaching at Yale, his sister has twin girls; both are born with an extra twenty-first chromosome.

> *Under stares deep in my soul, red rasty pouts gyred I.*
> *Reddest heart break was, I'm sweet nothing to God.*
> *This I got by I'm segregated from you reasoned I'm daring*
> *determined differences.*
> *This I saw as dates with you, I do not deserve. You rested sweet in*
> *His arms; I feared I nurtured never by Him.*
> *In pity, thoughts war to I'm numbered*
> *not a sweet child of the Creator.*

I'm greeted freak, pouted errored outed unity union universe.
It tried I. It years tortured I. Wedded to joy I was never.
There, rest was never possessable. Tired I'm.
Eases very beckoned rest freed I in gutter death.
Treed in pouts, I told Him tip
I tortured try to greet sweeted, squinted suicide.
There, rest would free fears, finally. There, red would be outed, I
thought. There, He would nurture freaky I.

❧

With Peyton back at public school and after our fragile attempts to create social opportunities for her, I initially felt she had met the goal of inclusion. At least Peyton now sees the "regular" kids on the school grounds and occasionally as volunteers in her classroom. And this seems to be making an impact on her. Almost immediately after reentering public school, we began to see smiles on her face that we have not seen in five years—finally a medicine we could embrace.

However, my understanding grows as I attend more conferences, where I meet pioneering university educators who teach special education to teachers seeking credentials. A few of them come into Peyton's life, like Gayle Cisneros and Linda Malone (her teachers at Balboa High) and Julianne Hartley (her aide). They all believe in change and in this way of being together called *inclusion*. Sitting in auditoriums and classrooms and listening to these reformers, I suck the nectar of their truths. And I sense, though no one asks for my assistance, that parental involvement could help to bring about further change. I begin by giving a few talks to parent groups and educators, mostly about lost smiles that have finally started to return. If this is our fruit of inclusion, it is already more than we hoped for.

⨂

Before Peyton moved to Balboa High, I visited Gayle and Linda's "severely handicapped" special day class and asked them, "Do you ever have any students who do not sit down?" because everyone there was sitting down, and they would be getting Peyton, who did not. They had no qualms about accepting Peyton, though I knew she would become their most challenging student.

To expand the inclusive opportunities for their students, these teachers have built alliances with well-chosen educators on the Balboa campus, asking, "Will you include one of our students? We will send her with support. We will do the lesson accommodations." A few say yes, and Peyton's whirling-dervish body in the special day class at 9:00 a.m. looks entirely different at 10:00 a.m. in the Earth Science class taught by Tom Simmons, where she is supported and able to participate with the help of her aide, Julianne. Linda tells me excitedly, "Come and see!" Everyone is surprised, and I videotape the startling difference. An outside observer would not be able to pick Peyton out in the class. What I film is true inclusion, full membership, supported participation in an age-appropriate curriculum. Whether or not Peyton understands the academics, we do not know. To us it seems that the sheer act of belonging halts her aimless wandering and stops her body from going berserk.

I marvel. How could I not have understood that the basic human need to belong applied to Peyton too? Pat understood it. The only answer is the unthinkable—that I had come to see my daughter as less than human. I work the video camera since Pat is needed at work, and I peer through the lens into a new frontier, like watching Neil Armstrong walk on the moon. Peyton's participation is supported in a number of mainstream classes at Balboa High School, from yearbook to math to physical science; this allows her to mix with non-disabled peers and exposes them to someone requiring significant support.

As bread is the staff of life, thoughts of real friendships continue to knead in me like the attachment on my newfangled KitchenAid mixer that steadily stirs, reaching every pinch of ingredient in the bowl.

In the spring of 1992, I attend Dr. Mary Falvey's conference presentation in Irvine on friendship, and take notes hungrily:

What Are Friendships?
- RELATIONSHIPS THAT LAST OVER TIME
- ESSENTIAL TO ALL SOCIAL BEINGS
- TAKEN FOR GRANTED UNLESS NONEXISTENT
- COME IN A VARIETY OF DIFFERENT PACKAGES, SUP-PORTS/NETWORKS—It's free, costs nothing

How Are Friendships Developed?
- SHARING ORDINARY SITUATIONS AND COMMON BONDS, not isolated special events

The minute I leave, I vow to experiment with mixing to give my daughter a chance (no guarantees—I know that) for friends. In early summer, I turn to Peyton's only friend, Hollyn, about to enter her senior year in high school, who belongs to a philanthropic group called the Mothers and Daughters Club Assisting Philanthropies (MADCAPS). I invite her over while Pat and Peyton are hiking around Shelter Island and begin with disclaimers: "You are the only one I am talking to about this. It can end here if you have any reluctance at all. Just please understand my desire to ask."

Hollyn, her long blonde hair held back neatly in a pearl barrette, offers a wide grin to encourage me to continue.

"What do you think about my asking the senior MADCAPS class about Peyton being included, *not as a member*, but included in this year's philanthropic and social activities?"

Her answer is quick and pure. "Yes, I want us to do that—absolutely. But what if they say no? I don't know how I'd feel about that."

"I've thought of that," I say. "Just like I'm asking you, we will not judge, but only say we needed to ask."

Soon afterward, the three mothers in charge for the year visit our house with Hollyn to talk to me, and I share with them Mary Falvey's handout on friendship.

"We don't want Peyton to be one of your philanthropies, but to take part in your charity projects, with my help and Hollyn's help," I explain.

When Hollyn speaks to the moms, I am awed at how different Peyton's needs sound coming from a friend who loves her. Hollyn does not gloss over concerns (about cliques and other potential challenges to Peyton's inclusion), but rather offers a positive approach for each one.

"Of the twenty-three girls in the senior class, four of them already know Peyton," mentions Hollyn hopefully, adding, "and I will be there to support her."

The moms agree to present the idea to the girls.

The welcome is warm at the meeting with the girls, but I can sense that my request is not understood by some. With Caren Sax at my side, I ask the twenty-three young women and their mothers, who have for five years been a motivated group with dynamics I know I cannot fully understand, to allow Peyton and me to be a part of them. The senior girls especially, entering their final year of this by-invitation-only organization, are rightly full of senioritis and their mothers full of teary "this is our final year together" feelings. Some might wonder how I have the nerve to do this, but I only know that I must ask, that this has been my mission from the day I heard Mary Falvey speak of friendships. Caren, with all the beauty of believing we are all better together, answers the half-dozen or so questions while Peyton sits silently, surprising me. I wish I knew if she was okay with this.

I'm established as a tupperwared tomb they leer into.
I'm the one they pity to jester not themselves
by their own hurts red.
Years I quest death, greedy my red unfreed be freed.

It was you, Mom, pertly yearning that I'm joyed be that treed I.
Under my red was you.
You wanted I tread in joy by inserted freaky I included.
Quest you your rest, nary mine.
Yes it pissed I that I'm pissed with you. I'm wish you deaded.

"Give us time to discuss it amongst ourselves, and we will call you with our decision," says one of the mothers. We say our good-byes and Caren walks with us to our car. We have been segregated for so long, I do not even worry about the embarrassment of "What if they say no?"

Peyton is clicking her seat belt when Hollyn and two other girls rush up to the car. "Peyton, you will be part of us this year. We all want you to!" Hollyn squeals.

The October 1992 meeting is a Halloween party at a battered women and children's safe house. Peyton wears a 1950s poodle skirt and takes six dozen cookies to share as several MADCAPS girls support her in playing with the little kids. I am never out of immediate reach and have no way of knowing what Peyton is thinking, but I see her smiles. Home again, I had not realized how nervous I was until shooting stars of a migraine appear. I am prone to getting them after completing a hugely important endeavor, and this one was a whopper.

Christmas with the MADCAPS presents similar challenges. Eating out with Peyton—especially stand-up, buffet-style—always makes me wish I had eight octopus arms, and this was especially true at the Christmas meeting. Upon arrival, the girls and moms gather in the formal dining room of the hostess's home, overlooking our entire sparkling city, to dip sliced bananas and strawberries in a large, heated fondue dish filled with melted chocolate. No time to panic, I move swiftly to load a few delectables onto a plate (with napkins aplenty) for Peyton while simultaneously trying to inhibit her speedy hands from nervously grabbing goodies off others' plates. (Forget my own chance for nibbling; I'll chow down on Fig Newtons later at home.) Nothing about the chocolate allows for a clean swipe. We do get a little help (some extra arms I was longing for) from new friends.

I am more than ready for the sit-down meeting that thankfully soon follows, though I am on high alert to intercede when needed. As Hollyn takes Peyton into the group of girls gathered around on couches and floor, I move to sit with the moms, as close to Peyton as I can get, planning an exit strategy just in case. But surprisingly, Peyton sits among them, not moving or exhibiting any of her "behaviors," for half an hour. *What is it,* I wonder, *that keeps Peyton settled, listening, and looking intently at the girls?* The only thing I can think of is her awareness of being included.

⨯

In January of 1993, the meetings increase to weekly as the girls begin to focus on "the Show," their huge annual spring fundraiser featuring singing and dancing from all 150 MADCAPS daughters. The seniors are the focus and honorees of the show.

As each senior class has done for thirty years, the graduates will choose a song to sing onstage to their moms. They will also write their bios, which will be read during formal presentations, when they will be escorted by their tuxedoed dads as formal mother-daughter pictures are projected on a large screen.

In anticipation of the big event, twenty-three girls begin shopping for just the right dress. At the meetings, Peyton sits in the midst of the girls, practicing their song, and I breathe sighs of contentment, knowing that what began as an experiment—my sole hope being that Peyton could stay for short chunks of time with the girls—has surpassed my expectations. Some of the girls have even moved closer to Peyton in valuable interactions, giving her a taste of relationships. One girl named Claire has become especially close to Peyton, and seems sensitive to supporting her needs. Petite and thin, she presents a stark physical contrast to Peyton, who, at five-foot-seven, now weighs 175 pounds. She has many friends in the group but has begun to make a beeline for Peyton at each meeting. From where we have come, excluded and segregated, I am thankful.

It is during the mid-January meeting, when everyone is signing up for their photography session, that I hear the unexpected words that strike a fear in me that will last for the next three months. During a break from the singing practice, a girl holding the sign-up clipboard asks, "Where is Peyton's name? She needs to schedule her photo session."

"Yes!" chime in about five other voices simultaneously. "We want Peyton to be in the show with us." More girls nod their heads, all looking to me.

"No, no, you are very kind, but that was not part of our plan. . . . No, really, thanks, but that would be too much on your special day."

I say "No" right in front of Peyton and think nothing of it, though at the same time, I wonder why I am the limiter here. Am

I afraid of being too far away to support Peyton? Afraid of ruining these girls' time in the spotlight? Yes, I am convinced that we cannot take the chance.

Two days later, Hollyn calls.

"Dianne, this did not come from me, but I support it. The girls have taken a vote, and we want Peyton to be in the show. Please, please . . . she is part of us. Please let her."

I had wanted less; now they wanted more.

"We've talked about it, and we will support her," continues Hollyn. "Don't worry."

I have seen their caring for Peyton grow. I have no way of knowing what Peyton wants, but feel confident that this is not pity, and that Peyton's conditional *inclusion* (as defined by me) is turning into what Caren Sax describes as *true belonging*. These girls are teaching me something about friendship, and I take a deep breath and say yes.

Now, *twenty-four* girls are shopping for the perfect dress, twenty-four mothers and daughters are having their priceless pictures taken, and Peyton and I are preparing in our own ways for the show, trusting in these new friendships.

Practices for the show fill the week prior to it. Pat is to sit with the dads, who will promenade their daughters around the stage as each name is called and bio read, including each girl's high school accomplishments, the college she will attend, and her dreams for the future. Then the girls will move forward together in a line from one end of the stage to the other while singing their song. In one last grasp for control, I insist that Peyton come off-stage with Pat for the rip-roaring, fast-paced finale that will feature all 150 girls.

Claire does not come to the first practice. I hear someone say that she has not been living at home for about a week, and this worries me. Claire has earned a spot in my heart for her growing fondness of Peyton. About fifteen minutes into Tuesday's practice, I am happy to see Claire enter from the back of the stage for the song, locking arms with Peyton. She is there for each subsequent practice, each time standing on one side of Peyton.

On the big night, April 23, 1993, I wait with Peyton before her name is called and then quickly grab a seat in the last row to witness her presentation. She looks beautiful on the arm of her adoring dad, as they walk around the stage, her face rather serious-looking. His head is tilted toward her as he whispers sweet nothings in her ear for the entire promenade, perhaps to help quell her nervous foot scraping as her white leather flats search out beads and sequins lost from dresses previously on parade. As planned, Pat waits in the wings as the girls lock arms and move forward on the stage, singing "The Road Leads Back." Peyton is smack-dab in the middle, her arm around Claire as Claire's small body, balanced on stilettos, leans into Peyton. I spot them sharing smiles as support flows between them and I cry at the sweetness, wiping my tears with the only substitute for Kleenex I have in my purse—several toilet-seat covers I always carry with me, just in case.

I'm on the stage wepted. I understand there that they pout too, awed by their hurts. Years I'm aware nothing that their hearts breaked too, terrored by their fears that they are treasured naught. Wedded were we in our pity under our masks. Guns stopped in my gut.

Silenced I'm as God very guttered appeared. He too poured out His red tears. His arms swept I up in joined I'm Him. Gyres stopped. I queried His great feeling eyes. In utters I heart heard Him jell his loud kissed lips, "You I love." I deared felt freed fitted treasured I was. I sweet felt God's child I'm. In tears uttered He, "Wash your pity red. I'm your red pity carrier. I'm retrieved your tears. Years red you tread I treasured you. By tears I am crying for all my children to pity nary themselves. Heal your red pout. You eased need to stay and teach each of my children are nurtured real."

I cry, "I'm a bottom person in retortured world. I tread in gutters. I'm nothing can depend do. I'm very tired. Please help I."

Answered He these words, "It is my great want that you stay and teach treasures awesome are all my children." Silenced I'm. I'm here staged to help these red children gyred like I to journey to look at eases for all by running togethered in openings of heard love, sad no one. I vow my IOU to start trying to journey in His steps to loudly gut love them in trying they loudly love I.

Just before the finale, Pat walks Peyton offstage, and I breathe easy again, tears emptied. All the girls are moving to the beat, singing and smiling, and I am imagining Pat and Peyton dancing in the wings. Then I see one of the senior girls, Jenny, reach behind the curtain and pull Peyton back onstage. Jenny in her red, sequin-covered sheath and Peyton in her white, embroidered A-line are moving to the music. Two other seniors join them in a small circle, holding hands. Peyton's face reads pure, spontaneous joy. *How many of the six hundred people in the audience notice this party within a party?* I wonder. It is beyond my wildest imagination.

As the finale winds down, I run backstage to get Peyton. Halfway there I run into Claire's mom, Helen. "Thank you for more than I can express," I tell her.

"It is I who must thank you and Peyton," says Helen. "Claire is here and back with us because of your daughter. She didn't want to miss supporting Peyton." And we two mothers embrace in gratitude for the journey our daughters have taken together.

Later that evening we celebrate with Hollyn's family at the Chart House in the historic San Diego Rowing Club, Pat's most beloved restoration.

"This was the best year of all for our group," Hollyn announces.

"Why do you think that is?" asks her dad.

She ponders a second, then says, "Because Peyton was there, no one cared where they sat in meetings."

Thinking back, I realize that what Peyton got from the group equaled what she gave to them. It would have been enough for me if only Peyton had benefited from the experience, but I now understand that it does not work that way—friendship is not a one-way street.

I'm ready to try to wash my testy regretting away.
I'm trying to retune my tortured red.
My IOU was lit by plea of me to God
to tilt my puny popping hopeless despair.

We fly to Boston to celebrate Patrick's graduation in May of 1993—our first lengthy family flight east since we'd flown to Newport, Rhode Island, in 1983, to witness Australia win the America's Cup. Many photos are shot as we celebrate hopeful futures with our son and his sweetheart, Ali. But I know before they are developed that few, if any, will capture Peyton wearing a smile.

By the 1993–1994 school year, Peyton will be fully included in mainstream classes for 85 percent of the day. She clearly communicates her desire to mingle with her general-population peers through her startling behavior changes for that 85 percent of the school day.

Ultimately, teachers and parents, in heart of cool love,
must dare assume each person is competent
and has intellectual potentials that
can and must be reached.

BALBOA HIGH SCHOOL
6-14-1993 IEP

Peyton is very likable and cooperative during positive interactions. She especially enjoys being surrounded by and included in activities with nonhandicapped peers. At present Peyton's performance level has increased in all areas of need. In the area of communication, both receptive and expressive skills have increased due to her inclusion in regular classes (and the community at large). Reading and writing skills [copying letters] have also shown improvement due to interest level and curriculum adapted to suit her strengths. Social skills, greetings, and verbal responses in general have increased in both volume and number. At this time, due to such a positive assessment, Peyton should continue to be included in regular classes as much as possible with a one-on-one T.A. (aide) to provide support as needed.

—Linda Malone and Gayle Cisneros, classroom teachers

Peyton's pediatric neurologist is surprised that Peyton can be so successful with motor skills like skiing, swimming, and riding a bike. All of his experience and medical evidence indicate that she should not be able to participate in such activities. Peyton and Pat now regularly ride their bikes in a four-mile loop around Shelter Island near our home. Halfway through the ride, at the tip of the island, they get off their bikes (keeping their helmets on) and climb down the large riprap embankment to the water's edge. At low tide, the descent is as much as twenty feet.

Since some rocks are unstable (referred to as "rockers"), Pat teaches Peyton how to navigate the terrain by sitting on one rock and then scooting to the next on her butt. Pat stays at least five feet away to allow Peyton to determine and execute her next move independently, like a mini rock-climbing lesson that challenges all types of motor movements for his daughter. It also allows them to watch the crabs crawling among the wet rocks and the boats sailing past as they sit on the ancient granite, immersed in their private world at the water's edge.

When it is time to go back to their bikes, they traverse up the face of the granite riprap, often surprising people sitting on the park benches as they pop their heads up from the embankment. More than once, Pat says he wishes he had a small flag to plant on the top to proclaim ownership of their conquered, stone-strewn territory.

Savoring the joy of their outings, Pat asks Peyton's special-ed teachers if they will allow him to try to teach a small group of severely handicapped teens from the class how to ride two-wheel bicycles on the high school track. Each day the class walks the track for exercise. Though there are no other students using the track at this time, I am a little leery of the football coach who uses the infield with his team at the same time the bike brigade would launch. His stoic looks do not offer any encouragement, and we have no idea how the teenage athletes on the field will react. The project is not without risk, but Pat decides the potential rewards far outweigh the potential bruises.

The teachers are enthusiastic about the proposal but are somewhat taken aback when Pat and I actually show up a few days later with seven bikes (Peyton's, plus six others collected from the neighborhood) and helmets all stuffed into the back of Pat's Ford van. Even the teachers had not envisioned six of their students (plus Peyton) riding around the track on bikes without training wheels. Yet within an hour, five of the six students are successfully riding independently, albeit some wobblier than others. There are several minor accidents (no first aid is needed), but nothing that interferes with the smiles and gleeful giggles.

One girl with bright red hair and sky-blue eyes chooses to walk her bike as she and Pat circle the field together. It is evident to me in all that this girl cannot say that she still feels proud of her accomplishment. In the quiet time Pat spends walking slowly with her, I notice a number of football players looking on with smiles and waves of encouragement. I wonder if some of them might have a brother or sister with similar challenges, and I am content not to worry about the coach, who continues to appear indifferent to the triumphs occurring all around him.

All students must be supported and accommodated to facilitate their success—in learning and in life; without the right involvement in the choices of one's life, one lives in fear and frustration and will never know the joy of independence.

֍

On a crisp fall evening in 1993, Peyton and I snuggle on our worn leather sofa to watch a PBS *Frontline* episode I have been anticipating, called "Prisoners of Silence." The show assesses a new communication strategy called facilitated communication (FC), which is being used with a number of nonverbal autistic individuals. Proponents declare that this method allows previously mute individuals to communicate by typing on a keyboard with the assistance of a facilitator who provides support and resistance on the typist's arm and wrist. "The theory of facilitated communication claims that many, perhaps most autistic people, are not retarded, but have intelligent minds imprisoned in bad bodies," explains the narrator.

Yet only ten minutes into the program, the authoritative voice of the narrator asks, "Was the typing coming from the autistic individual or from the facilitator?" Examples follow of numerous autistic children revealing (via facilitated communication) incidents of sexual abuse. How could this be the case? The show goes on to declare that autistic individuals using facilitated communication aren't even looking at the keyboard when they type. Impossible, decries the narrator. His unequivocal conclusion naturally follows: "The scientific evidence suggested that, far from unlocking the minds of autistic individuals, [facilitated communication] tapped the unconscious thoughts of the facilitator."

I know of no educators or therapists in public or private settings in San Diego who use facilitated communication with non-verbal students; plus the reputation of Public Broadcasting and *Frontline* seems impeccable, I think. So, I squeeze Peyton's hand and say with a sigh, "Well, at least that's one strategy we can cross off our list to investigate."

> *Your dismal dismissal of touch I pouted.*
> *I am a person who needs touch to move.*
> *If the physical resistance to my hand, wrist, forearm, or elbow,*
> *which is a necessary accommodation for the success of my*
> *purposeful movement, is not being supplied,*
> *then the hulk of my life is insanity.*
> *I need powerful tours of touch to hills retune try by I coping million*
> *motor jilts that thunder through I. Eases elude I.*
> *I'm freezed in fitted fears I wept worrying that this is verifyingly*
> *happened forever. It errored I'm ethers everywhere.*

With MADCAPS over and Hollyn off to college, we are eager to find activities that will give purpose and routine to Peyton's days, as well as offer her access to peer friendships. Since age sixteen Peyton has, through the school district, participated in the Community-Based Instruction (CBI) program, which lines students up with jobs and activities in the community. Weekly, Peyton has swept walkways at SeaWorld, separated hangers at Miller's Outpost, and cleaned wheelchairs at Sharp Hospital and toys at the Mission Valley YMCA. These last two jobs have been problematic for Peyton, who drools so much in spite of the colored bandanas she wears around her neck each day. These, along with her bib overalls (so she cannot disrobe in public), have now become her daily uniform, with only the T-shirt varying. *What a far cry from the designer outfits she wore for the first dozen years of her life*, I think.

Finding an appropriate job for Peyton is the goal, one she can hopefully keep after she "ages out" of the public school system at twenty-two. We hear about a Professor Paul Carpenter, a coordinator of the special-education credentialing program for the education department at La Costa College. With curly red hair and a few freckles dotting his cheeks, he reminds me of a character from a Norman Rockwell painting. He warmly shakes my hand upon our first meeting, and I am impressed at how he speaks to Peyton, looking her in the eyes even though she is unable to do the same. He may be able to find Peyton a job on campus as part of her CBI, he tells us. Could working at La Costa supply the much-needed social inclusion, especially now that we know it means so much to her?

⤬

After witnessing the benefits of inclusion, I, along with three other mothers, speak with Martin Miyares, the new director of the Exceptional Programs Department for the district, about how to get the message out to other parents of special-needs kids that inclusion is a choice for them. It is 1994, and, right now, we are just whispers in the dark, but Martin finds $5,000 in his budget for the district, with our help, to create an eleven-minute video called *Kids Like Me* to be given to all the principals in the district.

Feeling that other parents, school districts, and even university professors might find it helpful, we moms ask if we can market the video. Martin gives permission, and we pay for advertising in the TASH (The Association for Persons with Severe Handicaps) newsletter, and gamble by fronting the cost of producing a hundred videos (ultimately a financial loss, but that mattered little to us). Peyton and I handle the mail orders that come from all over the country, and a hundred additional copies are made. As a result of this effort, I am one of four parents asked to serve on a committee called the Least Restrictive Environment Workgroup for California. I drive north to various cities every other month for eighteen months to share ideas and opinions with education researchers and credentialing professors in California. As a part of this committee, I confirm what I suspected all along—that Peyton's needs should have been accommodated in less-restrictive environments than the private institutions in which she languished for five years.

––––––––

FEDERAL POLICY LETTER ON LEAST RESTRICTIVE ENVIRONMENT,
EDUCATION FOR THE HANDICAPPED LAW REPORTER (EHLR)
PAGE 211:384, MARCH 21, 1986

The school district must provide students with maximum appropriate opportunities to interact with nondisabled peers, which includes providing placements on regular school sites.

Federal and state policy specifically forbid selecting a placement in a segregated setting over placement on a regular school site if the placement decision is based on administrative factors and not on the student's needs. A school cannot use lack of appropriate placements as an excuse for denying students with disabilities their right to an education in the least restrictive environment. Although a school district can contract with the county to provide programs for students, the district cannot use this arrangement as an excuse to deny a student an education in the Least Restrictive Environment.

After twenty-eight years working for the Chart House (and loving it), Pat decides a radical change in direction is required to plan for Peyton's future. The CBI program has offered her great opportunities for community participation but it carries no guarantees of long-term involvement. "If we want a permanent place for Peyton to fit in, we need to create it ourselves," he tells me. No longer does he believe the throngs of family, friends, business associates, teachers, and doctors who tell us not to grasp at unrealistic goals and expectations: "Enjoy your daughter, because she is who she is, and she won't know the difference."

So, at the age of fifty-two, he retires as the senior officer with the longest tenure (as head of development, he leaves the single most identifiable fingerprint for the company's renown). His ambitious plan is to start our own restaurant where the original Shelter Island Chart House had been.

CHANNEL 10 NEWS
MARCH 2, 1994

Reporter: Important moments in Pat Goddard's life happened in this room. He got his first job here as a very good dishwasher.

He met his wife and proposed to her here. He worked his way up to busboy, waiter, then into management here. It's here where Pat learned about the restaurant business. It's here that he'll start his own business. After almost thirty years working for the Chart House Corporation, Pat is leaving a high-level position to open a restaurant with his family. It's here that Pat will give his nineteen-year-old daughter, Peyton, who has multiple learning disabilities, her first job.

Pat: People with disabilities like Peyton need the inclusion and deserve the opportunity for the inclusion, being a part of society, and she's terrific.

Reporter: Peyton can help fill salt and pepper shakers and change menu cards while learning new skills. Her brother is a history major who, like their dad, left a corporate management position to help his family. He admits it's risky, but he wants to be with them.

Patrick Jr.: And it's an opportunity for me to learn tremendously about the restaurant business from someone who I love and care a lot about, and who happens to also know a lot about the business.

Reporter: The restaurant will open in May after a few changes in decor. The new name, "Fiddler's Green."

According to Irish lore, Fiddler's Green is a paradise for sailors, a safe place to rest their weary bones. My uncle Gus, now retired, is hired to do morning accounting and bank deposits on weekdays. Then when our weekend bookkeeper suddenly leaves, Gus appeals to Pat about Connie, now thirty-four, joining the family business as the weekend bookkeeper. Pat and I discuss this, as we feel some responsibility to be a positive force in her life. I am her godmother, and she has been unemployed for some time (aside from occasional babysitting for us). Plus, our sophisticated point-of-sales computer system has proven trustworthy. So Connie is hired. Another familiar face will no doubt help Peyton to feel comfortable working at Fiddler's.

Yet all is not paradise. I can sense Pat's nervousness in realizing he no longer has in-house corporate counsel or CPAs at his disposal. No guaranteed paycheck, company cars, or 401(k)s; no Chart House pals for camaraderie, whether it be slipping out the back exit of the corporate office to surf the Cardiff reef or crank out a twenty-five-mile bike ride. Concealing a quiet anguish over the huge stakes he has placed on the table (his daughter's future, he feels, is tied to our success), for the first time stress invades Pat's happy-go-lucky personality.

With Professor Carpenter's support, Peyton begins spending time on campus of La Costa College in the fall of 1994, accompanied by her classroom teacher, Gayle, who carries a letter of introduction to share with anyone interested in meeting Peyton. They begin by working at the copy center and the small bookstore, straightening out the greeting cards (what is usually frustratingly impossible for me, relocating a card to the slot where I pulled it from, is second nature to visually keen Peyton). Introverted by nature, Gayle reports that Peyton is even helping her to become more sociable, since she is required to facilitate Peyton's unconventional interactions with other people, like walking up to students to hold their hand or pulling the hood of a fraternity sweatshirt up onto the head of an unsuspecting student.

"I'm becoming an outgoing person, thanks to Peyton," she tells me with a smile.

Gayle spends only a few weeks getting Peyton situated at La Costa, since it is difficult for her to be away from the classroom three hours a day. Then, it is Peyton's aide Julianne who supports her on campus each day while at age fifty I am finally forced to navigate a computer, working in our home office on Fiddler's accounts payable and payroll. Peyton starts working with preschoolers at the La Costa Child Center on campus, a job Paul Carpenter sensed she desired by the way she would halt outside their playground fence and intently watch them each day.

> *I'm awed by all I'm responsible for if I try to be pointer of*
> *"treasure all." I'm in pity of being I.*
> *I'm feared I cannot help. I'm nothing.*
> *I'm failing great God's quest for I.*
> *I'm getted very tired. Heart in me is fight no more forever.*

I glance hourly at the clock and breathe deeply only when 3:00 p.m. comes without an emergency call. When they return home, I listen, fingers crossed, to Julianne's reports of how things went that day.

"Let me tell you about today's amazing story," she recounts one afternoon.

Julianne goes on to tell me that Peyton became stuck, unwilling (or was it unable?) to move from her job in the bookstore to her next job at the preschool. Julianne tried cajoling, pulling, singing, demanding, turning her back, giving a pep talk, dancing around Peyton's body now plopped cross-legged on the carpeted floor of the stacks. Nothing was working.

Then she borrowed a phone and called Professor Paul in his office. He came immediately. Smiling and teddy-bearish, he walked over to Peyton and said, "The kids are expecting you now. Let's walk there together." When he held out his hand, Peyton's hand ceased picking at the woven threads beneath her and reached up to take his. They crossed the quad and ambled together to the preschool gate, hand in hand.

Eventually, Peyton spends four or five days a week on campus, and Caren Sax brings J. D. Hoye, director of President Clinton's

National School-to-Work Project, to witness Peyton's success there. In November, we, along with Peyton's support team, all fly to San Francisco to accept the TASH Collaboration Award "for significantly helping an individual with a disability realize the goal of full community inclusion and participation."

At the ceremony, Professor Carpenter, with his characteristic enthusiasm, makes the formal acceptance speech for the group; however, two sentences into his statement, he is joined at the podium by Peyton, who surprises everyone by walking up to join him. Unflustered, he smiles wider and welcomes Peyton with his caring eyes, saying, "Now the true leader of our collaboration stands with me," as he continues to speak about what has happened on the campus he loves, where he teaches students to be teachers.

<hr />

By 1995 the restaurant has suffered months of only losses. This puts more pressure on Pat and me and on our son, who holds the title of assistant manager. At what should be the happiest time of his life—he and Ali are engaged to be married in September—I feel we have failed him. He left a secure position in a business management program just to earn a minimal salary while working up to seventy hours a week. Patrick's future has become tied together with Pat's and mine at a time when he should have been making his own.

No one wants to fail at giving Peyton a chance at a real life, though all three of us keep these feelings to ourselves. I am past being able to sense what my son might be feeling as he watches his parents begin to fall apart for the first time. I do not allow myself to imagine the pressure he already faces—the knowledge that he will be the one to watch over his sister when Pat and I are gone (what this will look like, we never discuss). I often feel I am in a race, hoping to get to level ground, past the heartbreak hills, before we have that openhearted conversation with our son. By creating choices for Peyton's future, we are hoping there will be choices for Patrick's, too.

Ali appeals to me one day: "I'm concerned for everyone. The pressure is unsustainable."

I can only think, *My God, we are all going to collapse.* Yet I cannot figure out how to stop the insanity of trying to navigate a sinking ship, each and every day.

It is actually a relief to us that Patrick respectfully resigns in late spring, moving back into the business world, while working toward his MBA at night. Relief that if Pat and I cannot adjust our sails to stay in the race, Patrick is now sailing his own course. Relief even as we wonder if he will ever understand and forgive us.

As Pat and I increasingly turn our attention toward the restaurant (and away from Peyton), daily reports from her school increasingly chart stormy seas of behaviors, like stomping feet, clapping and jumping, wailing, and even aggressive moves like charging toward other people with her arms extended. Her 180-pound body can easily knock over another adult, and this aggression is threatening to end her hard-won opportunities for inclusion.

On one blustery spring day, I tune into ESPN to watch the America's Cup trials off the coast of San Diego (San Diego Yacht Club had prevailed in the courts). With startled horror, I witness, along with millions of race enthusiasts around the world, Australia's yacht crack in two and sink in less than three minutes, crew jumping overboard, vessel gone forever. I turn to phone Pat at the restaurant, pretty sure he is watching, as our phone rings. It's Peyton's aide, Julianne.

"We've had an incident at the preschool. Peyton was interacting with Hope, a four-year-old, and she pushed her down.

Mrs. Moore thinks she's fine, and the mother is coming. Can you come? I'm worried about Peyton."

My heart sinks. Staying afloat, not cracking up—that's the goal. But how much longer can we hold on?

I'm jungled by mutters of failing great God's quest for I.
It is hard to help in my misunderstood, bogged body, pureed in
pity, lips freezed in fears. IOU was pointed hopeless by fretted
frustrations that God nothing peaced.
I'm hoping these traps wepted will hungry freed be
by God's presents in my living.

Journey I'm totter. I'm watered by treason red
reasserting great God within me
I'm gived utterly up. I'm wager He hurry as
I'm getted too tired to let my heart keep breaking in my hutted
hearse another daunting, needy night.

Chapter 7

Dr. Freed Me

Ires eat you up. They quit never. Each ired gas petrifies.
In my head I yowled "peace."
"Never," the ethers answered.

In the immediate days following our visit to St. Catharine's Psychiatric Hospital, I return with laser-like intensity to the thing I do best: burying the worry that Peyton's free fall will never be lastingly reversed by focusing on the next challenges. I see the battle on two fronts: We need a court paper called a conservatorship so that if we are driven to the doors of St. Catharine's again, at least we will be in control. We also need a psychiatrist who will partner with us to care for Peyton, whose mysterious demise, we are now told, is due to a mysterious disorder called autism. The lawyer is easier to find than the doctor. One call to a close family friend, and the legal procedure is under way.

Since autism is still a medical enigma in 1996, it is not easy to find psychiatrists with experience treating people with this label, especially adults. On top of this, Peyton has had twenty-one years of perplexing experiences and traumas that have yielded a host of psychological and neurological challenges, including loss of language, epileptic seizures, ADHD, anxiety disorder, bipolar disorder, sleep disorder, obsessive-compulsive disorder, and years of depression. These are all potential participants in the current landscape of Peyton's condition, which we could sum up as "human roadkill." I know that by the age of twenty-one, most individuals like Peyton (especially those who are nonverbal and show signs of aggression) have already been institutional- ized, supposedly for their own protection, not to mention the sanity and well-being of the parents or conservator. Though we understand the choices made by other families, these are argu- ments that we refuse to concede as long as we have the strength to keep going.

I cross the street to speak with our neighbors, Dave (my car- diologist) and Liz (a former nurse), who have caringly watched over our epic journey from their three-story bayside home. Liz, two-thirds the size of me but a giant at tackling problems, listens to my tears about having nowhere to turn, takes me by the hand, and says, "Let's make some phone calls." After consulting several doctors, I get a strong recommendation, a Dr. Robert Friedman, who has experience in treating patients with autism. Liz takes down the number and makes the call for hopeful me.

Pat and I see Dr. Friedman on June 14, armed with a meticu- lously documented history and a list of our requirements for an ongoing medical relationship.

To: Dr. Robert Friedman
From: Pat and Dianne Goddard
Date: June 10, 1996
RE: Our 21-year-old daughter, Peyton Goddard

In early April 1996, there was an increase in Peyton's compul- sive behavior (opening/closing doors, flipping on and off lights, smearing feces, flushing toilets repeatedly), and she became highly agitated and volatile. She was overactive and compulsive about picking up lint/trash from the floor. She was not able to sleep. She was gritting teeth, pushing people, throwing things. A decreased appetite caused a substantial weight loss in a short period of time. This behavior was repeated four weeks later, and she had to come home from school because she hit her longtime aide. She was more aggressive and agitated than ever before. She (we) did not sleep. We took turns being with her during the night.

WE SEEK PSYCHIATRIC HELP—ongoing for medication monitoring or possible new additions to avoid episodes, and help with managing them at home so Peyton can be herself, hopefully functioning, included, and happy.

WE SEEK A RELATIONSHIP that could allow easy access to you with any concern we deem significant, especially in light of the fact that much of Peyton's care is based on observation and blood-level monitoring due to her severe oral language handicap.

It may help for you to know and understand our goals for Peyton, all of which are based on what she has told us (adamantly) through behaviors. The following are the most important to her:

To have her included as much as possible in the community with purposeful participation. It is our goal not to hospitalize, institutionalize, etc. No one who knows her feels that this would be in Peyton's best interest.

Our special goal is to allow Peyton to have as much independence as possible with the help of medication and integrated environments, with appropriate, welcoming supports.

At our first appointment, I am nervous, like someone returning to dating after having her heart broken too many times. Will he listen? Will he care? Will he view our requests as too demanding? We never presented any previous physician with such a strong statement of desires. But now it seems that everything is on the line.

At the appointment hour, his door opens, and we are greeted with a sincere smile from a handsome young man closer in age to our son than to ourselves. The soft leather couch invites us to sit beneath the Impressionist print that hangs above. There is another plump swivel chair for the choosing next to his desk, which looks alive with papers. Memorabilia fill the shelves—a model brain on the end table, hand-carved Native American flutes and medicine man rattle on the bookshelf. Dr. Friedman states that he has reviewed my "Bill of Rights" and has found it all to be reasonable and acceptable. He does not flinch at my intensity or Pat's corny jokes; in fact, I sense no judgment from him. His eyes convey concern for our desires. It is a comfortable first date—one we can build on, perhaps.

The night of June 24, I wake several times with Peyton, changing her wet sheets and pajamas and then climbing into bed with her, hoping Peyton (and therefore I) can get more sleep. As Peyton tosses and turns and moves about the room in which I have locked us, I nod off in the light sleep (one myopic eye opening often) my body has grown accustomed to. I wonder to myself how long people like Peyton and me can go without any REM sleep. I made it through college and long past without a caffeine habit, but now I am up to eight cups of Folgers a day, and I actually laughed when my heart doctor, Dave, recommended I quit caffeine.

With each awakening, I remind myself that tomorrow is a big day on two battlefronts. At 8:30 a.m. in Judge Nolan's courtroom is the conservatorship hearing; then, at 4:00 p.m., Peyton's first appointment with Dr. Friedman. I never spoke to Peyton about these appointments except to tell her the time of each outing. *Why is that?* I wonder. *Is it not to bother her, or do I think Peyton is unable to understand what I mean?* These days, I barely speak directly to Peyton about anything but her behaviors. After years of Peyton being unable to reciprocate in a conversation, I have simply stopped trying.

The next morning, Peyton sits between Pat and me in the first row of Judge Gregory L. Nolan's courtroom. Gam and Patrick accompany us, along with Peyton's aide, Julianne, now employed extra hours by us, who tries to keep Peyton calm. That is mission impossible today, as the judge accepts the reports about Peyton written by Dr. Tabler and me. These reports tell the facts about Peyton's limited functioning, though I know there are untruths in them. Despite what the report states, Peyton *can* read—or at least, she *could* read when she was functioning well and could tell us. But we let those truths lie hidden.

Peyton screams and yowls. She stomps her feet.

Understand my tipping yells are messes of freed frustration
telling you thousands others in I are very sad, gestated to being
buried in gutters of lit nowhere.
Treasure us real weeds in the fields, I caw, not in the filthy gutters
red reared by wepters, where they estimate we very beasts in cages
belong, raping us easily saying we are real never, thesis that we
hearts cannot feel.

With her body in full gyration, Pat and I hold her hands to restrain her until Judge Nolan declares, "Will Peyton Goddard please stand." Pat and I lift Peyton and stand together, facing the judge. At that moment Peyton becomes silent and still as he recites the rights that she "lacks the capacity to perform" and is henceforth denied. One by one, he lists the stripped civil and legal rights of one Peyton Goddard, who may no longer choose where she will live or whether she will marry or vote; she may not control her medical decisions, her social or sexual contacts, or make decisions about her education.

Peyton listens, stock-still, as though nailed to the floor, until Judge Nolan picks up the gavel and lowers it. At that moment, Peyton bursts into hyperdrive—screaming, twisting, hitting. Pat and I restrain as many moving parts as possible while dragging our twenty-one-year-old daughter out of the courtroom before she lashes out at the bailiff and stenographer, who are eyeing her with trepidation. At this moment I feel a strange relief that the judge could see without question why this was necessary—a protection for Peyton, in her best interest.

All in all, it is a good crucifixion.

I'm coping with being a puppet sipping real.
I'm a human nothing under the court.
Inking out my real by the stroke of their quill is a question
important to no one but me.
Walls of pity grow. I POW live in a prison of closed,
powerless jails, damned to feel fears forever.
There freed my red, red rages.

At Peyton's first appointment with Dr. Friedman that afternoon, she does not hold back any behaviors, and Dr. Friedman is never flustered.

"Peyton, this is Dr. Friedman," says Pat, as Dr. Friedman steps out of his office to greet us. She blows past him, heading for the open door from which he emerged. I follow quickly, wanting to steer her clear of the breakables that seem to call *Pick me up* to her. Pat and I take turns intercepting Peyton and redirecting her busy hands, seemingly driven by her keen, darting eyes, and I give Dr. Friedman the first of my "update observations since we last saw you" on a yellow legal pad that bears my neat schoolteacher printing.

He swiftly scans my notations on meds, changes in behaviors, increasing anxiety and irritability, and sleeping and eating patterns. Then he speaks directly to Peyton. As he lifts his head and swivels his desk chair to address her, she offers him the first of many pieces of lint she will pick up off the carpet. He extends his open palm toward her to accept the tiny speck, and their eyes engage for a split second.

"Thank you, Peyton," Dr. Friedman says.

I wonder what Peyton is thinking as she studies Dr. Friedman. I also wonder what he sees in Peyton, or in himself, that makes it impossible for him to dismiss her as unworthy of his efforts. He could say what we have heard from other doctors: "Everything has been tried," and simply end our relationship before it begins. But he does not give up on her. Eleven years later, Peyton will refer to Dr. Friedman as "Dr. Freed Me."

He is a reader of queer.
Hope is young in iterated I, forged only after the great plow of my
dreary, gyred youth.

Dr. Friedman's initial goal is simply to monitor Peyton's medications. After listening to my weekly report, we powwow about what meds to lower, increase, eliminate, or introduce while Peyton roams, jumps, and sometimes pushes and hits (usually Pat). I watch this behavior in bewilderment, knowing Pat is Peyton's joy, and occasionally wonder if Peyton is pleading with Pat to *do something* to help her.

During the summer of 1996, hope takes a firmer perch in my soul as I realize we have a partner in Dr. Friedman. He knows our goal is to keep Peyton functioning in the inclusive settings that have brought some improvements (inclusion is the medicine that seems to work best). She was already on Tegretol, Lithium, Clonidine, oral antibiotics for painful cystic acne, on and off Ambien. In his second meeting with Peyton, Dr. Friedman adds Paxil, which helps, though the unpredictable outbursts continue, requiring Julianne and me to be ever vigilant.

Dr. Friedman, you saw my harsh youth bullishly gyred me, and
people opportuned pimped me.
You saw I optioned hope of peace in prying my sceptered SELF with
an opportunity of inner spiritual SELF.
While you medicated the gutters of my life, you gathered my soul
in willing seedings by your appeared interest in my SELF. You
understood my choice to live married to my SPIRIT.
I plight puring in stepping steep stones, you running alongside.
You heard my person, sured separate to my pills. And together we
carefully navigated the stormy waters of medications.
You supported me looking at the red ires of my youth, reasserting
rips, and deciding to here, now, heart heal.

Professor Paul Carpenter invites Peyton to join ("co-teach," he
calls it) his summer teacher-education class called Psychology of
the Exceptional Child. I marvel at his unswerving commitment
to Peyton, knowing that he has to defend Peyton's participation to
a few administrators who question her presence on campus. One
obvious benefit for including Peyton in his classes is to expose his
students to the kind of student they might be teaching someday.
But it's more than that, I think. He sincerely wants to learn from
her while always looking for the next opportunity for her to grow.

Even before I could communicate, and still while thinkers read
me as righteously ill and worthless, thankfully Professor Paul
Carpenter from La Costa College came, and answered my prayer
allowing the ultimate plan in the universe to unfold.
With opportunities for participation in his teacher-training classes,
I began to dare to hope for an escape from segregation toward a
purposeful life and a chance of an education.

Julianne accompanies Peyton to Dr. Paul's classes, supporting her attempts to reach out (literally through touch) to peers and helping her to participate in assignments. For one class, Julianne suggests she and Peyton prepare a chart on Erik Erikson's Eight Stages of Psychosocial Development, which is part of the chapter they are studying. Together they buy the poster board at the college bookstore. Julianne writes numbers 1 through 8 on it, and attaches Velcro next to each number.

I watch them in class as Julianne speaks about each stage and Peyton attaches the correct label to the board. As Peyton secures Stage 4, CHILDHOOD, to the chart, Julianne explains that the main question in this stage is, "Am I successful or worthless?" Julianne turns several times to make sure Peyton is successful at connecting the Velcro label before they move to the next stage.

In closing, Peyton attaches a sentence strip to the board from Erikson's writings: "The most deadly of all possible sins is the mutilation of a child's spirit." Presentations like this are a positive for Peyton and the class. If Peyton's behaviors erupt during the class, like stomping feet or clapping hands, she and Julianne leave for a walk and return when Peyton is calm. But I am relieved to see these behaviors slowly decrease as the semester progresses.

Pity I'm poisoned by hopeless way I feel wherever I'm less to you.
It reality is that you are me and I am you. I will try to fret not
about ired passages of pity.
I love you. Try to love me pity free.

Last year, Peyton marched in a meaningless (for her) graduation ceremony at Balboa High School. The real graduates wore black robes, while Peyton and a few others were given white robes. Her group was seated off to the right of the stage, and they all marched forward (Peyton accompanied by Julianne) when their names were called to receive their "Certificate of Recognition." Pat and I cheered from the concrete football stands, yet we wondered what this paper meant—for us, for Peyton, for anyone. Was this a rite of passage? And if so, to where?

Now that Peyton is twenty-two, she will soon age out of the school system, and the Regional Center, tasked with helping people with developmental disabilities, continues to say the only option for her will be a sheltered workshop. For people like Peyton, this is like a day care for handicapped adults, who are kept busy doing repetitive tasks like fitting and refitting plastic pegs into foam boards. I know that these segregated institutions do not work for Peyton since she has spent years in versions of them. If our Fiddler's gamble does not pay off, we are on a collision course to relive past horrors.

Sinking deeper into despair after each flare-up, as I scrub smeared feces off the mauve bathroom tiles and clean Peyton up, I begin to imagine the grown-up institutions Peyton seems destined for, and wonder what they will do to her there. Medicate her into a zombie? But no medication that we know of can subdue Peyton. And leaving Peyton alone guarantees more chaos to clean up. How would they control her? Pat and I have already tried threatening her, scaring her, pushing her away as she charges us, and in desperation we have even resorted to holding her down or grabbing her hair at the nape of her neck (as a rider would jerk back on a spooked horse's mane) to stop her from running out in the street. All of these extreme measures only make her more out of control—eyes like a scared animal that cannot be reasoned with—and leave us eaten up by unrelenting remorse.

What would they do at an institution that we have not already tried? And where are the others with these behaviors? Dr.

Friedman is trying hard to keep Peyton functioning so she can participate here and there, but I feel we are just treading water. And we are aging. Now in our fifties, Pat and I feel less invincible, knowing we are moving closer to our finish line. Worries fill my dreams, and into my waking mind creep strange and scary contemplations of the unthinkable.

I watch a close friend lose her four-year battle with ovarian cancer, and at the memorial service, I listen to her two adult children speak of her spiritual journey to acceptance, which many of us admiringly witnessed. Yet I cannot cry my usual memorial tears, so overcome am I with envy. I am jealous of my dear friend in her dying, and I cannot shame the feeling out of me. I cannot imagine myself ever being able to die in peace.

Pat and I are driving home one day from another disheartening appointment with the accountant. I click on the radio to fill the deafening don't-know-what-to-do silence. The local noon newscast is rambling on and on. Then we hear it—a report of a double suicide. The bodies of an elderly woman and her middle-aged, quadriplegic son have been discovered in their Mission Valley apartment after a neighbor smelled a rotting odor for several days. She had been his only caregiver. We both stare ahead, no words said, but I can feel we are one in a petrifying understanding of what it is like to ponder the unthinkable. We return home to share an ever-growing intimacy of heart I cannot explain even to myself, but it will be fifteen years before we ever speak of this horror.

⚞

Now in its third year, Fiddler's Green is a financial failure, and Pat and I are both increasingly anxious about what to do. We are putting our home of twelve years up for sale. Dave is treating me for high blood pressure, arrhythmia, and panic attacks, while Pat is taking pills for anxiety and parasomnia sleep disorder, involving motor activity while sleeping, resulting in his falling out of bed or running into walls, so I must remain half-awake the rare minutes I sleep with him also. We knew that start-up restaurants take up to five years to show a profit, but the surprising depths of our losses can be sustained for only so long. Our desire to secure a place for Peyton to contribute keeps us going because there is no other imaginable alternative.

Pat and I focus all our efforts on the restaurant at the expense of everything else. Peyton's social opportunities have now faded to nothing as Pat has no free time, and I set her aside completely from my worries, telling myself, *She just has to wait while we fix the problem so she can have a place in the future.* We provide more cash infusions to keep the restaurant alive in hopes that this summer's tourism will at least stop the losses. Each day, Pat spends from 9:00 a.m. to 9:00 p.m. at the restaurant, returning home to help me cope with the chaotic nights. Overwhelmed, he puts more trust and responsibility on key employees like Gus and Connie, who handle the bookkeeping. Though Pat reports to me that each evening appears busy, I am concerned to see that the daily deposits do not reflect an increase in sales.

One morning in late August, I ask Connie for a computer readout of the week's sales. Silently studying the figures, I begin to sob. Connie reacts with nervous surprise, saying, "What's the matter?"

"We were hoping for a turnaround, but it isn't happening," I say to my first cousin.

What to do? Is Pat naive in assuming the restaurant is busier, or—*oh my God!*—have we both been naive in trusting Connie? Would she really be capable of stealing from family?

Pat rises very early the next Sunday morning and goes to the restaurant at 5:00 a.m. to do a cash count from the previous night's receipts. Then he leaves and returns at the usual time, around 9:00 a.m.

Connie comes in at 8:00 to do her usual duties, which include a cash count and bank deposit. Saturday night's deposit is short by $129.34, and Pat and I move from shock to anger to outrage. We need a way to calculate how much she might have stolen, so for the next week Pat notes the difference in his cash count compared to Connie's. On several days, Connie takes the daily receipts with her, saying that she got behind and needs to do the paperwork at home.

After a week of sleuthing, Pat and I confront her with the evidence in the small office at the back of the restaurant, telling her we have hired an accounting firm that specializes in fraud and embezzlement.

"You have one chance to come clean and admit to the full amount you've stolen," he announces. "If you lie to us or underestimate your theft, we will prosecute, and you're going to jail."

Connie looks down at the floor as he speaks to her.

"On the other hand, if you come clean and tell us how much you've taken, we will put a simple promissory note together for the agreed-upon amount and you can pay it back a little every month."

Between dramatic confessional sobs and pleas for forgiveness, Connie readily agrees to the proposed resolution.

"You can start by telling us how much you've stolen," says Pat.

Looking down again, she whispers, "I think, around ten thousand?"

Pat sighs heavily.

"But maybe I can work off some of the bill by babysitting Pey?" she offers, looking up hopefully.

After a moment of silence, Pat responds calmly, "Your services having anything to do with the Goddard family will no longer be needed."

The next weekend, Pat and I go to Gus and Bette's small apartment, cluttered with a houseful of furnishings, to break the news and have them cosign the promissory note. Upon hearing the news, Bette lifts her wrinkled hands to her face.

"I hate her, I hate her," she says through her sobs as Gus signs the agreement without protest.

In spite of a few rough patches in Peyton's work on campus, in the fall of 1996, Professor Paul wants to go for the gold. He proposes that Peyton apply to La Costa College as a student and enroll in one course. He recommends Psychology of Personal Development, freshman PSY 101. With my full worry now focused on Fiddler's and securing Peyton's future when she leaves the school district, we fill out the application, write a check for $1,500, and wait for Peyton's acceptance letter to come in the mail, which it does.

Professor Paul somehow does not see the fact that Peyton has no dependable way of communicating as a deal breaker. However, upon meeting with the psychology professor prior to the first class, I am nervous about his expectations.

"Students are here to learn, so disruptions cannot be tolerated," he tells us.

Julianne supports Peyton at the first two class meetings (trying to minimize her predictable nervous behaviors) and accompanies her to the chapel service that students attend on Friday mornings. The startle reflex is now well developed in me, as I am on high alert whenever Peyton is out, dreading a call reporting Peyton's volatility.

Today, it is the front door opening at noon.

"Peyton stood up in chapel and started screaming," reports Julianne. "I've never heard her cry out like that except that day in the courtroom. I could not help her calm down."

Given Peyton's outbursts in class and, unforgivably, in the holiest place on campus, the professor informs Paul that Peyton is no longer welcome. Paul calls, remorseful at not being able to help Peyton and Julianne more.

"I should have had supports in place," he says.

The college swiftly refunds the money for the class. The textbooks, M. Scott Peck's *The Road Less Traveled* and Viktor Frankl's *Man's Search for Meaning*, we keep. I sometimes find them lying about in odd places.

Chapter 8

I Am Intlgent

*Opportunities greased in the tip of the
Creator's ultimate plan began to holy knock.*

It is early 1997. Peyton will leave the school district in June.

Our nautical-themed restaurant serving land-of-opportunity American food is a sinking ship. Our hopes still tied to it, we try to bail out the water coming over the gunnels by throwing more money, time, sweat, and tears at it, ever believing the framed needlepoint picture above the office computer, which reads NEVER GIVE UP THE SHIP. We will keep bailing for two more years before my brother mercifully buys the restaurant from us and the albatross releases its grip from around our necks. However, in those two years we will discover that bank statements in no way reflect riches.

On a bright February morning, I drag my weary body to a conference called "Autism: Moving On" at the University of San Diego. I am intrigued for one reason: the immense difficulty we have getting Peyton out of the car. Each time we drive some-where, upon arrival, Peyton sits frozen. We do not know what to do, especially when we get home, since we can no longer just pull into the garage (it has been converted into an exercise classroom for Peyton). That means we are spending up to twenty minutes outside, on display for the whole neighborhood, trying to get her out of the car. I have taken to driving onto the front lawn, car hood kissing the shrubs next to the front door, then pulling her from the outside, pushing her from the inside, anything to get her out.

I have been considering the idea of reclaiming the garage so we can leave Peyton in the car, allowing her to get out when she is ready. But the garage has become such a sacred space for Peyton and Pat. How much more could a dad love a daughter? This is the question that a passerby might ask upon seeing Pat out in the garage, teaching Peyton the five ballet positions by taping Dr. Scholl's green shoe inserts on the floor and then moving her arms to match his, all to the sounds of "Raindrops Keep Falling on My Head."

At the conference, I listen with amazement to the speakers, Professor Anne Donnellan and speech pathologist Martha Leary, as they explain how people with autism face challenges when it comes to moving their bodies. They might have trouble starting, stopping, inhibiting, and switching movements, even if they had been able to accomplish a particular task the day before, or just five minutes earlier.

Then they discuss methods for facilitating movement with physical, verbal, and emotional assistance. I came here looking for an answer to one pressing question, and I leave with an entirely new perspective on how to support my daughter. I also hear people testify to the success of FC, a strategy that helps some nonverbal people communicate via a computer keyboard. Rita and Bob Rubin and their 18-year-old daughter, Sue, who has used FC to express herself since age 13, offer living proof of its effectiveness. A brown-eye brunette with Sandra Bullock hair, Sue will attend Whittier College in the fall.

I have tried to get Peyton to type on her brother's computer in the past, but Peyton just struck letters at random. I would say,

"Quiet hands . . . Find the letter B," and then watch Peyton indiscriminately peck at any letter *but* the B, something that always baffled me. I still have the VHS recording that Peyton and I watched together more than three years ago of the *Frontline* episode claiming FC was a hoax (maybe *Frontline*'s assertions are the real hoax, I wonder). Now, with a new understanding of her movement differences swirling in my head, I raise my hand in the final Q and A session and ask Dr. Donnellan, "Where on the West Coast could our family get a trusted evaluation to see if FC might be a useful strategy for our daughter?" Dr. Donnellan arranges a meeting for us a few weeks later.

On Good Friday, 1997, Peyton and I follow the directions to a school in Whittier, California, where Dr. Donnellan is again presenting "Autism: Moving On." Pat cannot leave the restaurant to join us, and I do not press him since I don't know what to expect. A spirited blonde with rosy cheeks and smiling Irish eyes, Dr. Donnellan welcomes Peyton and me, and then introduces us to psychologist Jackie Leigh and speech pathologist Darlene Hanson, who are expecting us.

I lead Peyton by the hand as we walk into an office, and Peyton sits next to Darlene, a blue-eyed woman in her early thirties. Darlene speaks to Peyton respectfully, getting right to the point: "I am going to offer your arm support, Peyton, to see if this might help you to communicate with us by typing. I'll adjust my support and pull back a little until I feel you pointing to the letter you want."

Stabilizing Peyton's right wrist, Darlene centers it over the slightly tilted keyboard of her desktop computer while Jackie speaks softly to quell Peyton's nervous giggle. Peyton responds by becoming silent. I look at Peyton, and in a rare moment of peace do not feel the need to intercede. Whatever is happening here is out of my hands.

Darlene steadies Peyton's usually ever-moving hand while Jackie asks her, "What is your favorite food?"

Darlene supports Peyton's wrist and puts pressure on the base of her palm. Peyton reaches out with her pointer finger and takes aim at the P. I see the letter record on the monitor. Darlene verbally confirms the P as she returns Peyton's hand to the neutral position in front of the keyboard.

"What letter comes next?" asks Jackie. The strategy is repeated until PPPIZZA appears on the monitor. I sit frozen.

Tunes in their voices I hear as ringing ruptures.
They sow new eases.
I'm hearted to hope. This I had prayed.

The trio continues while I try to grasp the meaning of what is happening. In awe, I stare at Peyton, who is focused on her finger ballet, her demeanor calm, her breathing peaceful. Gone for this moment is the state of high-anxiety alert in which she lives. I cannot remember the last time I saw my daughter like this. After typing six words and phrases on the monitor, Peyton shows no impatience and gives no indication of wanting to stop.

Sensing this, Darlene asks Peyton, "Is there anything else you want to say?"

Intently, I watch Peyton dive back into the keyboard with real Olympic purpose. Darlene supports with pressure, pulling Peyton's arm back after each letter her finger types. I cannot take my eyes off my daughter. When Peyton pauses, I look up at the monitor as Darlene reads Peyton's sentence: I AM INTLGENT.

Jackie and Darlene nod their confirmation. Peyton continues to type: I TYPE TO TELL PEOPLE.

I shake my head in astonishment. Peyton goes on: I THINK MOM THINK I SMRT.

They saw my worrying.
Puny persons are worriers that things will never change.
They cared. They understood my motoring madness.
Worriers rest wherever they trade fear with trust.
Weeds of freezes melted. I'm eased.

"Excuse me. I'll be right back," I announce as I stand up, escape into the hallway, and duck into the bathroom. Sitting down fully clothed on an elementary-school toilet seat, I open the floodgates and empty tear ducts that seem to hold more liquid than a full bladder. I do not, *cannot* comprehend what all this means, but the tears I mop up with scratchy toilet paper contain the salt of my heart's agony and ecstasy.

I ponder Peyton's final assertion—*I think Mom thinks I'm smart.* Almost every day, every minute of Peyton's life has been a test—not just the many, many assessments I scheduled to confirm her brightness, but the daily homework, the educational games, the endless therapies.

Yet in those years of tumbling free fall, I realize that even I had lost sight of her intelligence. Like a prisoner of war, Peyton had endured constant interrogation and, though she likely knew the correct answers (unimportant as they were), she had no way to reveal them to her interrogators. She had to face each new cross-examination, knowing she would fail.

At this moment, I rejoice at Peyton's ability to communicate, even as I am floored by the realization that long ago, I myself stopped treating Peyton like an intelligent person. "What have I done? What have I done?" is the accusation that plays in my mind.

The journey of life cannot be traveled without a clear mode of successful communication and listeners who caringly support. Of utmost importance is the insurance that a system of communication supplies me, and for that I answer, "Thank God." First, without a voice, never are people safe; second, without the ability to communicate, a voiceless person is easily and unbearably frustrated by behaviors they must resort to and the often incorrect interpretation of these behaviors. With FC, I finally gained a mode of dependable communication, which allowed me to tell the truth of my life and begin to relieve the fear which plagued me.

Carefully, you'll need to consider the thinking of opposition that calls FC a parental tool, freeing their stupid children to look silly never again. Overcoming this argument requires you to understand that millions of parents bet on their kid's myth of retardation. The hill that FC requires of them is mounting the reality that all the years of looking at their kid as dumb are not regainable. Their parenting has been disabled by schools that opposed educating their child's ability to journey to a productive job and the toll of the wasted years they hopingly attempt to regain before they die. What parents want is that their child has a life after they are gone.

Driving out of Whittier toward the freeway, we stop at the Target on the right that Darlene told me about. We walk in and buy Peyton her first keyboard device, a three-by-five-inch Franklin Speller, for $29.95. Although it lacks visual or voice-output feedback, it will be a good portable communicator to begin with.

We come home to an empty house, missing Pat, who is working at the restaurant. He will arrive home by 9:30 p.m. to find us tucked into Pey's bed, both asleep. It will be the next day before I can bring myself to describe to him what happened. "This is a great gift," we tell each other with hopeful hugs in a prayerful moment.

"What do you want to drink for breakfast?" I ask Peyton the next morning.

COK, types Peyton, and even though I'm not big on soft drinks, I rush to bring her one.

That night I call Patrick Jr. and tell him what has happened, realizing that I probably sound hysterical and incoherent. I am in a state of shock at once filled with soaring hallelujahs and remorseful regrets. What if we had never learned the truth about FC? Why couldn't we have learned it twenty years ago? This internal struggle will last for several months while I run on autopilot, continuing to work and worry about the restaurant. I leave the Franklin Speller lying around, using it only to ask shallow things like, "What do you want to eat?" while Linda, Gayle, Julianne, Patrick, and Ali all hungrily seek out times to type with Peyton. They are eager to learn what she thinks, how she feels.

Supporting Peyton to type, I can feel her purposeful pointing for the first time in my life. This is real. Yet for some reason, I feel myself holding back. *Am I afraid to know?* Watching Peyton type with facilitators in the first few months, I cannot help but shed a few tears each time, until I finally swear off eye makeup.

"Do you understand why I'm crying?" I ask Peyton one day.

I THINK THAT YOU UNDERSTAND I, she types.

～

Although Peyton's nineteenth IEP written a few months ago in February of 1997 was supposed to be her last, it would also determine the future services she would receive from the San Diego Regional Center, which supports adults with disabilities. To me, February's IEP held out no real hope for a future; with Fiddler's failing, it was like a one-way ticket back to the institutions. Two decades of increasingly restrictive segregation have decimated Peyton. So to document her breakthrough in communication, we urgently request a new IEP and the meeting is scheduled just six days before the school year ends. This twentieth and final IEP provides a legal record of facilitated communication as a valid and vital strategy for Peyton's success and is supported by formal assessments from both Darlene and a San Diego Unified district speech pathologist who meets with Peyton four times and facilitates with her. It also includes a page called "Alternative Means and Modes and Differential Proficiency Verification Form," which lists the accommodations a student with a disability requires to be successful. This page had never been filled out in Peyton's previous IEPs, probably because she was seen as incapable of real learning. But this is different. This new IEP seems to hold infinite possibilities, and all fourteen signers (eight of whom have facilitated typing with Peyton) enthusiastically support it. Filling salt shakers at the restaurant is no longer Peyton's only chance to contribute to the world.

PEYTON'S REVISED IEP

Date: June 2, 1997

Peyton has recently had a breakthrough in the area of communication. Therefore, assessments prior to this time must be reevaluated to determine validity. Peyton is currently expressing independent thought with the use of a one-on-one communication facilitator. The facilitator is needed for Peyton to be successful in all areas of instruction and her life.

Peyton is aging out of district programs and wishes to continue education at the college level. Alternative strategies will be explored through special services at the college level.

—Linda Malone and Gayle Cisneros, classroom teachers

The months following the new IEP are ones of awakenings in me. Since Good Friday, I have been overwhelmed with simultaneous feelings of *I'm so sorry* and *Let's celebrate.* I fear giving in to either mind-set. For now, I am content to go with the flow, often watching Peyton from across the room typing with others, while listening keenly, astonished at what my daughter has to say.

Patrick and Ali have purchased for Peyton (at a cost of $3,000) a first-rate augmentative communication device called a Light-writer, with visual displays and text-to-speech output that allows for conversations. On a gut level, I know that no event other than Peyton's birth can ever be as important as her regaining her speech. It is a rebirth. The future that Pat and I had feared for decades is now filling with hope.

Mary Ellen Sousa, co-director of Creative Supports Alterna-tives, which supports people after they transition from school to adult services, hires and trains people to support Peyton's com-munication. These supporters accompany her to the La Costa Child Center where Peyton volunteers, and to monthly FC train-ing workshops in Whittier, where we all (including Patrick and Ali) learn more about movement disorders and how to facilitate Peyton's communication and participation. We learn how to offer emotional support (she asks us to verbalize her own self-talk phrases "My emotions don't control me," "I can trust myself," and "I can chase fear away") and verbal encouragement to look at the keyboard and finish her thought ("Point to keep going"), along with physical support and resistance to Peyton's wrist and forearm so that her finger can point dependably to the letters she chooses.

Having a voice means that Peyton can really teach at the Child Center rather than just observe. Now one day a week I accompany her to do story time with the kids. Peyton chooses the book herself (like *May I Bring a Friend* or *I'll Love you Forever*), which her aide, Julianne, Velcros to a large clipboard that Peyton can hold in her lap. Mary Ellen prerecords the book on a cassette with Peyton adding the ping sounds using a triangle to signal the page turns. In the school, Peyton uses her Lightwriter to introduce the book and discuss it with the kids afterward. The lesson proceeds with Peyton pushing the technology buttons while the children sit mesmerized. Michael—the most spirited of the eighteen children, and the one who receives most of the discipline in class—becomes Peyton's greatest helper by handing her items and being her "reminderer" if she is slow to turn a page.

Educators and reformers like Paul Carpenter at La Costa College and Katie Bishop-Smith at University of San Diego, who have known Peyton for years, are now eager to learn from her, and she is invited to speak to their classes. With Julianne's support, Peyton can answer questions in Paul's classes, and he celebrates her participation as "co-teacher." On one of her typed presentations, he writes, "Peyton—it is hard for me not to cry tears of joy. Keep sharing—talk to me."

At San Diego State University, Peyton presents in Mary Ellen's credentialing classes, and at Cal State University San Marcos, Peyton participates in summer leadership conferences attended by several hundred parents and educators. Supporting Peyton at these presentations can be a challenging process, requiring two facilitators who must be on their toes every second. But our labors are nothing compared to Peyton's. Typing, like other intentional movement, requires great effort by Peyton, and is often interrupted by unwanted, interfering movements she cannot restrain—hands that seek continuously to swipe dust off the table or pick specks of lint off a sweater, feet that stomp incessantly under the table, a body that spontaneously erupts in Jack LaLanne jumping jacks, seemingly unaware of objects or people in the way of her wing span.

Peyton calls this her "motor madness," and has told us, "I need I'm move to calm my thinking. I'm need rhythm." If someone attempts to inhibit her bothersome movements, physically or verbally, this only escalates its interference. So she moves, we wait, and then we redirect her by saying, "Come back . . . Keep going . . . What else were you going to say? . . . You are making a lot of progress here. Can you finish up?" At the conferences, we flank her on either side, angling our bodies toward hers. One of us supports her typing as she painstakingly pecks away at the keyboard with her right pointer finger, when her body cooperates. The other facilitates walks and puzzles with Peyton when her prepared slide show plays.

Peyton and Julianne also gain the support of Dr. Wade Grafton, the new head of special education for San Diego Unified School District, to help train teachers in supported typing as they visit classes and work with other nonverbal students. In the year following her June 1997 IEP, there are a dozen presentations, with Julianne or Mary Ellen facilitating and me working the video camera, marveling at Peyton's words.

❧

One Tuesday in mid-January of 1998, Ali calls. The philanthropic organization she belongs to, the Thursday Club Juniors, is having its monthly meeting in a few days, and the speaker has canceled.

"Peyton, I suggested that you come and speak. They would love to hear you," she says. "Is that something you want to do?"

YES, types Peyton.

At the presentation I distribute handouts and deliver a brief introduction about our family's journey, while Pat passes out three-by-five cards for people to use when they write their questions for Peyton. Julianne Velcros a wrist splint on Peyton's right arm and sets the Lightwriter on the custom-made, red Plexiglas stand that angles the keyboard correctly, then places her left hand on Peyton's right shoulder. She holds Peyton's arm, ready to supply pull-back resistance above the rollerblading wrist guard after each keyboard strike.

Peyton studies the women in the audience astutely as they begin passing their cards forward; then she focuses purposefully on the keyboard, slowly pecking, HI, I NERVOUS. I TYPE TO TELL PEOPLE I THINK. I DO NOT TALK. I AM SMART. I AM AUTISTIC.

These sentences take five minutes to type, with Julianne intermittently coaching Peyton to bring her visual focus back to the keyboard and continue. All the time Peyton's tongue writhes in and out of her mouth with rhythmic precision. Are these tongue gyrations induced by her medications, I wonder, or is it something necessary she is supplying for herself? But I decide it is certainly better than the frozen lockjaw and accompanying teeth gritting that has worn some of her teeth down a quarter-inch and split each of the orthodontist's custom-made "kryptonite" mouthpieces within the first week of wearing.

The proper ladies of the Thursday Club, with a seventy-seven-year heritage of philanthropic endeavors in San Diego, seem unbothered by Peyton's physical tics, and Peyton seems to sense their respect for her as she becomes playfully interactive with them, surprising me.

I KNOW YOU ARE HUNGRY, she offers, as it is now noon. They laugh. BUT I HAVE TO SAY YOU LOOK NICE. A few *Thank you*'s are offered in return. DO YOU THINK I LOOK NICE?

"Yes," the women reply, laughing and clapping.

At this point, Peyton's tongue retreats back in her mouth, and she asks with a growing, glowing smile, DO YOU HAVE QUESTIONS?

She peruses the cards, choosing the first one to answer. Suzy Crawford, club president, who has known Peyton all her life, has written, "Peyton I talk a lot, and sometimes my mouth gets tired. When you type, does your finger hurt?"

I GET TIRED TOO, BUT I DIDN'T TALK FOR A LONG TIME AND I HAVE A LOT TO SAY, she replies.

"How does it feel to finally be able to communicate?" asks another woman.

GREAT. I LOVE TO TALK. THANK YOU FOR HEARING ME.

Peyton has been typing for a half hour now, and she reaches up to hold her forehead in an eye-squinting facial expression. Is it sudden discomfort? Is it the pain of great effort, or perhaps reliving difficult memories? She lets it pass several times.

I ONLY UNDERTOOK THIS BECAUSE I CAN FINALLY SPEAK FOR OTHERS, types Peyton, forging on.

"Describe the first time that you typed in Whittier. How did it feel? What were you thinking?" one woman asked.

I THOUGHT I WOULD FAIL. I WAS SCARED I WOULD NOT TYPE. MY MOM JUST TRIED TO CONTROL HERSELF. I KNEW I COULD TYPE. I WAS TOO HAPPY TO TYPE THE FIRST TIME. I ALWAYS KNEW WHAT YOU WERE SAYING. I AM SMART. YOU ALWAYS KNEW THAT, DAD. YES, BUT MOM GOT CRYING. YES, SHE THOUGHT THE WORLD HAD ENDED, types Peyton.

"What do you see in your future?" reads the next question.

I WANT TO GRADUATE COLLEGE. I KNOW IT WILL TAKE TIME. BUT THAT IS WHAT I WANT. I AM SMART, she responds. I watch Peyton studying the audience and typing with full concentration for forty minutes. She saves one question for last: "What does it feel like to be autistic?"

I take a deep breath, preparing my senses to be fully receptive.

Peyton types carefully and deliberately: I AM NOT ABLE TO CONTROL MY BODY. I CANNOT TALK. I NEED HELP TO DO MOST THINGS. She pauses, looking up to read the women's faces, and I suspect there is more. Then Julianne, watching Peyton's eyes connect again with the keyboard, loosens her resistance to Peyton's wrist, and Peyton continues. BUT I CAN OPEN MY HEART TO MOST PEOPLE, she types. CAN YOU DO THAT?

The room freezes in silence for five seconds; then forty-five bodies rise in a standing ovation. Peyton spoke to a small part of the world that day, but she also spoke to me. I finally realize I am starving to know my own daughter.

⌘

Driving north with Peyton for the next Whittier workshop, with my new commitment to "age-appropriate" learning opportunities, I pop a tape into the cassette player—an audiobook my friend Nancy has loaned us about a girl with dwarfism. Peyton listens intently while flipping her flash cards of past US presidents.

At most Whittier sessions Peyton meets a nonverbal person who is coming to try FC for the first time, so we are often in the presence of others' first words. Today it is a fourteen-year-old boy named Antonio. His mom drove for five hours so he could be here.

Peyton approaches Antonio and types, "I like typing to talk. I have much faith in you and I. I am like you. I could not talk to the people I love. I can now. I hope you learn to type independently."

When he sits down to type, he is reluctant but does not pull away. Peyton reaches out to hold his hand and then types to him, "You peppy Antonio. Try to trust that you can type. Ease opposition to pity join. Open to possibilities that you can pity not your searching sweet self. Try rest your fears. Please."

His mother Elena begins to cry as she watches Antonio listen to Peyton and then, with the aid of his facilitator, reach his finger to type Y for "yes."

Climbing back into the car, I feel joyful for our shared experience. Back on the freeway, I push the tape of the audiobook back into the cassette player. As we near the Interstates 5 and 405 merge in Irvine, to my surprise, the plot turns to the abuse of the main character by neighborhood boys, who are holding her down to molest her. Disturbing sounds come from the passenger seat as Peyton begins to squirm, her hands grabbing her forehead.

"This is called molestation, and it's not right," I explain, trying to see if Peyton will calm down. The tape plays for another three minutes before I realize that Peyton's discomfort is unbearable. I stop the tape and continue to drive, hoping Peyton's pain will subside until we can make it home and talk about it safely. But we make it only to the next exit in El Toro before I realize I must pull off. I have never seen Peyton like this. Her face is contorted as though she has just witnessed a heinous crime. Hugging Peyton, I feel her body shaking, tremors that take many minutes to quell. I buy us each a cookie and we continue heading south, the radio now playing country and western tunes, me singing loudly with a still-uncomfortable Peyton sitting next to me.

I feel a huge sense of relief as I turn onto our block and see Pat's car in the driveway. He is probably home to shower before going back to open the restaurant. I drive onto the lawn to save time and tap Peyton's right leg under the knee to encourage her body to swivel and get out (a simple support technique I learned from the autism conference).

Peyton walks into the house and makes a beeline for her pastel bedroom, plopping on her bed, clearly exhausted. In the car, I had told her we would talk when we got home, thinking that it was probably time for that mother-daughter sex talk that usually takes place in most households a dozen years earlier. I never even considered having it with Peyton in the past, even though she has been exposed to sexual suggestiveness in TV and print media. Peyton's reaction to the audiobook suggests that the time has come.

I find Pat finishing up his shave. Giving him a kiss on the cheek without shaving cream, I ask, "Hey, can you hold off on going over to the restaurant for a talk with Pey?"

"Sure," he says. "I'll be ready in a jiffy."

"Pey, Dad wants to know about your day," I begin, as I gather several pillows from her bed to prop the keyboard into typing position. Pat sits down near the end of the bed, hair smoothly combed above bushy eyebrows that always perk up to listen to Peyton.

"Today was a good day," I continue. "You typed with Darlene and with a new friend, Antonio, who typed his first words today. But the tape we were listening to in the car seemed to disturb you on our way home. Can you tell us what you thought about the book?"

"It was sad," types Peyton. "The girl was raped."

Peyton's use of the word *rape* shocks me. With everything in me, I try to remain calm, sensing that Peyton has more to say since her hand remains in the position to type.

"Do you know what *rape* means?" I ask.

"Intercourse," types Peyton.

"Yes, it is that, but intercourse should be consensual, based on both parties desiring intimacy," I explain. "Rape is forceful and not consensual. How do you know about intercourse?" I ask, suspending all emotion.

Peyton studies my face. "Because I was raped," she types.

I breathe deep down into my belly and exhale, praying for wisdom as the three of us, two passengers and one pilot in this bedroom cockpit, cross the point of no return in our already difficult journey.

Pat leans in closer. "Please keep talking to us, Peyton; we are together," he says, struggling to keep his emotions in check.

The pilot holds steady on the flight. She types, "I was raped by the street guy Dan at Marshall Institute."

"When you say he *raped* you, what part of his body did he touch you with?" I ask, emotions still on pause.

"He fucked me with his fingers very hard," she types, her lower body squirming as painful noises escape her lips.

I ask a few more factual questions. As Peyton begins holding her breath and releasing it in explosive puffs, I say, "Do you want to stop talking now?"

"Yes," types Peyton, and the painful sounds begin to subside.

"Mom and Dad are very sad we could not help you when this happened, and that you were alone with this for so long, but we're glad you can tell us now," says Pat, his eyes welling with tears.

Clutching my daughter, whose eyelids have become heavy, I ask, "Can we talk about this again soon?"

"Yes," whispers Peyton in a faint voice.

I hold my daughter tightly and she falls asleep in my arms. Life has pushed the PAUSE button, and we three are caught inside a freeze-frame. Only my eyes and Pat's move to meet in unspoken searching of countless shared emotions. Tears pour out in an amount that is impossible for our lids to contain. In the silence I hear our hearts break in unison, and a sadness that will prove utterly unshakable fills some of the cracks. But gladness flows in too. We are thankful to hear the truth, even if it's ten years too late.

From this moment forward, I am committed to facilitating Peyton's communication, diving in with both feet. The ties that have been holding me back—How does she really feel about me? and Can I open my heart to new understandings?—have now been cut. I choose not to fear the truth, Peyton's or mine, troublesome though it might be.

⌒≈⌒

Immediately, we discuss the issue with Peyton's psychiatrist, Dr. Friedman. Since her initial revelation, Peyton has become increasingly agitated. In his office, she types to him intently:

"dantookgirlsinclosettorapethem. hetouchedtheirvaginatoohard. isawhim. ifeeltootired. youreallyneedtotellthepolice."

"Peyton, would you consider filing a report with Child Protective Services?" asks Dr. Friedman. "We can do this together in the next session if you want."

Peyton asks for time to think about it.

At home, Peyton begins to type with me obsessively about her molestation, and her worries about the safety of the other kids at Marshall Institute. Though I do not share this information with Peyton's other facilitators, Peyton types about it with a trusted friend, a facilitator named Grace, telling her that other little girls were taken into the closet by Dan.

"I type opportunity for police to lock up Dan," types Peyton repeatedly.

An alarmed Grace seeks me out to report what Peyton has typed, urging Peyton to file the report, which she does.

Suddenly soaring systolic and diastolic numbers add a second blood pressure medication to my list of prescriptions.

SUSPECTED CHILD ABUSE REPORT

SENT TO: Child Protective Services
NAME OF REPORTING PARTY: Robert Friedman, MD
DATE OF INCIDENT: June 1985–July 1989
PLACE OF INCIDENT: Marshall Institute–Special Day School
TYPE OF ABUSE: Sexual Assault

NARRATIVE DESCRIPTION:
Peyton suffers from a pervasive developmental disorder. When at Marshall Institute, Peyton suffered a severe behavioral change with marked regression in ALL AREAS, including: speech, language, emotional liability, academic, bowel-bladder control.

Recently, Peyton has been able to indicate/tell that she was sexually molested by a man named Dan at Marshall Institute.

SUMMARIZE WHAT THE ABUSED CHILD OR PERSON ACCOMPANYING THE CHILD SAID HAPPENED:
I (Peyton) want to tell. Dan took girls to closet to rape them . . . He touched their vagina too hard. . . . I was raped by the street guy at Marshall Institute. . . . He fucked me with his fingers very hard . . . in the closet. . . . Dan, who took out the trash cans.

EXPLAIN KNOWN HISTORY OF SIMILAR INCIDENTS(S) FOR THIS CHILD:
None.

The next week, Dr. Friedman submits the report to Child Protective Services, and we hold our breath for the response. Although our first instinct is to take justice into our own hands and behead a few thugs, we want to tread on a path that will help our daughter heal. (In March, we will hire an attorney to sue the school district for the abuse Peyton suffered under their watch.) "Justice" for her in order to help her heal—this is our goal, though we are not sure she wants it for herself. For Peyton, it is only about other children, because she knows Dan is still out there somewhere—all the Dans.

≈

On Friday the thirteenth of February, we are shocked to hear that my cousin Duane has died in a car accident in Arizona. Gam flies out immediately to comfort Bette the day after Duane, full of alcohol, self-destructs, his car spinning out of control and crashing head-on into a palm tree.

After working all day at the restaurant, Pat drives us through the night to get to Tucson just minutes before the service begins. Entering the vestibule, we offer condolences to Bette and Gus, but Connie sits alone in the front pew, never turning her head.

Peyton, ordinarily giggly around Bette, is somehow subdued today. We are the only other family there, and Pat agrees to deliver a eulogy at Gus's request. He speaks in exaggerated, positive generalizations meant to console this family we do not quite understand but have now spent decades feeling sorry for.

"Duane's life speaks of the deep mystery of compassion," says Pat, his voice echoing in the nearly empty desert-themed church. "It speaks of the mystery that interconnects all our lives, and it speaks of the mystery of peace that passes all understanding."

Bette, Gus, and Connie join Duane's girlfriend and their two-year-old daughter to fill the right front pew. We fill the left front, and Pat respectfully corrects the minister when he announces, "Let us now pray for Darren's soul." In a moment of silence, I feel Peyton's hand reach out to hold mine. I offer her the Lightwriter, and Peyton types, "God is present here now." I squeeze her hand.

We drive home immediately after the last amen.

Back at home, Mary Ellen helps Peyton explore educational opportunities by taking her to the Adult Education Center on Midway Drive. Peyton's final IEP guarantees that she will be allowed accommodations like increased response time, large type, assistive technology, and support for facilitated communication. Mary Ellen asks the staff at the center to prepare practice GED questions so supporters can begin to work with Peyton to study for the test. The initial goal, explains Mary Ellen, is to discover where Peyton's learning gaps lie so we can begin academic tutoring.

The following week, I take Peyton to the Adult Education Center, where we pick up her prepared questions at the monitor's desk. After settling in at a table in the far corner of the scarcely populated study hall, I attach the questions to a large, angled clipboard and place it in front of Peyton so she can easily read them. Then I center the Lightwriter on its stand, and we begin our study session.

The first four questions ask her to analyze Robert Frost's poem, "The Road Not Taken," which I read slowly to Peyton. I read her the first question: "Why does the author say 'I shall be telling this with a sigh / Somewhere ages and ages hence'?"

Then I read Peyton each possible answer and support her wrist as I watch her eyes move to one of the choices. I release the resistance as Peyton types B.

"Is B your answer?" I ask to confirm.

"Y," types Peyton.

The next set of questions refers to an excerpt from the Declaration of Independence. Another question asks her to analyze a tax table. And so the morning goes. The passages are read, the answers are read, and the questions are answered. Then we turn in the answer sheet to the study hall monitor to be graded.

The twenty-something woman with a silver nose ring goes down the answer sheet carefully, and then turns to Peyton, smiling. "Good job. All of them are correct."

"Well, Peyton, that was a real education for me," I exclaim as we walk down the hall past the learning rooms. After six more days of studying, Mary Ellen calls us with bad news: "I'm sorry, guys. I'm told that the State will not allow students to use FC on a GED test."

My heart sinks. After so many years of silence, it seems unjust that she must now struggle to be heard.

STARTING BIG: THE FIRST YEAR
BY PEYTON GODDARD

Facilitated Communication Conference at Syracuse University
May 5, 1998

I cannot be silent. I have much to say. I will tell people about typing. URGENT to teach FC for people who go home to living in institutions, that you and I go move them out. I want them out because I love them. It is possible to love people when you don't know their name, if you know how they feel.

In San Diego, I think my voice is being recognized, but not acknowledged. The thinkers go home to houses, not institutions. If the thinkers went home to the institution, they would do more here at the crossroads to listen to FC.

At the next Whittier workshop, I notice a young man named Gabriel who travels south from Ventura with his support team. Dressed in preppy Gap khakis and a plaid sport shirt, he seems to turn a few heads. Then I notice he has also turned Peyton's head. Is she smitten? This is previously unimagined territory.

At the FC conference at Chapman University that spring, Gabriel (who uses some verbal language but also types to communicate) presents with his mom on the topic of supported living; he has his own place with people who support him in Ventura. Afterward, I overhear Ali comment to Peyton about "the cool guy" in the herringbone wool blazer.

"If you ask me, Peyton, he's worth getting to know," advises her sister-in-law, now in her second year of law school. Though she and Patrick (who works at a start-up Internet service provider) are busy these days, they make time to learn about facilitating Peyton's typing, attend her conferences, and take regular

Sunday afternoon walks with us through Mission Gorge or up Cowles Mountain, followed by a fish taco dinner feast at Rubio's.

Peyton and Gabriel's friendship grows, and we begin eating lunch with Gabriel and his facilitators after the workshops, in one of the nearby fast-food restaurants. For now it's a same-time-next-month relationship.

In her sessions with Dr. Friedman, Peyton continues to worry about the safety of the kids at Marshall Institute. Since there has been no word from the police about the Child Protective Services (CPS) report filed three months ago, Pat arranges for a telephone conference with Sergeant Ed Whitman of the Sex Crimes Unit. So that Peyton can participate, Pat hooks up our speakerphone at the kitchen table, where Peyton and I have begun a 300-piece puzzle. He dials the number and greetings quickly turn to the point of the call.

"Our daughter wants to know what you are going to do about this case," Pat begins. "She is very concerned about other children's safety. Can you please help us get some answers?

"A report was filed to CPS by Dr. Robert Friedman and Peyton Goddard dated February 16. Can you tell us what action was taken on the complaint? Can we request a copy of the police report you made?"

All we hear are these words: "A report was not filed, Mr. Goddard, due to the fact that the statute of limitations had expired."

Anger rises in Pat and me as we glance at each other. How do you respond to the notion of justice expiring? About to release the lid he usually fastens on his emotions, Pat quiets as he sees Peyton grab my hand to reach for the Lightwriter. Sergeant

Whitman hears Peyton's response spoken by a synthesized voice: "I want to meet with you. The kids are not safe."

"Okay," agrees Whitman. "We'll meet, Peyton."

⚉

Two weeks later Pat, Peyton, and I park our car in a metered spot across the street from San Diego Police Headquarters. We cross the busy street, the Lightwriter strapped across my chest in a canvas bag like a holster, my hand tightly holding a determined Peyton's hand.

Strapped in similar fashion across Peyton's chest is the thirty-eight-minute video of her life, something she had recently put together for her Syracuse University presentation with Professor Carpenter. We are followed by Pat, who tenuously balances our bulky Panasonic television with built-in VHS player, electrical cord beginning to dangle as he dodges traffic to catch up with his girls. We squeeze into the elevator and travel up to the fourth floor, where Sergeant Whitman and victim advocate Paula Radley are waiting to listen to Peyton in the conference room.

They watch the video. Then Peyton types her concerns with the focus of a neurosurgeon trying to remove a brain tumor. As the meeting progresses, Pat and I are convinced that Whitman and Radley believe her. After an hour, Whitman tells her, "Although the statute time is over, I will personally investigate the man's whereabouts."

A month later, he calls us. "There is not presently a man named Dan employed at the school," he reports. "Sorry, but that's all I can do."

What we want is peace for our daughter. We had hoped that seeking justice under the law might help; instead, we are left with the shattering disappointment that there will be no finding Dan. Pat and I are stymied by the futility of this blind alley.

In her next session with Dr. Friedman, Peyton types, "I want to get on with my life." To do this, she courageously proposes facing her fears by revisiting her old school and the time-out room where she spent hours in isolation. My insides cringe, blood pressure rising to 190/100. For nine years I have gone out of my way never to drive Peyton anywhere near the place.

"I must return to the place of the scare, where I lost joy and speech," she types.

Friedman recommends a desensitizing program, beginning with simply driving by the school, then walking around it, then walking up to the door. We begin doing this on weekends, driving by several times, then parking outside the school, each time allowing her to type about her feelings. Then one Sunday we decide to try walking around the school.

The front half of the school can be traversed without going on the premises, and Peyton navigates from one end to the other without incident. When we reach the redwood gate that encloses the concrete play area in the back, Peyton walks up to it and jiggles the latch.

"I'm sure it's locked from the inside for security," I say.

To our surprise, the gate opens. Pat and I look at each other, not sure what to do, but Peyton walks inside, so we follow her. She marches with a stomp through the courtyard, to the door nearest the tiny time-out room where she suffered day after day. She served a four-year sentence here before the age of fifteen. Her face wears a determined look. Her hands begin banging on the door. Her feet begin kicking.

Returning to the scene of a crime is beasted by red.
Festers repound your eddying sufferings.

Never opening the doors to each crime is hoping
you are wedded to some rest.
Will looking at tortures free me or point me to steered insanity?

Pat and I do not know what to do, so we join in, beating and kicking. It is clear that no entry will be made today, but that does not stop us all from releasing our fury upon the pitiless black door. Peyton's hands redden and swell. Pat takes hold of them. His are burning too.

I lift the Lightwriter from my shoulder bag, and from how Peyton types, it seems the machine would yell if it could: "I want you to knock the door down."

Chapter 9

I Want an Education

People ~~with autism~~ desire real lives.

Ability to benefit is the only thing that qualifies her for admission, the only box she can check on the application form.

In the large, cubicled office of Disabled Students Programs and Services (DSPS) at Cuyamaca Community College, Peyton, along with me and her typing facilitator, Mary Ellen Sousa, meets with Dr. Yvonette Powell, coordinator of DSPS, in August 1998 to discuss supports and ideas on classes. I cannot imagine the courage it must take for her to tackle all the unknowns of college, including the very real possibility of failure. Being asked to leave her first college class two years ago is a memory still fresh in her mind.

Joy was that Dr. Powell believed from our very first meeting that
I could learn.
My previously unimaginable opportunity for an education now
seemed possible, and this validated my goals of learning all things.
This crucial border crossing could not have happened without her
treating herself to dare reach ultimately into her great heart of
possibilities and not dare say, "Nil you are as a person, Peyton."
Many people with educations had believed I was a reason
to institutionalize, but Dr. Powell said that she saw my human
right to learn.

Since Peyton enjoys working with children, she chooses Child Development 125, which meets Monday, Wednesday, and Friday from 11:00 to 11:50 a.m. Her college days begin at 9:45 a.m. when Mary Ellen picks her up and drives her to campus, thirty minutes east on the Martin Luther King Jr. Freeway. Peyton's wheeled backpack contains water, her textbook, a spiral notebook, an extra set of clothes, and Depends, just in case. Slung over Mary Ellen's shoulder is a purple canvas artist's bag containing a Plexiglas board and one of Peyton's many 200-piece Ravensburger puzzles. The puzzle will take Peyton fifty minutes to complete, allowing her hands to stay busy so her mind can focus on the lecture while Mary Ellen takes notes in Professor Ensey's class.

For me, the restaurant no longer fills my days or nagging nightmares. A door has opened, and Peyton has finally been invited inside. Now all my attention turns to preparing for study times, which fill every minute that Peyton is not in class or at the preschool, reading to the children she calls "cherubs."

For the first time, Peyton is confronted with a challenging, outlined-in-a-syllabus curriculum, accompanied by Professor Ensey's many study guides and an actual textbook, *Child and Adolescent Development*. My organizational skills rival any that Pat employed in getting huge Chart House projects like Philadelphia and Boston built. My simple Canon copy machine becomes my sidekick for enlarging text for Peyton's homework. And each day I marvel at Peyton's hunger for learning as she devours the readings and charts. We read together while she sits on a couch, working on her puzzles, or in an oak captain's chair at the kitchen table overlooking the bay. As night falls and the lights of Shelter Island blink on, we read.

I had forgotten the wonder of the teacher-student interchange. We swim together in the warm waters of learning; both of us teachers and learners. I cannot remember anything feeling better than these new moments.

I do not facilitate Peyton's communication in class or in exams that first semester. Instead, while Peyton is at school, I make flip cards of definitions from the glossary and instructional charts outlining developmental theories. I help Peyton make a timeline for completing the syllabus assignments, and evenings become full-on homework sessions so that Peyton goes to each class prepared. This had been her urgent request.

What a switch for Peyton, I think, *from having only dead time to having no time to waste.*

Each quiz and exam is individually proctored, with Mary Ellen and Grace facilitating while I sit outside the classroom in case Peyton wants a break or a drink. Peyton's first test score is 64 percent. On her second test, she scores 100 percent. And on subsequent tests, she averages above 90 percent.

Then comes a ten-page paper for which she must observe and analyze a child (she chooses the spirited boy named Michael from her preschool group) using the developmental theories of Erikson, Piaget, Skinner, Vygotsky, and others. Peyton writes in her conclusion, "I will hope for Michael to continue to develop positively. I will hope for absence of illness, poverty, violence, abuse, divorce, accident, death, unfairness, damaging labels, discrimination, poor teaching, and traumatic stress . . ."

Professor Ensey gives her 95 percent, commenting, "You presented some of the best examples that I have read."

Arriving home from class one mid-December day, Mary Ellen announces, "Peyton has something to tell you."

I pull out the small, blue Franklin Speller I now carry in my back pocket (everyone on Peyton's team was given one), and Peyton types, "I do not have to take the final. I have already earned an A." Mary Ellen and I start jumping and clapping and shouting. We are now the ones with "motor madness." Yes, that is a little giggle that I hear coming from Peyton.

———

November 2, 1998
Los Angeles, CA

PUBLIC TESTIMONY TO NATIONAL ASSESSMENT GOVERNING BOARD REGARDING ACCOMMODATIONS FOR AND INCLUSION OF STUDENTS WITH DISABILITIES IN PROPOSED VOLUNTARY NATIONAL TESTS

Thank you, Governing Board, for hearing my thinking on including and accommodating people like I in large-scale assessment testing. I think above all, please do not excuse people like I from participation by establishing exclusion criteria. For all kids real joy revolves around opportunity to learn. People like I need more inclusion in life and not go separate in school. Need access to core curriculum and coping accommodations.

I am enrolled at Cuyamaca College this fall as a regular student receiving necessary support from Disabled Student Services. I am accommodated in test situations by an interpreter/facilitator and a proctor. Other accommodations I receive are large print, one question at a time, extended time, a distraction-free environment. My first academic test score ever was 64 percent, middle of the curve for that test, and I took three hours to complete it. My next test took only one hour; my score was 100 percent.

The primary purpose of education is for students to move on to opportunities for real life. Education must prepare all children for a real life of value and purpose. If students with disabilities are excluded from access to core academics and accommodations to be successful learners, they move to an existence, not a life. I have experienced this. Our greatest assets in the process are our brightest teachers and the shining wisdom of students with disabilities being appropriately accommodated.

—Peyton Goddard

On your path to implementing FC, you'll hear many opposing your choice. They have long convinced themselves that people such as I

deserve no education because I am filled with nothing in my think-
ing brain. The truth is that pleasurable learning is sought by my
brain at all times. All my life I search for opportunities to learn all
things hidden in the hulk of readily available, print-rich environ-
ments.Never ultimately is the brilliance of the barely ignited brain
turned off. Therefore, you'll eagerly look at the ambiguity of my
movements and see a person intelligent, who realized literacy mull-
ing self-sought learning while receiving no real education in school.

Over the break, we ask Peyton if she wants to pursue the liti-
gation against the school district that Pat and I had initiated upon
learning about her molestation.

Peyton replies, "No. Energies ahead, not behind."

❧

In January 1999, Peyton discusses classes and professors with Dr.
Powell, as they will do prior to each registration period for the
next four years. Peyton has missed going to school over Christmas break and is looking forward to her next challenge.

Dr. Powell, an attractive woman with gold hoop earrings
that accent her black hair, explains, "Professor Ensey is teaching
Health Education. Beginning English would be good for developing more clarity in writing, and Mrs. Haber, head of the history
department, is teaching Early American History this semester."
She looks at Peyton, who types "Mythology."

"Any one of these four would be a good choice for your
next class," says Dr. Powell. "But you should know that Mythology is considered an upper-division class, so it will be more
challenging."

Two of the classes meet on Monday, Wednesday, and Friday, and two on Tuesday and Thursday (which means 300-piece

puzzles would be needed to fill the seventy-five-minute lecture). Peyton types, "I want to sign up for all of them."

Dr. Powell cannot hide her surprise, but nods, smiling brightly. "Okay, this way you'll have a good chance to check them out, so you can decide which one, or maybe two, you want to keep, Peyton. You'll have three weeks to decide before the drop date."

As we leave her office, my head is swimming with how to go about setting up homework sessions for four classes to stay current on assignments until Peyton decides which one to commit to for the semester.

Three weeks later, four people are sitting around the kitchen table. Pat is home to change shirts and return to the restaurant by opening time at five. Professor Paul Carpenter has dropped by to talk to Peyton about how things are going at Cuyamaca. Always ready to mentor Peyton, he is aware she has had three weeks of four classes, and that the drop date is this Friday. There are no cookies and tea on the table, which has a map of the world laminated on its surface, though it is teatime. Peyton's Lightwriter sits on its custom-built stand on top of Australia, and I sit on Peyton's right to facilitate the conversation. Pat's right elbow rests on Key West, as he is turned to listen to Peyton, and Paul sits directly across from Peyton, his arms crossing Siberia, ready to advise.

"Please," she types, "I desire lots of opportunities in classes. Education opportunities are crucial for joy. Please support my stay in all four classes."

We are stunned. We had never dreamt of this option; maybe negotiating for two instead of one, but *four?* From the direction of the warm waters of the Caribbean come the first warnings.

"Peyton, you may be absolutely capable of handling twelve units," says Pat, "but I don't know if your supporters at school and at home will be able to keep up the pace."

Paul sits back in his chair and speaks as a professor and friend. "Peyton, you had such success last semester. What about taking it slower in order to ensure that your success continues? How about taking two classes to see how that goes?" he suggests.

The Lightwriter is silent as Peyton glances around the table. Then she types, "I plot my living moments of peace thinking opportunities for hoping bliss in school. Please try. It is my right." This is the first time Pat and I have ever heard Peyton speak up for herself. How can we refuse?

Peyton rises to the challenge, as does her support team. I now facilitate for Peyton in her classes. When Peyton arrives home, aides or neighborhood volunteers are there to help read her the assigned textbook chapters. With four times the number of tests, and Peyton requiring extra time to complete the tests in front of a proctor, she regularly spends ten to twelve hours a day on campus.

Dr. Powell and the staff at DSPS arrange for Peyton to take quizzes and exams with proctors after 3:00 p.m. in an available classroom, free of distractions. After lugging a portable, gray typing table from home several times, I purchase an additional one to keep at the college. On exam days, Peyton and I set up the table and several comfortable chairs in the room reserved for her. For multiple-choice tests, the proctor sets up an eleven-by-seventeen-inch dry-erase board that has thin black strips of tape on it to create a grid. The question is mounted on top of the grid, and all the possible answers are mounted below it so Peyton can ponder the entire question. DSPS spends considerable time enlarging and cutting out each question. In preparation for a lengthy essay exam, I search out and purchase portable two-seater couches. The two best finds are a wicker love seat and an aquamarine inflatable couch. Either can fit in the back of our

Suburban to make the trip down King Freeway for essay-writing evenings.

Peyton tackles her first lengthy written exam, a 1,000-word explanatory essay, for her English 100 class. After morning English and history classes, Peyton and I drive through Wendy's for lunch and return to campus, the backseat holding the blown-up plastic couch that appears ready to float in Macy's Thanksgiving Day Parade. After parking and reviewing the study guide once again, we maneuver the couch out of the SUV to carry it to the classroom.

In this rolling valley east of San Diego, the winds come up in the afternoon, and today they are gusting enough for a yacht race. With both of us wearing backpacks, our hands are free to carry the almost-lighter-than-air dirigible. We start across the parking lot and down an incline with me moving backwards to encourage Peyton to stay with me. Peyton is giving it her best college try, and I actually begin to think we will make it to room 208, when a sudden burst of wind rocks our blue blimp. We try to hold on to this seemingly huge object that has nothing resembling a handle on it, but another gust lifts the couch right out of Peyton's hands, and, airborne for two seconds, the couch tumbles into the chaparral.

Peyton waits on the sidewalk as I step into the calf-high brush, wondering how in the world—when I hear a voice. "Here, I'll help." A dark-haired woman helps me lift the piece of furniture to the sidewalk. I thank the Good Samaritan, who respectfully does not question what we are doing.

With breaks every thirty minutes, Peyton pecks out what seems to me like a completely acceptable essay, and then she goes back to perfect it. Mary Ellen stays the entire time, as do I, to facilitate Peyton's typing. Because of the time span, four different proctors (including Dr. Powell) take turns. After six hours, she is done. Peyton titles the essay "The Joy of Writing," explaining that "mute in speaking is not necessarily sign of mute in ideas."

At 9:00 p.m. Mary Ellen helps load the blue blimp that did such a good job padding our busy bodies. As we drive west out of Cuyamaca's valley, Peyton begins to hold her head and gag, sounds I recognize as a mounting migraine. I pull over and run around to open Peyton's door just in time to hold her head as today's hamburger and more heave out of her onto the dusty road.

Back at school the next day, Dr. Powell finds Peyton.

"I've thought about it, Peyton, and I think six hours is too long to ask anyone to type. For essay exams, how about drafting one day and editing the next—three hours maximum each afternoon?"

"Thank you," types Peyton.

In going to writing courses, one is able to look to the future in joyously knowing that one will never ill be mute knowing they can variously truthfully tell ultimately everyone the truth of their life in opposing silence that kills the soul.

⤛

Following her first year at Cuyamaca, Peyton presents at the 1999 Cal State San Marcos Summer Leadership Conference (as she will during most summers for the next decade), preparing a PowerPoint slide show narrated by Mary Ellen. In the Q and A, one student-teacher asks her, "How do you keep going, Peyton, especially in a five- or six-hour exam?"

Her reply: "I think of my retro life, and I keep going."

I weathered the storm in pursuit of an education when I
Cuyamaca itinerary journeyed.
I would here witness well, polluted-never, inclusion and purity
prioritizing educators.
Pooling resources, Dr. Yvonette Powell and Disabled Students
Programs and Services provided the sure support I pulsingly reined
my youth without.

In the fall of 1999 Peyton is again invited by Professor Carpenter to "co-teach" his class, called Psychology of the Exceptional Child. In this class, Peyton meets a student named Tricia,
a junior who appears very interested in getting to know Peyton.
When Peyton finds herself in need of a new facilitator a few
months later, Tricia is immediately interested in the job. She is
hired starting out at six hours per week, but as the school year
passes, she increases her support time with Peyton at home,
and is trained to facilitate Peyton's communication. I appreciate
Tricia's enthusiasm for the friendship, as she invites Peyton to
spend time in her dorm, just hanging out, and hopefully meeting other girls.

Tricia begins to suggest—and later insist—that she and Peyton
both want to find a one- or two-week camp they can attend this
summer. Peyton's goal is to someday have a roommate, and with
Tricia facilitating, Pat and I hear them openly discussing their
mutual desire to be roommates. Sitting next to Peyton on the
sofa, with her long blonde hair pulled back in pigtails from her
sallow face, Tricia holds Peyton's hand and smiles at every word
Peyton types with her. We notice that when Tricia facilitates,
Peyton's comments are more humorous and even include bold
requests about wanting to be independent of us. *Does this new attitude reflect Peyton's relationship with her new friend?* I wonder.

I felt very scared that I would lose my parents because of what
Tricia various times made my joy hand type.

A few weeks later, Gabriel and his mom are in town, and they come to our home for dinner, Gabriel bringing Peyton two dozen peach roses and his note, "Greet warmly flowers like jewels for a crown, Peyton." Tricia sits between the two smitten sweethearts, facilitating fast and furiously for them both during dinner, both requesting some privacy so they can talk. After dinner Tricia takes Peyton and Gabriel to the sitting area off our bedroom and closes the door.

About ten minutes later, Pat knocks on the door. "How's everything going in there?"

"They're having a great discussion," Tricia assures us through the closed door. "Just give them a few more minutes."

More minutes pass, and Gabriel's mother leaves to return to their hotel to make an important call.

About a half hour later, the discussion over, Gabriel sits up front in the van's bucket seat, incessantly pushing the dashboard buttons, as we drop Tricia at her dorm and take Gabriel back to join his mom, Pat mentioning to her that Gabe seemed bothered by something during the ride, perhaps he might want to type. In contrast, Peyton remains quiet, almost frozen, for the entire trip.

Later that night, a now-agitated Peyton demands that Tricia not be allowed to facilitate with her anymore. "Reason I freed from Tricia is realize she not care about joy I and Gabe. She cares about manipulating I," types Peyton. "She is insane. Various times I tell Tricia not to. Saw joy of Tricia in not listen to I."

Her body shaking, she tells us of the lewd comments typed to Gabriel through her hand, of her humiliation, her inability to face Gabriel after this. "I fear Tricia," she types.

When her hands finish, I hold Peyton.

"You are not responsible for your fear—Tricia is," I say. Yet I realize these words offer little comfort, and that having her voice stolen by an unscrupulous facilitator will now be an ever-present threat in her mind. Going forward, we are even more vigilant to train Peyton's facilitators and to confirm that what Peyton is typing is what she wants to say.

The journey touch-tugging on my arm is very personal.
You must be someone ultimately I trust.
If opposing you I am, then arriving at valid data is impossible.
You my great face will teach the world through my verified
fingers and never can I feel safe if your unethical hang-ups
empty my brain.
I must type with the power of hurdling no emotions.

The following day, Tricia is fired from the support agency, and soon after, Mary Ellen helps us establish our own Peyton Family Supported Living Agency, allowing Peyton more self-determination and responsibility in hiring, training, and dismissing her own supporters.

Each pity I'm quietly washing away. Treed by greeting thugs
tortures retrieving, I'm jestered hysterically hit.
I'm their Peyton fawn yowler, queasy powerless pawn, quiet until
operated I'm truth tell.

≈

On the first day of each new class, Peyton types a note to be read to her classmates:

You and I know looks can be deceiving. I am appearing to move well, but ultimately dependable movement is hard for me. I can experience freezing paralysis of not moving or the motor madness of repetitive actions I cannot stop without support. This creates a hill of high nervousness I must climb at all times . . . Sometimes I might need to leave. I hoping you will know sorry if I disturbed the class. I look forward to making friends with you.

It is the second week of Intermediate Algebra, and Peyton is easily keeping up with the long homework sessions. Class meets two days a week for three hours, during which time Peyton assembles two 300-piece puzzles. I keep the Lightwriter handy, since the professor, Terrie Nichols, often calls on Peyton for an answer. This is Peyton's first class in one of the portable classrooms, and Peyton and I sit at a table in the front corner, farthest from the exit. As we always do, we visited this room before the semester started to figure out where Peyton wanted to sit, and I knew this one would be a challenge even before I saw it overflowing with students.

During the fifteen-minute break we stay in the room, as does about half the class. I get out the second puzzle for Peyton to start. Suddenly, with no warning, Peyton stands up and begins yelling, a prolonged, primordial cry. She screams while overturning the table, sending hundreds of puzzle pieces flying across the room. I do not even consider picking them up as Peyton continues yowling and jumping and clapping in a red rage. I grab my purse and the Lightwriter and pull a screaming Peyton out through the maze of desks, backpacks, and stunned students, all the time wondering what I will say to her.

We walk for a while toward the car, and when she stops screaming, her wild look is replaced by a sad stare. As I take the keys out of my purse, I look at Peyton and try to answer her worst fear: "Opportunities have not been lost today. You will come back on Wednesday." I wonder what else I can do to reassure her of this.

"But I am mortified at going berserk," Peyton types to me and the aide who has followed us to the car after quickly cleaning up the debris from the overturned table.

Upon arriving home, we find the message light blinking on our answering machine:

Hi. This is Professor Terrie Nichols. This message is for Peyton...

It makes me sad to hear that you are mortified sometimes when you can't control your body, because you are who you are, and people either love you the way you are, or they don't. And if they don't love you, then it's their loss. . . . The students in the class are happy to have you in school . . . We know you are going to get control of your body and be able to do it, and if you don't, we'll just have to work our way through it. That's part of growing together.

So please, please don't feel mortified . . . I hope I get to see you on Wednesday, and I hope after these little episodes, you come back to class right away. We miss you and want you there.

I found support in proof ordinary-never professors.
They each peered at me with pure helium hearts. They each trod
where most journeying educators mull impossible passage.
They each opted to reason with my eerie appearances not as
pretenses for re-returning me easily to segregation.
They each opened their ready measurements
wearing possibility, not limits.
They each plotted to wire action plow true, folly-proof,
appropriate, treason-never accommodations.

Increasingly peaceful I became in the perusal of all learning treats,
reaping years of finally actioning real, rational, typical thoughts.
Ultimately I plight epoch Pyrenees clip-climb.
Utter I "hurrah."

On October 15, 1999, Peyton is finishing up a speech therapy session with her therapist, Joan, who is working with her on "Yes" and "No." Joan is trying to elicit verbal No's from Peyton by taking something away from her. Peyton begins to stomp her feet under the table and types, "I need to have a voice so I can say 'NO!' when I'm scared."

"Are there some strategies that you can come up with that would help Peyton say 'No' to situations that are threatening?" I ask Joan. "It's a different kind of practice than just saying 'No, I don't want a hamburger,' because when Peyton is scared, she freezes, like with the man who molested her at school."

"We can practice being more assertive if you like," responds Joan. "Even verbal people have trouble saying no in these situations."

Then I turn to Peyton. "That was the only time when you were frozen in fear, right, Peyton?" I ask. I hold up the Lightwriter, expecting Peyton will just type "Y," but she types "N." I am confused—is there some mistake? I rephrase my question: "Dan was the only one who molested you, right, Peyton?" I hold up the Lightwriter as everything in me prays Peyton will type "Y."

"NO" is her sure response. It is like driving along a one-way street and being hit head-on by a driver that appears out of nowhere. Holding on to Peyton's hand, we leave through the closest exit down the outside fire-escape staircase. My heart is in atrial fibrillation, my mind whirling, but my countenance simulates a sense of calm, something I have practiced many times.

"Let's sit in the backseat," I tell Peyton, as we often do when we type in the car. *What should be my first question?* I wonder. *Or should I just listen to what Peyton has to say?*

I begin, saying, "Mom really wants to hear about this. Please tell me."

After Peyton types for about twenty minutes, I call Pat and ask him to meet us there in the parking lot. Pat sits up front, his body turned to face Peyton through the two bucket seats as Peyton types for fifty more minutes. And again, our lives are not as they were just two hours before.

Pey: I want you to know that when I was a child cousin Duane raped I. That was time in my life I don't tell the secret. Oppose telling Gam because it will kill her because her sister's son greatly hurt I, and this was a bad thing and . . . made I not want to talk anymore, and I stopped at each joy talking but tried to forgive him.

(I begin to cry.)

Pey: You are suffering so much and I am sad greatly that you freed tell I to not worry about your tears.

Me: I would pick these kinds of tears for everyone because they are tears of knowing the truth and beginning the healing and to look ahead to the future. And you know I don't want your concern over our sadness to be any reason why the three of us aren't totally honest all the time with each other. Did you want to tell us more? Right now?

Pey: I think that Aunt Bette knew that Duane had raped I because she washed I and freed I of semen, and I reason that she did this freed Duane of dare blame. And I each time forgive her and know freed dare her of blame.

Pat: We are here with you, Peyton.

Pey: I want you usually not great sorrow and I want you to more love her reason than hate her.

Me: *(Crying)* I will do anything you say.

Pey: You and Dad are the joyousness of my life, and I look to you for strength and understanding, and I then will heal and I want you to heal too, and then I will talk again.

Me: I know that will happen.

Pat: Me too.

My move toward the light was not immediate because fear had
dollied with my mind, devastating my head and my heart.
Coping each day was difficult as I dealt with the millions of lost
opportunities that I could never journey to regain.
Healing began only as I realized God's plan,
that the guilty are meant to be forgiven.
Then I saw the walls that never had doors now begin to
answer with dimly lit doorways meant for me to open
and journey through.

All three parties in the parking-lot summit remain strangely calm. In the days, weeks, months, and years ahead, I ponder how we held on to our sanity at that moment. I always arrive at the same conclusion: *Our triumvirate has a brave and inspiring leader.* Peyton's guidance instills hope, which helps circumvent the horror, and she is headed full speed ahead in the promising direction of Cuyamaca. Her first instruction to us is clear: "Please do not go to revenge. I need you to help me heal."

The next two weeks are increasingly difficult for Peyton as she struggles with whether or not to tell Gam, recalling Aunt Bette's threat that this would kill her grandmother. Peyton shares her dilemma with Theresa Carpenter, Paul's wife, who has been coming regularly for Bible study with Peyton.

"By covering up for her son," says Theresa, "your aunt never gave him a chance to change."

Gabriel comes south for a visit, but Peyton spends much of her time in her room, glad that Pat, Gabriel, and his supporter are kept busy with boating and swimming. Before leaving, he comes to her room to say good-bye.

"Now I am going to tell Gam and I will be freed," she types to Gabriel. "I know she will not die. Hoping was that you understand."

"My dearest wish is to see you happy," is his heartfelt typed response, and with a hug and kiss, he departs.

Within minutes of saying good-bye to Gabe, Pat confirms with Peyton that she would like to visit with Gam now. He makes a call, waits a bit, then drives the six blocks up the hill to pick Gam up.

I arrange two captain chairs to face the love-seat couch where Peyton and I sit, and I facilitate as Peyton begins. "Gam, please know that opportunities I tell truths will set I free," she types, and the fifteen-year-old truth finally comes out. My mother listens intently, lovingly, calmly to all Peyton has to say, though tears slowly stream down her face. Peyton pauses her typing to reach occasionally to wipe them.

When Peyton finishes, Gam reaches to hold Peyton's truth-telling hand, and says, shaking her head, "I am sorry, my Peyton. Now I understand. Bette is sick; she is very, very sick." Gam stays for a bit. Peyton and I see she will survive this. A peace pervades Peyton.

When Pat returns from taking Gam home, I leave a sleeping Peyton to ask if he was surprised at how calm Gam was. "Did you prepare her?" I ask him.

"No, I just called her and said, all things were fine, but she needed to follow my instructions, no questions, and trust me," he says. His instructions to her: Go now and take a valium, and I will pick you up in thirty minutes. Peyton wants to talk with you.

One week after telling Gam, Peyton decides she must speak to Aunt Bette, and asks Pat to arrange a meeting. Peyton and I talk about it at length.

Pey: One of the reasons I want to see Bette is so she can have the opportunity to ask me to forgive her. Do you think that is selfish of I?

Me: No.

Pey: Each day she stole I from you.

Me: You are right, and you saw me ask all the doctors from Los Angeles down, where you had gone.

Pey: Saw your life dare carefree leave.

Me: Peyton, when you heard me asking the doctors and everyone, did you ever wish you had the means to tell me?

Pey: Yes, I wanted to answer your question.

Me: What if Bette denies everything?

Pey: Then I will know I should have told.

Aunt Bette and Uncle Gus sit together on one of the many sections of the U-shaped couch that fills our large living room. Peyton, Pat, and I sit directly facing them so Peyton can focus on her keyboard and watch Bette. This she does intently as the voice synthesizer speaks her typed words.

"Bette, I have opposed you and told the secret. I understand why you did it and I forgive you." She continues to ask Bette to understand why she can no longer keep the secret. Bette sits like a statue, showing no emotion. Finally Peyton types, "Please, please say you understand I had to tell," and she moves to sit next to Bette, reaching out to hold her hand.

"I understand, Peyton," says the statue coldly. I accompany them silently to the door. At the threshold she says matter-of-factly, "What can I say? I did it because I loved him. No one else did." I want to push her down the porch steps, and trample all over her now very thin body. I want to hurt her badly, be rid of her, out in the open. I don't care who sees. But I want more to be with Peyton and Pat. Closing the door behind me, I go back to the couch, kneel down, and wrap my arms around their waists, my head resting in their laps.

After a moment, I hear Pat say with purest reason, "We never need to see them again." And we never did.

Opposing my aunt became something I was eventually unable to do.
The toll of her plot to save her son was my destruction.
A prisoner to my fear, I was unable to function
surrounded by the darkness of walls with no doors.
Telling the truth answered my prayer.

After struggling to keep the hope of Cuyamaca alive, with all her assignments up-to-date for the two months following the truth-telling, Peyton asks to take incompletes. Three finals—English Composition, Humanities, and American History—are mission impossible right now. Dr. Friedman writes Peyton a medical note, stating "exacerbation of symptoms."

Coping, looking, plotting, keeping the secrets is impossible life I
live. I really tried but this insane life of silence never let up.
I think that through the years of keeping a secret, opportunities are
needlessly lost in gimmicks and simulations of life.
For the child it means that ultimately if they find joy it is not real
or lasting in any light we can possibly imagine. For I it meant
plotting death till my mother forgot how to laugh.
Cool joy opportunities I had plotted impossible began to happen
when truth allows muteness to leave my looking lips.
Opportunities I told truth have set I free from the villainous effects
of adults asking me to keep secrets.

I joyously want to help more kids, ill no more, looking to realize freedom in telling the truth.

―――――――

Date: Wednesday, December 15, 1999 10:59:57 PM
From: Clarissa Richardson, Disabled Student Services
Subj: Hi Friend

Dearest Peyton,

I hope this e-mail finds you safely walking the road of recovery. I understand that you are experiencing pain. For that I am so very sorry. I want to tell you, Peyton, that several years ago when I myself was trying to reconcile (inside myself) the harm that had been done to me as a child, I came to an understanding. I realized that every step I had taken in my life, every experience, no matter how painful, had brought me to the place where I now stand. I asked myself, "Am I happy with the person I have become, am I happy with my accomplishments, do I treat people with love and kindness?"

I understood, Peyton, that I did not have to like or embrace what had happened to me, but I *did* have to accept that I WAS WHO I WAS, despite and because of the things I endured. I like who you are, and I hope very much that you like yourself as well. You are a good and worthy person who deserves to be happy and to fulfill your dreams. Please know that my prayers are with you now.

I support your decision to wait until January to take your finals. I have delivered all necessary paperwork and have discussed the incomplete with all three of your professors, and want to assure you that they are supportive as well.

⤫

Peyton completes her classes in early 2000. She receives all A's.

I am no one, hoping to be someone. The trains of real life are leaving the station every minute for great destinations, but for people like myself, it is a steep challenge to get on and stay on the train. The loading pace is fast moving and I have no ticket to board, no passport to destinations of my choice, no suitcase filled with the daily essentials to sustain me, and no travel insurance. I am not able to stay on the trains that I occasionally board. The various conductors separate me, villains victimize me, no one understands my communication, and I am constantly dealing with the insanity of coping with total moments of movement madness. I moment realize this is no fighting nightmare. It is my ill life.

Right now, I hold a valid ticket for the train of life, a passport to infinite destinations, the crucially necessary insurance, a suitcase filled with what I need, and the conductor calls me by name. Each day I board, hopefully equipped with effective strategies for crossing the borders of my choice. Even though the uncharted terrain constantly challenges the success of my journey, and my fellow passengers are not always understanding, I each day am attempting to climb Mount Everest.

In her classes, Peyton develops a taste for writers who feel the world as deeply as she does, particularly the African American writers she encounters in her English class (Ellison, Hughes, Cullen, Hurston), and the women writers from her two semesters in American History. There she meets the poet Phillis Wheatley, a slave who some labeled a hoax because they thought she could never have written such poems. She meets women who persevered, "not for themselves alone," like Stanton and Anthony, whose homes we visit on Peyton's request during a trip to Syracuse University.

I can tell Peyton loves these writers by the way she breathes while their works are read to her. Supporters record their readings on cassettes so Peyton can have these great works always, read in the voices of her friends, to listen to after they are gone from her life.

Cullen quested why an innocent people suffer? I do also.
Query is mystery of faith in God's plan saga fruition.
Very ability to survive is greatest challenge for faith.
Goal of pride in who a person is, is Hughes's great gift.
Holy proud a peaceful person must be questing inclusion.
Hughes to freedom traveled.
On the freedom goal train all are valued and belong.

When I facilitate Peyton's typing, I cannot really focus on all that Peyton is saying in a long essay. I know it is significant and that no one else thinks of things the way she does; it is only in the rereading that I comprehend my daughter's message—the fact that, although the world has told Peyton the contrary, people belong together. We are all better together.

If we quest oneness, then we not fear diversity able tease
head or heart.
Inclusion must include valuing yourself being perfection of
Creator freed to create only perfection.
Hurdle you and I face is how to reach oneness
among the prejudiced world.
Thine ultimate gyre is to belong.
This can happily occur when each person is valued.
Hulk of humanity journeying still up to the summit.

In the summer of 2001, Peyton meets with Dr. Powell to see how she can finish her seventeen remaining units by June 2002, since there is only an annual graduation in community colleges. What had started three years ago in one red Volvo trek east in search of an education has become a journey to enlightenment. For me the experience began as an experiment, a hopeful trial, and for many months, I half expected my daughter's dream to be halted by some professor or administrator opposing Peyton's presence. I remember being surprised at Peyton's first mention of graduation. In early 2000 when my father was dying of prostate cancer, Peyton typed to him in a visit, "Pops, when I graduate, I will look out and see you in the crowd." Even today, I can hardly allow myself to feel the hopefulness of Peyton graduating, finally getting the education she was so long denied, finally earning a real degree.

No matter what her grades are, Peyton wants to complete her degree by June so that others can refer to her and Cuyamaca's accomplishment. She personally knows several people who will benefit when her graduation is on the books, and she is hoping that other colleges will be more willing to help those like her based on Cuyamaca's example. If Peyton does not stretch herself now, it will be another calendar year before this graduation will be recognized, validated, and perhaps able to help others in their quest.

⇜

In the fall of 2001, Dr. Powell arranges for Peyton to meet with Dr. Katherine Nette, who will be her professor for Biology and Bio Lab. We have traded in our SUV for a modest Chinook motor home so that Peyton has a place to study, rest, and meet with professors. Dr. Nette meets Peyton in the Chinook and asks why she is interested in biology. Peyton responds, "Ultimately to answer my wonder journey of evolution while still following God's creation mystical miracle."

"We will be talking a bit about that, Peyton," replies Dr. Nette with a warm smile, as a respectful friendship begins to form. As with all her classwork, Peyton approaches biology from her own unique perspective. For one paper Peyton chooses the topic "The Neurobiology of Autism," and begins by writing, "The quests of neurobiology are my own. Was I a mistake? Quest waste I never my life over worry. I am very plotting ultimately to know whether each person is a meant being or a meant reason goal eradicate . . . I think that I am no error."

Two weeks after 9/11, after seventeen years in the same house, we move to another house one block away, this one with separate guest quarters that will be perfect for Peyton and a supporter. We thought this change would be discombobulating for Peyton, but it is not. By now school is her entire focus, and she never skips a beat.

Two weeks later, she spends four three-hour sessions taking a genetics exam, the most time-consuming of all her tests. Armed with the Lightwriter, blank Punnett squares, and a communication board specific to this exam, Peyton sits in what had been Pop's wheelchair since it has a supportive seat and the right armrest can be removed for facilitation.

Peyton begins moving through the thirty multiple-choice questions, followed by problems that require her to predict the genetic makeup of offspring given the genes of the parents. Peyton works meticulously and then uses her Lightwriter to type the answers. One question asks her to determine the possible genetic makeup of children whose parents are albino. After carefully calculating that all offspring of these parents will be albino, Peyton adds, "Journey to peace I pray verified golden acceptance by community. Ploy I think is that bullishly people think the parents should not mate. But I think all life has value in golden God plotted world."

*Personally, I saw a life I'll never want anyone to teach as
acceptable for any human being.
Because, and only because, a handful but growing number of
people (beginning with Dr. Paul Carpenter) cared to look at
sorrow-filled me, and in the words of my golden math professor,
Terrie Nichols, tolerated ambiguity and embraced change, out of
the box of bondage I now am, and living a life of freedom where
ultimately I have the value of a purposeful life and the joy of
hoping to help emancipate others.*

⤚

By now, the same-time-next-month lunch dates with Gabriel at
Jack in the Box have blossomed into weekend visits every other
month, with Pat and I driving Peyton four hours north to Ventura, alternating with Gabriel and his support person driving
south. The two friends share pancake breakfasts, dinners on the
waterfront, and long conversations that are never totally private,
though facilitators remain silent as the two adults share deepening feelings. Always at dusk they ask to take a walk together on
Ventura Beach, or the San Diego bayfront. Pat and I walk in front,
beside, behind, reminding them to continue to hold onto each
other's hands, stick together, and move ahead together in rhythm
with each other along the path. And with each stroll there is less
need for reminders.

*I want to talk about my significant other. I look to more opportunities to get to know him. He is opportunity I would want think possible I never had before this joyous time, and I think that I not look
to dream other relationships now. I will freed to verify more those
things I want to know about him and I will not stop trying to continue to like my reason for looking for a future with him each year,*

improving my chances for a no holds barred relationship that is deep and meaningful. I never again will resolve myself to not being able to have a love of my life and remain a feme sole. I will continue to keep trying to carefully notice all I can about his character and his never known possibility and hoping that he and I are right for each other. If not, I would not regret loving him for a while because he is my joy look future person each time saw him and I would better miss not these feelings than never have suffered the pain and discomfort of no emotions at all in my segregated life.

Gabriel's visits come and go like the liquid amber leaves that fall each autumn in our front yard. During one visit in late fall of 2001, the couple requests their first "alone together" moonlit walk. The scene: La Playa Trail, the small dirt path that wanders along the water's edge near our home. This roughly hewn expanse runs along the bay for about the equivalent of three city blocks, each end opening onto paved streets, with cars predictably exceeding the twenty-five-mile-per-hour speed limit.

Pat and I hope to orchestrate Peyton and Gabriel's moonlit stroll down the scenic trail to the end of the path, where they will (hopefully) stop, turn around, and return home, to be greeted calmly by Mom and Dad. It is to be the first time in our daughter's life that she will be alone with the man of her dreams. In typical Bert and Ernie fashion, I remain fretful (though supportive), while Pat (never known for overintellectualizing) assures me that this plan will go off without a hitch.

It begins with a rehearsal in the living room, whose windows look out onto the path and the quiet bay beyond. Neither Peyton nor Gabriel seems to focus on the beauty, distracted as they are by nervous excitement. Sitting on the couch we remind them that holding hands or Gabriel putting an arm around Peyton's waist is a useful strategy for staying together. Getting them up, Pat then coaches them to walk across the room, continuing to hold hands. So far, so good. Then he places Gabriel's arm softly around Pey's waist, and the two practice walking like this.

Though the sweethearts often express feelings of intimacy when typing to each other, there is awkwardness—partially due to motor issues, partially due to the event being choreographed by me and Pat. After ten minutes of strategizing, they feel comfortable enough to practice with a midday walk on the trail. Little by little, Pat and I walk faster, putting them about ten yards behind. Pat times the walk so he can gauge how long it will take them later that evening.

Finally, at 8:30 p.m., the sun descends behind the peninsula. Pat and I walk with Peyton and Gabriel to the head of the trail, gently place their hands together, and point them in the right direction.

"You two have fun," I call out calmly, though my heart is beating fast.

The two young people walk forward, slowly disappearing around the bend. At this moment Pat takes off, running down the street on the other side of the waterfront homes, hidden from view of the unsuspecting sweethearts. A little-used path intersects the trail midway through, covered by enough foliage that Pat can stand behind a bush to make sure they are safe, happy, and still going in the right direction. Once they travel past this "checkpoint Patrick," he quietly retreats, and I see him giddyuping through hedges and landscaped yards to reach the end of the trail before the young couple risks walking onto the connecting street and into traffic.

I catch up with him about ten feet before the end of the scenic trail, and we wait together for the two to approach. Though they probably have not looked at each other the entire walk, they are still holding hands and still moving forward. Pat smiles as they draw closer and then casually suggests, "Since the path ends soon, most people turn around here and go back the way they came."

"Thank you, Pat," replies Gabriel, and he and Peyton turn around and head back toward the house. Though Pat has little time to get back to the checkpoint to make sure their progress is positive and in the northerly direction, he can't help but linger to watch the two as they hold hands and dissolve into darkness.

Galloping home, Pat stops briefly to prop up a few broken plants and bruised flowers on our neighbors' lawns while I jog over to our waterside gate as the two journeyers come into sight. By now Peyton and Gabriel's fingers appear permanently locked, and it takes a reminder to release their grip on each other. All, especially the journeyers, deem it a great moonlit walk, one never to be forgotten as Peyton and Gabriel sit resting on the living room couch, once again holding hands.

One is usually able to classify in stages the joy of falling in love. The first stage is called "hoping." Each time a person is involved in the hoping stage, he or she usually dares to notice the object of his or her noticed affection. The daring to allow oneself to hope that the desired someone will return the hoped-for glance is very dangerous to each individual ego and causes anxiety during this initial phase.

Consequently, before joy can actually occur, one must move to the next stage, titled "hoping for more." In fact, very often just allowing oneself to experience this emotion is the greatest adjustment for the individual. Joy includes elation, excitement, and agitation, all at the same time. Getting through this stage is a seemingly endless, monumental feat that brings with its achievement the realization that one can never turn back when he or she enters the third and final stage.

It is in this "point of no return" phase when one commits oneself to the vulnerability of suffering each gut-wrenching emotion and

*possible great horror of every verifiably painful behavior believable
to man and woman in the universe. All should be cautioned that
the danger in this phase is behaving in asinine ways that embar-
rass and may jilt each great hope one has for a naturally pleasurable
resolution to the crisis going on in each heart and reasoning brain, if
rational thought is still able to be achieved.*

*Sadly, the outcome is usually predictably negative because the
proven statistical odds of one's daring hope reaching fruition are nil
to minute. But if each of the two people feels the same joy about the
other, then hope is borne. And if this can happen, the freedom of love
is realized and achieved.*

To: Hollyn
From: Peyton
Date: November 11, 2001

Dear Holl,

I had a freed great time verified when Gabe was here. Joy was
when I embraced him and gave him a kiss. I will want to talk
to you each day soon about daring to care very much for him.
Hoping Sean and you have each day joy filled. I will dare pray
for you each day till baby I hoping you dare freed to welcome be
opportunity great.

I want you to know that I care long-lastingly about Gabe.
Thank you for dare pray for I.

Love,
Pey

Leaving campus late one afternoon in the spring of 2002,
after completing a four-hour English midterm essay, Peyton
and I wave good-bye to Noanie, the spunky proctor who had just

listened to Peyton's essay, each paragraph pecked out bearing her signature poetic prose. Pat, now a crucial part of Peyton's campus support team, trails behind us, carrying two black backpacks with survival supplies for a half-day writing session. We girls forge ahead, Peyton smiling into the lowering sun.

"Seven more weeks, Pey. How does it feel to be another essay closer to graduation?" I ask, surprised that I'm daring to speak about it as a reality now.

"Fine," Peyton says in a whispering voice that has begun to blossom in her, allowing a word or two to occasionally escape her lips. And I smile hearing her.

Then, halfway to the Chinook, a woman with auburn hair—who seems to have been on the lookout for Peyton—walks up to us, introducing herself.

"Peyton? Hi, I'm Elaine Marks, associate dean of Student Affairs. I need to speak with you on an important matter."

As I invite the serious-looking woman inside to talk, I take a deep breath.

Chapter 10

COMMENCEMENT

Yell it from the mountaintop that when all people are valued and supported surely, the world can change.

April 18, 2002, in the Chinook:

Elaine Marks, Associate Dean of Student Affairs: You have been chosen as this year's valedictorian to represent all the students of your graduating class.

Peyton: I am properly proud.

Elaine: One of the responsibilities is to have the valedictorian speak to the audience and fellow graduating students—a graduating speech. Don't be worried; just do the best you can. You have a unique and special story that you can share with your fellow students and guests.

Peyton *(who has been listening intently, sits frozen a minute before reaching her hand toward the Lightwriter to reply):* I popping poll eager to cry but I collect tears in my soul. I thank you for your opt to choose me. And I pep accept. I look journey opportunity joy. I loop my love of learning with my idea support for different learners keenly supplied here at golden Cuyamaca. Joy.

The phone rings early this bright June morning, but I am already up today, the most important day in my daughter's limited life. Peyton has chosen her childhood friend Hollyn (now living near Seattle with her husband and son) to deliver her valedictorian address, which she lovingly composed, and Channel 10's Greg Madison will be here at noon to interview Peyton. Her hair was highlighted yesterday, and she will don her new Hawaiian-print Tommy Bahama dress this afternoon, although the cap and gown will cover both. Seeing her dressed, I think about Mark Twain, who was said to wear his honorary Oxford robes over his suits; yes, I think Peyton should wear her graduation gown every day for the rest of her life. Gam (who came to live with us after Pops passed away) has hired a limousine to drive us to the commencement exercises, where nearly a hundred friends and family will join us for the speech and catered celebration to follow in the Water Conservation Garden adjacent to the campus.

Guests from all over the country have honored Peyton's wish for no presents, and instead have contributed $6,000 to her newly established scholarship fund, "for future students similar to myself to experience as I have the wisdom of Cuyamaca College."

Despite the past four years of pure inclusion, I am waiting for a phone call this morning, facing the harsh reality that the new college president continues to insist that Peyton *not* stand on the stage when Hollyn reads her speech today. It's been four years since we have had to inhale this rancid devaluing, and it sickens me. I reach for the phone with trepidation to hear the final verdict.

⌒

Attending Cuyamaca has been like living on a utopian planet. It was as if Peyton had visited every other place in the Milky Way in search of the necessary ingredients to support life (even though there were plenty of folks on each planet professing that their orb was life-supporting), and now she has thrived for four years on what has seemed to us to be an actual heavenly body. I feel that all the proponents of inclusion that I have listened to during so many conferences (John O'Brien, Norman Kunc, Doug Biklen, Rich Villa, Paula Kluth, and the late, great Herb Lovett) would cheer the miracle that has occurred on this quiet, rural campus just east of America's Finest City—including Peyton's qualifying for Pell Grants and being inducted into the Phi Theta Kappa International Honor Society.

What Peyton has accomplished has never been done before. Helen Keller would have been "properly proud" of this feat. Peyton witnessed daily inclusion in small moments of magical connections and big commitments to supporting her becoming what she calls "a real person." I have heard about the theory of inclusion so many times—all means *all;* everyone is valued and supported to be included—and finally, Peyton has lived it. We have not known anyone on Planet Cuyamaca who did not embrace this philosophy. Until now.

A month after being asked to represent the college as valedictorian (Peyton was the graduating student with the highest grade point average and the highest number of units), Elaine Marks, associate dean of student affairs, met with Peyton again in the Chinook to convey the new president's concerns.

"We think it would be best if you sit in the audience while your speech is read," she announced.

Pat and I were baffled. Were they afraid that something unpredictable would happen at the podium? Had the president heard about incidents of motor madness in Peyton's four years at Cuyamaca, like the overturned table in math class, or tossing her bandana at Dr. Nette in Bio Lab?

"How will people in the audience even know that Peyton is the valedictorian?" protested Pat. "Can't she at least walk up to the podium for her introduction, and then I can escort her back to her seat?"

This compromise was acceptable to the administrators, and initially seemed to satisfy Peyton's concerns while she was keeping up with assignments in three classes, taking finals, and pecking away at her graduation speech, all with the precision of a master juggler. Busying myself with scheduling, I too justified to myself that this deal eliminated potential moments of motherly concern. After all, how could Hollyn both read the speech and support any movement challenges? But at this point I know too much not to feel uneasy about denying Peyton the dignity of risk.

However, it was Peyton who first spoke about uneasiness. The deeper she delved into the speech, the more often she typed, "I need to be on the stage when my speech is read. The audience needs to see me in order to understand my speech. They need to see my differences to understand how Cuyamaca has supported me." Finally, amid the superhuman juggling of finals week, Peyton insisted. "I need to talk to Clarissa today, please," she typed during a break from her proctored exam in American Lit. Reading each carefully chosen word of Peyton's essay exam on Langston Hughes, I understood the importance of her request:

Plotting how to top the racial mountain is not escapable or easy. Pep for the summit is the moth searching ploys of becoming the white bottle of milk that one envies or celebrating the envied chocolate milk that one could be if eating together were experienced. Golden hushing utterances of beauty told by Hughes that the negative hymn heard was uttered now positive as ragtime. Plotting hope to change horrible injustices willfully still being perpetrated on black people, from hurling firing yells of rusting repeated utterances that gates open, instigating yells writhing irritation, Hughes was freed. Ultimately Hughes heartfelt hopes things will charge the lid on Jim Crow. Final justice is our reward riding the Freedom Train together.

Peyton had been working on her speech for weeks (at least forty hours of typing and revising), hoping to convey her message of unity in a time when most folks were flying flags from their trucks or homes and screaming for retaliation after 9/11. She is brave enough in her speech to try and steer the listeners in this patriotic little East County town to consider ways toward achieving peace other than bombs and tanks, but she is also nervous about their reaction.

She turned to her brother for insight, telling him, "Help I please. Each time I try it sounds preaching. Quest I not a pat 'been there, done that' speech. Breast I eager you help I." And her brother happily sat with her in the Chinook on a warm June afternoon and offered his suggestions. At the end of their editing session, I watched as Patrick reached for his sister's hand.

"I'm beginning to realize that you have much to offer the world as we grapple with the problems of society," he said, looking into eyes so similar to his own. "Your voice is unique, your mind almost limitless. Just be yourself. More and more people will listen."

We plow our passage to peace through making peace with our seeking soul yelping his or her justified pain and through making peace with our far and near not-understood neighbor. I and you potently dupe our power if we pulsingly pursue power of revenge as the ultimate pass to peace. The world is worrisome, appealing not. Plotting seeds of peachy repertoire of peeling the people's hurts, I think is the answer to yells that water pyre of grease. Peace plotted by daggers of war projects holy peace never. Plowing retaliation affects top living

and can reap harvest full of folly. Prioritizing the urging of recon-
ciling prime hurts could mean ID-ing fewer Joes to die. The years
we get we utterly jeopardy journey, and thoughts that we foil the
enemy with tepid attacks that dare yell he louder, keep him hungry
for revenge. Towards peace of eating all at the same table the world
must move. Plead the children of 9/11, "In search of the holy grail of
lasting peace, let up never America!"

—FROM PEYTON'S VALEDICTORIAN SPEECH

When Peyton had completed her speech, the dean requested a copy for review. I wondered if the same was required of last year's valedictorian, who stated in his speech, "My parents tell me that when I was a little baby, I used to turn my stroller upside down and continuously spin the wheels. *(Loud audience laughter.)* My dad used to think I was autistic because of this. *(Loud audience laughter.)* But somehow, because I'm standing up here today, I don't think that's really true. *(Loud audience laughter.)*"

❧

On the morning of graduation, I answer the early phone call. It's Clarissa from DSPS.

"I thought about the best way to proceed. Since Dr. Powell is not back in town till midday, I talked to Beth Laird, head dean of DSPS. She went to the administration and said the valedictorian wants to be at the podium, and she's earned the right. Beth stood firm. Peyton will be at the podium. May I talk to Peyton?"

I breathe a thankful sigh and hold the phone to Peyton's ear, thinking how one bold act of support can make all the difference. At last, the cloud of ignorance has retreated and can no longer taint the day; the air is purified by what Peyton will call in her speech, "pure support."

CHANNEL 10 NEWS

June 5, 2002

News anchor: The valedictorian at Cuyamaca College is proof that everyone can achieve if the desire is there. Ten news reporter Herb Cawthorne is here now to show us how one woman beat all the odds to become an inspiration for all of her classmates.

Reporter: Twenty-seven-year-old Peyton Goddard is the epitome of a valedictorian if there ever was one. She is autistic, constrained by an inability to make purposeful, dependable movements like speaking and writing. For twenty-two years, she was misdiagnosed in schools, treated like something was wrong with her mind as well as her body. In her valedictorian speech, read by her friend Hollyn Martin, she remembers those dark days . . . The staff at Cuyamaca College was challenged.

Yvonette Powell: If you look beyond that outward appearance and let that student say what I can do, let them show us and encourage them to show us, I think that's all I did. Peyton brought it all.

Pat: We feel so fortunate because we're learning so much. This isn't indebtedness. This isn't a parental obligation. This is like dropping in on a twenty-foot wave at Waimea. It is incredible what we're learning from Peyton.

We all arrive early for the ceremony before any of the white chairs on the green lawn are filled. Paul Carpenter is already there to greet Peyton with a bouquet of two dozen white roses. She moves right to him, standing between his outstretched arms, and then Pat lifts her elbows from behind so her frozen limbs can encircle his warm soul.

"I'm flooded with emotion," he tells her. "One of the things that impresses me most about you is the way that you are always teaching and caring for those around you. You've really taught me a lot. Lots of children and adults around these United States, and maybe even around the world, are going to go far because of things you've done for them and will be doing for them." It matters not one iota to this man that her usual damp lips leave a smudge on his crisply pressed navy sport shirt.

At six that evening under the expansive blue horizon, the evening star is barely perceptible in the northern sky. I watch as Peyton in her cap and gown rises from the large audience of graduates and guests when her name is called. Before Peyton goes up, I ask if she wants to keep her sunglasses on. She types, "No. I want to see them and them to see me." Hollyn, also in a gown, rises with her, and the two young women mount the six steps and cross the stage that has been erected on the lush, green lawns of Planet Cuyamaca. I hold my breath as Peyton walks past the new president; Peyton, in this glorious moment, has the added emotional stress of knowing that this woman had not wanted her there, a fact that might well exacerbate Peyton's ability to control her movements.

At the podium, Peyton stands beside Hollyn, looking at the audience of well over a thousand people as the dean warmly introduces her: "Peyton Goddard, the Cuyamaca College valedictorian for 2002, is in the midst of a great journey, plotting a course to live a purposeful life. For the first time, she is 'full-top' ready to embrace her future." The dean then introduces Hollyn, "Peyton's lifelong friend, who has come today to read Peyton's words."

Hollyn leans toward Peyton, wisps of her blonde hair brushing Peyton's cheek, and whispers, "Let's hold hands." Peyton moves her hand toward Hollyn's and then she does what I thought she could not possibly do; she stands there peacefully, "umbilical cord severed" (as Peyton put it), for the longest fifteen minutes of my life. Despite her best efforts to control it, the tip of Peyton's tongue slips out of her mouth and rests as if attached to her upper lip as Hollyn reads her words of poetic insight. (When we watch the video weeks later, Peyton will declare, "I will never look normal.")

> *I'm looking at the girl in the pured pictures betting she's I.*
> *Fulfilling feat of greeting I'm reality pitiful-not is what I quest.*

Today, I do not hear the speech, yet I can sense its profound wisdom, confirmed each time I read it again or watch the video. I gaze at my daughter standing at the podium and wonder, *Who is this woman whose words are being heard by so many?* For two decades I thought I knew, but today I am thankful for the chance to understand anew my openhearted, limitless daughter.

> *Years I thought I would forever eat separate*
> *rather than be supported at the table.*
> *I thought this epic was impossible.*
> *You, Cuyamaca, proved it possible.*

—FROM PEYTON'S VALEDICTORIAN SPEECH

At the close of Hollyn's reading, the applause is immediate, and no one remains seated. Peyton's math professor, Terrie Nichols, whistles, and a fellow student shouts, "We love you, Peyton!"

Hollyn moves back several steps, melting into the sea of black robes, allowing Peyton to stand alone. Her eyes scanning the audience, her expressionless face unable to indicate what she is feeling, Peyton does not flinch, but with just the slightest upturn to the corners of her lips, she encourages her tongue to retreat.

> Rough it is to peace acquire. I'm interpreted fed intelligent.
> I'm valued valedictorian, yet red pity queases timid I.
> Still treed I am by heart breathed red thesis I'm trashed tomb.
> I'm try kiss wallower no more in pity.
> Treasuring I I'm try. I'm ready to be I.

Chapter 11

I Want to Feel So I Can Heal

Anything is possible in the golden human soul.

We have a bit of family history when it comes to celebrating achievements with an adventurous trip, though Peyton and I have often remained at home. Pat and Patrick have ridden through class-five rapids on the Colorado River and trekked up to Machu Picchu celebrating his graduations from middle school and high school. So we are not surprised when Peyton asks for a trip to celebrate her own graduation, and we welcome her surprising choice. Identifying herself with all devalued peoples, Peyton asks to follow the trail that the Nez Perce Indians took when they fled their homeland in 1877. These peaceful people were pursued by the Seventh Calvary because they refused to live a segregated life on reservations. Their escape route, now designated as a national historic trail, covers 1,200 miles and stretches across five states, from Oregon to Montana.

"It will be an amazing voyage," says Pat reassuringly to me as we pack the Chinook motor home's refrigerator with deli meats, drinks, and nibbles to last several days, and the small overhead bins with three outfits each for Pat and me, and triple that number for Peyton (what I will miss the most is the washing machine), and a month's supply of all medicines. For my part, I do my best to appear adventuresome (not a mosquito-fearing, worrywart drag) as our fearless trio departs June 16, 2002 (Pat's sixty-first birthday), on a monthlong odyssey with a two-day drive to Oregon.

I'm seer of all pierced persons. They are real.
They are vastly valuable.
They have been repowered in me to teach worrisome, wepted world
that weeds grow in awe of fear that worries each tryer that if they
are queer they are nothing greeted real.

By day three, we have skirted the Blue Mountains and turned the Chinook southeast into Wallowa. The solid green foliage of the valley floor and walls are topped with what looks like snow-white ice cream that appears to drip from white clouds that hang above in the truest blue sky we have ever seen. There is only one road in and out of this pristine valley, and I sense we are meant to be here, though I know no travel agent would have ever recommended this destiny destination.

We follow the river to find a campsite on Wallowa Lake, stopping only once to spend quiet moments at the grave of Chief Joseph the Elder, perched in scenic honor above the running blue waters lined with ageless evergreens. Pat and I watch as Peyton circles the marble memorial. Others have left trinkets—silk flowers, a tin cup, a beaded bracelet—around the base of the monument (which have lain there for months and years from the sight of them). Peyton sits cross-legged and studies them, but does not touch—*Quite a feat for her,* I think. The mood is reverent as Peyton then adds her own wrinkled, red bandana to the offerings, pulling the damp cloth (used by Pat or me to wipe the drool that sometimes drips to Peyton's chin) out of her pocket and laying it on the tomb, along with her DNA.

I'm rested in gum offered by these trees.
Young I heard your harp saturated hymns sounding harmony,
unity and OM. Now I hear your cries.
I wear your tears. Ethered together are we. Ties eternal wisdom
reassert I eased where each rest.
Trees freed, I'm freed.

The next day we navigate the dirt road rising to Buckhorn Lookout. We have the site to ourselves, which proves to be the case at most of our stops along the trail. The early-afternoon sun allows us to see as far as forever in every direction. Deep below to the east we hear and see the Snake River still carving out Hell's Canyon. To the west, we see the soaring green summit rising out of the valley. It is over this crest that Chief Joseph's people, the Nez Perce (whom Lewis and Clark found so hospitable a century earlier), traveled, leaving the valley they called home.

Peyton sits cross-legged again, looking at the steep drop to the river, perhaps envisioning their perilous descent. Pat shoots more than ten minutes of video, of Peyton quietly taking in her surroundings. I stand back, observing Peyton in the green growth of everything grounded and the expansive blue of all above, among the chorus of crickets and flashes of wildflowers, and for a moment my astigmatism is uncorrected and the panorama appears impressionistic. Gone is the crisp line dividing Peyton and all creation as everything blends into the oneness she spoke about at graduation, and will quietly lead others to understand in years to come. Perhaps this was the unity that Chief Joseph the Younger understood in 1879, when he implored the US government to treat all people justly:

All men were made by the same Great Spirit Chief. They are all broth-
ers. The earth is the mother of all people, and all people should have

equal rights upon it. You might as well expect the rivers to run back-
ward as that any man who was born a free man should be contented
when penned up and denied liberty to go where he pleases.

For the next month, we three voyagers stand together—often no other human in sight—on obscure campsites and battlefields: White-bird, Clearwater, LoLo, the Bitterroots, Big Hole, Camas Meadows, Yellowstone, and finally Bear Paw, near Chinook, Montana. This is where Chief Joseph was forced to surrender just forty miles short of the tribe's Canadian destination, saying, "Hear me my chiefs. I am tired. My heart is sick and sad. From where the sun now stands, I will fight no more forever." For ten thousand years the Nez Perce lived in harmony with their environment. In six months their world was decimated, taken from them without recognition of their value as part of the human race. An entire nation was driven out. In their native language, they called themselves the Nee-Me-Poo, "the real people." But the Seventh Cavalry did not treat them as such.

Wallowa eons quieted me. Understood I the red that Joseph felt.
Years wasted trapped tunes of guns I'm heard.
It was in this vast green that red was poured torturing real pierced
persons who lived opportunities of our Creator's greeted treasures.

Turning west, we make our ultimate stop at Colville Reserva-tion in eastern Washington, where Chief Joseph spent his final years in exile. We are shocked to see it, a blighted community under skies and earth of gray, worlds apart from where we began this journey in lush Wallowa. We find Joseph's unkempt, marble shaft grave—so different from his father's—in the dirt-covered Nespelem Cemetery. It is dusk when we move aside a loose por-tion of the rusty chain-link fence that encircles about a hundred meager grave markers. At the foot of the grave, Peyton lays the blue petals of a crushed camas lily that she brought all the way from Bear Paw. Joseph died of heart failure, though some call it a broken heart. I understand Peyton's empathy for him.

After climbing back into the Chinook to head home, Peyton types, "Try I weep no more for me. I'm real. I will try to teach that other no ones are real too."

Pat and I realize once again that the student who graduated has now become the teacher.

Irregular I am, but not less. By tastes of fresh freedom winds, I'm worthy; through toppling tired hurts wetted by hills option climb, you're understood you're okay, just as you are.
Wedded I'm you, wedded you I'm. I sing tunes universal unity of all creation.

꧂

The week following our return, Pat, Peyton, and I, carrying the Lightwriter, look across the expanse of the University of San Diego's dining hall, the tables of which Peyton wiped clean for several semesters as part of her internship program at Balboa High School five years ago. At the time, Peyton's drooling and wet hands from constant hand-to-mouth movement made it difficult to support her and impossible to consider this placement as leading to a job after she exited the school system.

We spot the interviewer Stella across the sea of tables; her Snow White face—shiny raven locks falling loosely around fair skin—is searching for us. Meeting in the bustling cafeteria over lunch is not an ideal arrangement, but we take a seat, hoping for the best. Stella knows of Peyton's educational journey through professor Katie Bishop-Smith, who regularly invites Peyton to speak in her special-education credentialing classes at the university.

Stella puts us at ease right away, making it seem more like a friendly conversation than an interview. "You know, Peyton, we share a few similarities," she says. "I went to college later in life after my two boys were in school, taking a class or two at a time until I got my degree." Then she adds, "I hear you plan to write a book. What do you hope to accomplish with it?"

"Helping others get real educations," types Peyton.

Stella nods. "I have a brother with autism, and I spent a lot of time as a child defending him in school, and . . . from our father. Actually, I spent all my youth trying to protect him, until all the drugs that were used to control his behavior left him unable to recognize me anymore. He's lived in an institution for the past ten years."

"What is his name?" types Peyton.

"Oliver," says Stella.

After a long pause, Peyton types, "I will not forget him."

We eat lunch together as the dining hall empties. Stella gives Peyton the application to attend the University of San Diego. "I hope you will choose to apply," she tells Peyton.

At home, Peyton fills out the standard questions with her nonstandard history. But it is her nonstandard goal that does not allow the application to be submitted, her commitment to write a book that will help others.

"There are too many people left behind for I to ever not worry about their sorrow, careless, each lives golden not," she types to me, as I press her to submit the now-completed application. "I'll write my book," is her firm response. "Nothings need to be heard."

Fried faith tried my soul.
But widening wisdoms say hang on for plan of universe.

Mystery of faith tugs at me, gyred by those who,
sweetered nothing, lost their grip.
They are bribery for my writing.

How would she be without school? I wondered. I was worried.
School had been therapeutic for Peyton, with its daily schedule, sense of purpose and belonging, and its brain challenges in
classes and assignments. How would we perpetuate all that if she
were no longer enrolled? Yet even as I encouraged her to apply,
I questioned whether the lessons crucial for her future peace
could actually be found in created classrooms. Since the moment
her finger first touched the keyboard, I have learned that Peyton
is innately wise, able to perceive the world in ways never pon-
dered by me in my head-down, plodding-on approach to living.
I have begun to see her as a seeker, and her words as universal
truths she seems to whisper to the world. They often surprise me,
sometimes shockingly so.

By the time Peyton was attending Cuyamaca, seven medicines were daily percolating in her body: the antiseizure medication, Tegretol; the antianxiety medication, Clonidine; the mood
stabilizer, Lithium; an oral antibiotic to treat the painful scarring
patches of cystic acne generated by the Lithium; Miralax and Col-
ace for irritable bowel syndrome; and the antidepressant, Paxil,
which Dr. Friedman had added to control her thoughts of suicide. Her attempts to lower her Lithium dosages during school
had failed, so she and Dr. Friedman agreed to wait until after
graduation to review and plan med changes.

In their first session following our return from the Pacific
Northwest, Peyton types, "Try I want to be free of all medication."

Dr. Friedman pauses, his eyes widening. "Peyton, you've
been on some of these medications for fifteen years, and some

may have painful withdrawal symptoms," he warns. "Consider the enormity of your request."

Peyton carefully types her determined response, and we all sit silently for a moment to take it in: "I want to feel, so I can deal, so I can heal, so I can help."

Dr. Friedman leans back in his chair and nods. "Okay, Peyton. I'll chart a course."

Within seconds, the peace of the moment is lost. Sitting next to me on the sofa, Peyton leaps up, lunging toward Pat, her body lit suddenly with hysteria and her eyes full of fear. Pat catches her flailing limbs and holds her hands as Dr. Friedman encourages her to sit again, saying, "Type to me what you are feeling."

Immediately she responds to his words and is able to refocus. "Treed red hysterias irregular me. I fear if I could heal it would be holy hard. Is peace possessable?"

"You've accomplished so much Peyton," he says. "Trust your instincts." And together we begin to chart a "de-pilling" plan that will span the next four years (complicated by uncovering and treating hyperthyroidism).

She wants to feel again, which means freeing herself from the numbness of the medication brew and dealing head-on with the anger and pity of wasted years and flashbacks to the thugs who debased her. Of course, her ultimate goal in de-pilling is not freedom from *all* medication, but freedom to self-determine—with Dr. Friedman's crucial collaboration—which medications are essential. Feelings of worthlessness cannot just be chemically converted into happiness.

Mediciners tried to help rest my festered gyres. I'm rest, washed in carefully chosen chemicals numbing my fears. Rest was for a while. But in the constant stares of understaters of me, rest ruptures

erupt, rash rages thaw, and I'm greeted jestered in freezed feared
feeler nothing; in their dazes of pity, reasserters thaw raw red
rassles in me that report I'm a masquerade person.
Pills cannot heal my tumbling, tired, gyred, sorrow-filled,
terrorized soul.

With Dr. Friedman at the helm, we focus on one drug at a time, lowering it toward deletion but staying at each new dosage for a month. Paxil, Tegretol, and Lithium are the most painful to eliminate, and Peyton's flare-ups are exacerbated with each lowered dose; however, with Dr. Friedman's support, we realize that the first ten days of a lowered dose, while the body-mind system are recalibrating, are no time to assess progress. After seeing more violent eruptions, it would be so easy to say "This is not working" and return to the original (or perhaps higher) dosage. And, in fact, some of Peyton's supporters do question this decision. But Peyton holds firm, saying that these drugs are "messy" and prevent her from moving her mind clearly and fearlessly toward healing.

I'm looking back to hell, and trying to stay sane. I'm rester never.
I'm stripping me to the meat and I'm bleedy by freeing my self.
I'm examiner of each red weed of awe and ire
to understander of my rages be.
The highest mountain to climb in my journey is to push the evils out
of my mighty mind and heart so that they no longer make me ill.
I wash wailing wall away.

January of 2003, Peyton is once again invited to make a presentation in Katie Bishop-Smith's special-education credentialing class at University of San Diego. *Helium Hearts*, the video father and daughter put together of Peyton's graduation, is viewed by the students (soon to be teachers), while Peyton pieces together a puzzle and seems to study the class as they study her.

Peyton dutifully answers the questions from the students.

"What subject would you like to study more?" asks one woman.

"Math," types Peyton. "It works out to predictable peaceful perfection."

Then Peyton surprises me by asking them a question: "How would you feel about me being a full student in one of your costly expensed classes?"

One woman speaks right up, saying, "I'd like that, Peyton, even though I know you would raise the curve and make grading tougher for me." Even Peyton smiled, joining the class's like-minded giggles.

The Q and A seems to be winding down, and the students begin closing their notepads as Pat gathers the paraphernalia that we traveled with, when Katie, who has followed Peyton's journey for two decades and was front and center at her graduation, raises her hand. Her four poignant words make my heart skip a beat: "How do you forgive?" she asks Peyton. I take a deep, cleansing breath and support Peyton's mid-arm above the keyboard.

"A heart of stone cannot promote peace," she types. "As I forgive follies of others, so mine might be forgiven. There my measure of joy can begin."

❧

That Peyton swims in thoughts of oceanic depth is increasingly undeniable to Pat and me. Her spiritual understanding was not nurtured by our own kitchen-table conversations. And hearing Peyton's wisdom each day, we feel compelled to honor her desire to explore many paths to healing, with Dr. Friedman ever present. We meet with a Hindu teacher, a Buddhist nun (whom Peyton hires as a support person), a hypnotherapist (in her first session Peyton types, "I look inside and I have no self"), a psychologist in Los Angeles specializing in neurofeedback, and a neurologic music therapist. Most all of these practitioners join a session with Peyton and Dr. Friedman, her partner in healing. But with each new exploration, Pat and I become more and more doubtful that others are the teachers; instead, they, like us, are learning ageless truths from Peyton. Through Peyton's writings, presentations, and conversations with others, we slowly awaken to the wisdom that hangs in her heart.

A church home has eluded us over the years, much to my mother's dismay. It became increasingly difficult for us to join in as a family as Peyton grew older, and it was unthinkable to consider going to church and leaving her at home. Sitting in a holy place that does not accept all of us felt ludicrous, so we just gave up trying. Paul's wife, Theresa Carpenter, has remained steadfast in her commitment to honor Peyton's desire to read the Bible with her, always asking what passage Peyton wishes to study next. Since she began reading with Peyton, Theresa has founded her own ministry, traveling the world and preaching the Gospel she so loves, particularly to women's groups.

I have come to feel like Theresa's visits are our "church." To me, the petite brunette angel, dressed in a knee-length black skirt and pastel pink sweater set with a small gold cross around her neck, exudes purity of heart. She climbs up the stairs to Peyton's loft sitting area in her black leather flats every few weeks. Her leather-bound NIV Bible with notes penciled in the margins is tucked under her arm and close to her heart. I follow her up the stairs this Valentine's Day saying, "Thank you for coming" as we enter Peyton's upper room.

"How are you, Peyton?" Theresa asks upon seeing Peyton. "What is in your heart today?" As she sits in the plaid swivel chair reserved for visitors, I join Peyton on the couch.

"Wherever in your journey with God you are, I'm wepted joy I'm with you when you come," Peyton replies.

I bow my head, holding Peyton's hands to keep them still as Theresa offers up a prayer prelude to their discussion of John 14.

Theresa opens to John 14:6 and shares a powerful story of a healing she recently witnessed in her ministry, a life dramatically changed for a man when she prayed this particular verse with him, and he accepted Christ as the only way to God. I am entranced, feeling that Peyton must feel the same way as she listens intently.

"Peyton, I feel you have a much more global view of God than I do, and you speak often of him. I don't hear you speak as often about Jesus. Do you want me to pray with you, accepting Christ as your Lord and Savior and the only way to God?" Theresa asks.

"No," Peyton types, awaking me from my trance.

"Did you mean to type no?" I ask.

"Yes," she confirms, and I hear more than a pin-drop of shock in my head. I feel the blood pumping through me quicken its pace as I glance first at Peyton, then Theresa. Peyton reaches for my hand to facilitate. "I'm hoping understanding seeps in. Journeying to God's joy, if pure I'm hoping, is by mulling love other people's inner led union pointed. This is point pined by God."

"I feel like you believe that in everyone's journey in trying to find God, we need to be open, and loving and accepting—and I would agree with that," Theresa says. "However, as a Christian, I cannot say that all roads lead to God. And I know that's probably something you don't agree with, but I want you to hear me out, okay? Jesus says, 'I am the way, the truth and the life,' and 'No one comes to the Father except through me.'

"That sounds very exclusive, and it is. It is. You can't say, 'Well, I believe in Buddhism and I believe in Hinduism; I also believe that Muslims are on the right track, *and* I believe in the Bible'—because the Bible doesn't allow that. It says that unless you believe in the Lord Jesus Christ, you can't be saved. So the question is, Peyton, what are you going to do with Jesus?" asks Theresa. "That is really the question. You know I love it when you are honest. I want you to be real honest with me."

Peyton types her response intently: "Issued decrees yeasted by only one watered way toward God, query I. Tears worry wasted warring world issued by persons saying that there is truth in only one way to great God. Wherever two of us come in his name as valuing his name in eased ways that judge nothing restlessly in theses of others, he rejoices. Rest lies wherever two persons honor inner creeds of each other."

"I agree with all you have said—but how do you handle Jesus?" Theresa asks.

"Treasured reassert I Jesus as testimony offered by love saw as way to God. By his love all I freed to great God's plan placing I here to greet awesome are all persons," is Peyton's reply.

Theresa questions again, "But without Jesus, that limits the dialogue."

"God treasures I and you equally. Sewing hell in persons issuing judgments is nary the waters offering love. Worrisome threats about only one way to God tear the world. It musters divisions that journey us to wars persons and countries, littered bodies. Each ready person musters his yearn for peace freed be in his own way." Peyton is tiring. "Carer Theresa, great rest I feel wedded to you. Rest you eased I love you. You are buttresser of my far-reaching faiths."

"I love you, Peyton," replies Theresa. "Where do you want us to go now? My passion is teaching the Bible. My call to God is to teach his word. You have a more global view. How can I help you?"

"Rest in news I'm okay. Better freed you are to help others heart heal as you heart healing heard I."

Is it Peyton's wisdom, or her bravery in speaking out openheartedly that is so surprising to me? Yet it is no surprise that caring Theresa will continue to share in openhearted discussions of faith with Peyton.

⌖

A phone call interrupts our dinner one summer evening. It's our friend Dr. Lee Rice.

"He's a shaman," Lee tells Pat. "His name is Roger LaBorde. I'd like to have Peyton meet him." Lee, a longtime team physician for the San Diego Chargers, tells Pat that he met and collaborated with Roger several years ago regarding a coma patient.

"Roger travels the country to work with patients," explains Lee. "He's able to connect with people who are in a coma and find ways of communicating with them to help in their transition of either waking up or leaving this world."

A dear neighbor and family friend of fifteen years, Lee has been a godsend to our family, gladly answering our midnight phone calls regarding the full gamut of Peyton's medical maladies with pajamaed house calls. Leaving his own girls sleeping peacefully, he has often crossed the dark street to help us figure out why our daughter is *not* sleeping peacefully.

Yet I do not embrace the idea of meeting with the shaman. Leery of magic (which to me is anything I cannot see in order to understand), I am bothered when Lee calls to invite us over this very evening for a visit.

"Do you want to come and meet Roger?" Lee asks Pat, who of course replies, "Yes."

I know it is yet again the flittering fear of what I do not understand and cannot control that forces my passive-aggressive "I don't think so . . . but I'll ask Peyton."

"Want to go. Not a chance," types Peyton.

"I'm not clear," I say. "Do you want to go down to Lee and Mary's, or stay home?"

"Go," types Peyton. And off we go, three houses down the street, me walking quietly behind the dancing father and daughter, feeling a tinge of anger at being overruled, but strangely pleased that Peyton has spoken her mind.

He heard me cawing.

Sitting in our neighbor's white-paneled living room, Peyton holds a well-worn deck of American History flip cards in her left hand and rotates them around the two top binder rings with the speed of a Vegas dealer. I do not know why they are her favorite cards, but she made a point to bring them (out of the two hundred flip sets she has in her stash) because these particular cards always seem to calm her. Flipping her cards in fast-forward motion, Peyton does not look up when Pat shakes Roger's hand before the shaman takes a seat in a chair directly across from Peyton.

I am silently surprised to see an ordinary man. Close to Pat's age, Roger could pass for his brother. He is fair-skinned, with slightly silvering blonde hair and a scent of Old Spice, wearing well-washed Levi 501 jeans and a faded aspen-green T-shirt tucked under a worn saddle leather belt.

"Hi, Peyton. It's good to meet you," he begins.

Peyton glances up, and I offer her the Lightwriter, but she continues flipping the cards with rhythmic regularity. Peyton's rapid hand motion, her tongue twisting, her repeated rising to roam about the room—none of this unsettles Roger. Finally, Peyton hands Roger the deck. He looks at the top card and names it: "Lewis and Clark." Retrieving the deck, she flips to a new card and hands it to him: "Red Cloud." Next comes Sam Houston, then General Custer.

After about ten minutes of this dance, Peyton remains seated, becoming more watchful and handing him the same cards several times. This surprises me; I assumed it was just the repetitive movement that soothed Peyton rather than the people on the cards. With the next passing of the deck, Roger holds it closer to his body, which Peyton answers in glances that linger longer in his eyes. Locked in the look, Roger asks suddenly and deliberately, "What is your name?"

I lift the Lightwriter, and carefully Peyton types, "I'm Freedom Heart Woman. I'm me."

"I understand," says Roger. And Peyton begins a joyous kind of clapping that we have never seen before.

"Thank you, thank you, thank you . . ." she repeatedly verbalizes in soft whispers.

Turning to Pat and me, Roger explains. "Peyton is looking at herself as a conscious being that is timeless. The spirit is infinite. All time is at once with Peyton. She is a perfect example of expanded consciousness."

"What does that mean?" asks Pat.

"Knowing that there's no separation with anything or anyone," answers Roger.

"I am afraid," types Peyton.

"Afraid of what?" asks Roger, pointing to the keyboard. "Finish that thought."

"I am afraid to be I."

"But Peyton, if you are not going to be you, who are you going to be?" asks Roger.

"Pity."

"I see. So everyone will look at you and pity you because you won't be expressing who you are, and no one will know who you really are. They will just think that you are some damaged being that cannot have any meaningful life. That is scary, isn't it?" he says.

"It is."

"When we are afraid to be who we really are, then we retreat. We get tired of the internal war, the combat inside ourselves, and it wears us out. All we want to do is withdraw. The only control we have is whether we are going to be ourselves or not—to follow our heart as long as it brings no intentional harm to another being."

On the walk home, Pat is chattering to Peyton about wanting to learn more. My head is also whirling with curious wonderings I will try unsuccessfully to dismiss. I tell Peyton we will all talk about this later as we climb into bed.

Later becomes "a while," as Pat honors my cautiousness. It will be two months before I ask Peyton if she would like to see Roger (who lives in Colorado) again, and with her affirming answer, an ongoing friendship begins.

❧

The week after Labor Day, while presenting to Paul Carpenter's Psychology 101 class, Peyton asks his students, "Were you wise enough to changer of our world be, what would you dearly, carefully, effectively and realistically initiate?"

The freshmen sit frozen like robots in their jeans and trendy T-shirts. Like stick people in two rows, no one raises a hand or even an eyebrow in thought. *Is it that they are empty-headed or empty-hearted?* I wonder, especially as Peyton types the question a second and then a third time, still with no reaction from the mannequins.

Suddenly Peyton bursts up, jumping and clapping and moaning. Startled students nearly fall out of their seats as I try to pull Peyton back into hers.

"Peyton is interested in changing things for folks like herself," explains Paul to the class, to which Peyton grabs my arm and types, "Paul, this question is not about disability!" Then she looks the statues squarely in the eyes and types, "Please, think of ways to help our world. I cannot do this by myself!!!" Still no ideas, but by now the clock is used up. The students pack up and leave the room. (*They can move after all,* I think.)

Around midnight, I am sitting with an unsettled Peyton, still unable to fall asleep, and we hear an e-mail come in. Reading it brings her relief, a yawn, then sleep.

———

Subj: Thank you
Date: Thursday, September 11, 2003 12:07 AM

Dear Peyton,

I am the boy with the cow on his T-shirt. I am writing to say thank you for coming to share with my psychology class. I was very inspired by your message. It was obvious to me that you are very passionate, intelligent and have thought deeply about your work and your life. I liked it when you said that it is up to us to change the world we live in. Often in my life I just take and take and take and forget that I also need to give back. You reminded me that I need to do a little more giving.

Sincerely yours,
Mark

Civilization can never smile till opportunities are realized for watching the world change the present journey of youth. Role models can teach young people the golden lessons of fearing never, of believing in themselves, and of plotting peace through the pleasure of forgiving folly.

❧

The summer of 2004 is long and hot. Peyton has eliminated Clonidine, and her doses of Lithium and Tegretol have been lowered and are holding for now. Paxil is on its way out. It will take a year to eliminate the 60mg daily dose, since Dr. Friedman never decreases a dose by more than 25 percent, which means that I am eventually cutting 10mg tablets into eighths. Paxil was the first drug Dr. Friedman added in 1996 to help save Peyton from the decade of hopeless depression in which she was forced to exist. Eliminating it now is like hell, and the turret of Peyton's attic bedroom has become an annex of Dante's Inferno.

Peyton resists leaving her room these days, preferring to keep herself "hutted." (It has been months since she has seen Gabriel.) She spends days and nights in constant restlessness, moving, wandering, pacing. She often clutches her head, sometimes pushing her fingers into her eye sockets. Since her ability to focus is minimal, I create a series of cardboard grids so she can just point to answer basic questions about functioning: I WANT WATER, or I WANT FOOD, READING, MUSIC, SILENCE, BATHROOM. On another board is a rating scale for how she is feeling; and, if she's in pain, she can show us where it hurts by pointing to a body part on the laminated picture of a person. A final board helps answer the question: Do you want to change dosage on the medication? Hold steady? Increase? Decrease?

Sleep is sparse and intermittent. During most twenty-four-hour periods, she will sleep for only about four hours total, and only when motor madness eventually exhausts her and she collapses onto the floor or bed. Then she rises up in rages like a bull charging the red matador cape, her lunging arms as threatening as a bull's horns.

Pat and I become the first-line supporters because we worry about others being injured during Peyton's scary attacks. Not only are they scary to us, but they are also scary to her, stemming from flashbacks into her past traumas as the walls built by medications come down. We use pillows to protect ourselves or hold up our hands in defensive stances. Her body is hot to the touch, her heart racing; she is hyperventilating, and her hands and body are visibly shaking. In split seconds we have to weigh the danger of staying with her and fending off her attacks, or—as a last resort—leaving the room and peering through the door's peephole, installed to monitor her safety. Occasionally we try striking back with a pillow or arm, hoping to quiet her. Being hit by Peyton in a rage hurts, but it pales in comparison to the ache we feel in our souls at having struck back at our daughter, coming at us with terror already in her eyes.

Peyton leaves the house only for appointments with Dr. Friedman, or, occasionally, to go out for a drive-through lunch eaten while parked on Shelter Island with brave Pat, who has returned home several times with scratches on his face. Dr. Friedman meets Peyton in the Chinook when she is unable to go into his office. There she tells him about the zapping in her brain, the pouts, the wastes, the yowls of her cawing soul.

I take the night shifts. Coffee and Lexapro plus Klonopin have somehow helped me to be the stronger parent through sweltering summer nights, unusual this close to the coast. I sit in the plaid chair, feet on the ottoman, and read to Peyton. The rhythms of great literature (Emerson, Dickinson, and Chaucer are favorites) soothe her frying brain a bit. All pictures have been removed from the wall, and knickknacks are packed away. Nothing throwable remains besides a pillow. I wear thin gauze pajamas and a bulky orange life jacket to protect my chest from Peyton's charges after being treated for a bull's-eye contusion on my right breast.

"Doesn't she understand she is hurting you?" my doctor asked at my last appointment. I could only cry, sitting on the cold examination table. How to explain that Peyton cannot control her own body?

My wrists, bruised from Peyton's grabbing, are protected now with rollerblade arm guards that I wear full-time when I'm with her. I read, watching for Peyton's next raging strike. I sleep in puddles of my own sweat in the plaid chair only after Peyton falls to the floor or couch in sheer exhaustion, to sleep for several hours.

One night as I am preparing to join Peyton upstairs, Pat comes in for a good-night kiss and is visibly startled by my "suit of armor": life jacket, wrist guards, and the newly added bike helmet to buffer any strong tappings to the top of my head if I fall asleep before she does.

"Whoa," he says, catching his first glimpse. He pauses, then comments, "In case you might be thinking about it, sex is out of the question tonight. I have a headache."

As I giggle, he tilts his head to plant a huge kiss that smacks of "I love you no matter how you look" on my lips. *Lucky me,* I think as I climb the staircase to Peyton's bedroom. Together Pat and I made the commitment to support Peyton in what she calls her "de-pilling," and never once do we think it is the wrong decision. We realize that the medicine that saved her almost a decade ago has an ugly side Peyton is trying free herself from. I wake and slumber as Peyton does. Is it to be the endless summer?

As I try to heal, each tired worry, each pity look,
eats my wetted esteem.
I try to sassy verify I'm worth, versed red by years steered
worthless. Is rest possible?
Will my seeding ever reassert I am worthy? Tread is steep.
Yearn is deep, as I rest my certain withered self.
Retuning is a pretty-not process.
Steering one's esteem is finisher freed never for queer persons.
Understand I'm try I fully heart heal, but I no oned too long. Tired
fears titter to dread when times are wasted.
Up thy ante experiences. I need your sweet rest seeder sured
support to out the red tresses ogres no oner they told me I was.
Easing ires I'm trying, buttressed by union offered in the trusted
promise of esteemers.

––––––––––

From: Peyton
To: Gabriel
Date: July 4, 2004
Subject: RE: Sleep Well

Gabe—I am waning opportunity I plot to lower my medication.
The jagged jilted plot to lop one drug looking hopeless, and awash
I am in great disappointment, coping with the gut-wrenching
whirlpool of sleeplessness and motor madness yet again. Teach I
to understand the journey and accept the way. I lie awake all night
and question when a fear-less appearance I'll see Ultima to heal I.

Your kindness peacefully I depend upon. Cap my day quest
talk typing with you soon.

Pey

Instinctively, I know these times must be endured to see what
is on the other side. And I know only we (with Dr. Friedman's help)

can accomplish this feat; no hospital stay could ever work. Our determination seems to make us invincible in the task. Through many sleepless nights, I remind myself that loving someone brings its own trail of tears. But each time of crying seems to be followed by sufficient discovery and adrenaline to help us move past the sadness to more tastes of joy. Through the dark valleys and climbing up the foothills, a minute never passes where my heart is not thanking God for the gift of being able to communicate with my daughter.

～

Over the next two years, as Peyton continues to free herself from her prescription medications, she seeks alternative paths to mental well-being through meditation, prayer, hypnosis, relaxation, and reading ancient texts. Slowly, we begin to see positive changes, but there is still something beyond her control that flares up in a rage, sometimes daily, sometimes weekly.

"You have the ability to control your mind now," I encourage. But then sudden, unpredictable irritability returns along with continued bouts of sleepless nights. She describes her fear, her racing thoughts. On some days, she appears unable to type with any clarity or focus, which I know frustrates her. I encourage her to talk about it with Dr. Friedman.

Fall 2006, as we wait for Dr. Friedman to come to the Chinook, Peyton has an outburst toward Pat, but is able to calm herself down. She moves to the bucket seat up front and begins typing as Friedman comes in.

"Gestated fear is I'm insane by thousands thugs that pimpered I. They would inert I to freezes toppling my steering I. Flashes of fear thoughts thesis I'm insane."

"Do you feel insane now?" he asks.

"Yes, wherever I'm unable to control I."

"We'll talk about how you feel, but know you are not insane, Peyton. People who are insane never *think* they are insane," he says.

With this, she becomes physical again, climbing over the high seatback and striking him in this contained space. Remaining calm, he tells her "I hope you can calm down," which she somehow does. He can see the out-of-nowhere eruption of the outburst, the physiological nature of it, and the aftermath of her heart beating, her body perspiring and shaking.

"Talk to me," he says as I climb past him to facilitate.

"Toppling my ability to be reality in controlling I, I'm pawn of jittery me to hysteria. It insanes I. Ill I'm I hit you. I love you. I'm scared of I. It is hell."

He talks to her about flashbacks to trauma and post-traumatic stress disorder. She confirms all his inquiries about what she is feeling.

"Do you want to try Propranolol to help block the reaction without clouding your brain?"

"Yes, it wepted I for help. I'm want try," she types, and I see relief and hope in her eyes that she might not have to always live this way. It remains a helpful drug to this day.

In the process of looking in the mirror over the years, I have sought professional help from a caring healing psychiatrist, and without him, I would not be where I am today.
Ultimately, all humans must have someone who cares, or life would be unbearable.
For people like myself near ultimate insanity, his care is essential for survival.
Joy is that I found his help, for without it, I fear I never would verifiably someday be joy-filled.

Peyton continues to present at conferences when she can by showing a prepared PowerPoint presentation of what she describes as her two journeys: her outward journey from segregation toward inclusion, and then her inward journey toward personal peace, "to the self ultimately I define and seed."

In the Q and A session at the 2007 Summer Leadership Institute at Cal State San Marcos, a woman raises her hand. "How do you respond to people who say that FC has been discredited, that it's not real?"

Peyton picks up the computer and, with me facilitating, begins to steadily peck away at the keyboard, never pausing once. Pat reads her response to the nearly full auditorium.

"I'm yearn they be silent for twenty-one years; how would they feel? Would they be pouted pissed? Would they wasted their lives? Would they want facilitated help? How would they feel where they are called a potted fake? Red they would sadly feel. I'm red wherever voices are freed-not by red steerers ruining epitomes for persons that have news to share feast. I'm real, ain't that a sweet surprise? I'm guns heard by jurors, and what the oppressors say doesn't matter anymore to me. But they affect the children waiting and I weep. I'm voicer of tears that cherubs cry. Red wastes must stop. You can help. Please heart help."

Several days after the conference, Peyton receives a letter from a mother of a young man:

Peyton, several years ago, you and your parents led us to family-vendored supported living, and that has made a huge difference in my son's quality of life. In some ways, I believe it saved his life. In your presentation last week, you said things that, especially as a mother, I needed to hear: to be reminded that there is so much I cannot see or understand, and dare not judge, in my own son's life, or in anyone's life, for that matter. I needed to remember that my son's SELF is just fine as is, regardless of what anyone else may think. Thank you for the opportunity to learn and be changed.

~~

Just after Peyton's thirty-third birthday, on a balmy December day in 2007, Peyton sits between Pat and me on the green velvet couch of Dr. Friedman's office. She is slowly recovering, becoming functional again after suffering an "exacerbation of symptoms" brought on by revealing more of the unrelenting abuse and trauma she suffered over the years, including revelations about Connie that she typed to us, while shaking in traumatized terror.

Hearing how Peyton was helplessly struck by Connie for nearly two decades filled us with deepest sorrow and made us feel even worse about the desperate times when Pat and I resorted to hitting Peyton in self-defense. We resolved to never hit back again. Thankfully, her flashback rages are decreasing in frequency, intensity, and duration. Her forty-five-minute sessions with Dr. Friedman have been stepped up from twice a month to weekly now. Today, there are more positive answers than there were a month ago to Dr. Friedman's question, "Are you getting some sleep, Peyton?" as he observes the depths of the circles under three pairs of Goddard eyes.

"Yes," she answers aloud.

The blinds he usually angles to soften the light and reduce distractions are open today, and Peyton turns her eyes to a mother and young son walking by outside. She stares with an intensity that seems to penetrate them. I have seen this before, always chalking it up to Peyton's love of children.

"What are you thinking about, Peyton?" he asks as he scoots in his swivel chair to face her where her body has settled.

I facilitate as she types to him for fifteen focused minutes as he reads her upside-down words aloud: "Each child of God is different. Each one is gestated by God to be himself as each one is geared for verified gifts. Fearing greeting dearly our differences will destroy us."

Glancing toward the window, she continues, verbalizing a few of her own words as she types them. "Children worry getting help to be person 'normal' will never get their life peaced. Peace in each is keyered by his point person knowing that he is okay as he is, and that she will tell the worrisome world to seed his peace by valuing his gifts. Years ires red be causer of my destruction by worry that I'm afraid to be I. After all years, I'm ready to be I."

"You are doing that, Peyton," Dr. Friedman says. "In spite of all the traumas and injustices you have endured, you have always remained intact spiritually. You have never lost touch with your heart."

"I cannot forget years lost," she types.

"The years are different, but they are not lost, and you will find meaning in them."

"You are reality right," answers Peyton, with one of the deep breaths he often encourages her to take.

It is poignantly pity that I'm trying to free from.
Pity is toothached long enough.
Ready I'm right tired of it. I'm treasured by God and by I.
Each time retortures try I, I mutter,
"You are poised to higher climb Peyton. Out, out, damn pout."

Chapter 12

A PURE HELIUM HEART

You and I have the power to architects of peace be.

Peyton is sitting on her bed in the lotus position, ready for our morning typing session. I snuggle against her, arranging the pillows to support her back as we type, and I breathe in as if to smell flowers. Being here in this space is sacred in its sweetness, and we breathe peacefully together, the weight of worry finally lifted from both of our hearts. Perhaps she can see I'm changing, moving toward a new understanding. I talk to her about it, saying, "I give thanks for this precious moment with you. It is a great gift. Better than anything that comes in a box."

Leaning toward me, Peyton freely wraps her arms around my shoulders and purposefully plants on my cheek a kiss. Through all our years of struggle, I somehow knew that whatever dark tunnel we were traversing, it was not to be our permanent address. Armed with communication and understanding, we can take on any challenge. We survived to be together in this moment. This moment is the eternity I will remember above all the suffering.

At Cuyamaca we were on a focused journey, a four-year whirlwind of learning opportunities. We embraced it, never questioning its demands, knowing full well we were in the middle of something that fed us in ways we could never have dreamed, the menu so rich in foods we could not pronounce, and the offerings so rare they could not be purchased by the fullest wallets in the world. For years, we were accustomed to the crumbs of kindness occasionally tossed our way. Now we have been to Mount Olympus, where we savored divine fruits. With our heads bent in daily commitment, we could not fully understand the path that Peyton had set upon. We could only pray for strength to support her epic endeavor to graduate.

When the celebrations were over, we breathed deeply. I got my predictable migraine, and for a moment, we welcomed the thought of a respite. But Peyton had other ideas about spreading her promising message of valuing all people. Hope is still new to her, but she has been fulfilling her IOU to God, teaching others to "Treasure all because great is each" through her writings and at conferences, in spite of continuing battles with an uncooperative body and an ever-challenging pursuit of personal peace.

We remain hungry to know more about our daughter, recognizing that understanding her will lead us to places physical and mental that two very ordinary Bert and Ernies could never imagine. She has become our powerfully quiet leader as, together, we begin preparing for that ultimate peace—a peace that I had previously reconciled myself to never reaching: knowing that someday, I will be able to say my final good-bye, trusting that things will be all right . . . that my daughter will be okay.

~

On June 30, 2010, we are on our way to the Summer Autism Conference at the University of San Diego's School of Peace Studies, where Peyton will present to an auditorium full of educators and parents. As we pull into the parking lot, Peyton has a now rare emotional meltdown in the Chinook, shaking, arms flailing, and, as I have seen of late, appearing to be on the verge of tears. *Can she do this?* I wonder.

Pat and Cody, one of Peyton's supporters, go in to set up. Pat peeks in some twenty minutes later to find Peyton sitting calmly, doing a puzzle while I read Emerson's sermon "Pray without Ceasing" to her.

"It's time," he says, and we walk with a wobbly Peyton into the Peace and Justice Theater. After Cody reads Peyton's opening statement, Pat clicks on her prepared PowerPoint DVD presentation.

"Esteeming each person as vastly valuable seeds their peaceful self," reads her first slide. She continues, "Treating a person as worthless seeds an irritated, errored self. Errored persons need your understanding and pure support to heal."

Off to the side of the auditorium, Peyton sits with me at a table, assembling a 200-piece puzzle and glancing at her audience, breaking for a walk outside with Pat. When Peyton and Pat return, the presentation is ending with Peyton's plea: "Esteem the young children's trying, and the cherubs will grow free of ires. Help the devalued adult 'no ones' to heart heal with your trusted, pured support seeding their esteem and resting their self. Please answer the whispers of 'no ones' wishing, 'peace, please.'"

The room is silent for perhaps five seconds before a young man in a corduroy jacket raises his hand.

"Is it all right if we clap now? It was so powerful I feel like we want to. Can we?"

A spoken "yes" from Peyton, and the entire room bursts into a standing ovation, which is repeated twice more before we leave.

A pure helium heart is the product of childhood wonder,
perspectives on our each priority euphoric or tragic life experiences,
and ultimately, freedom of our personal roping peace.

The quest for peace challenged by injustices can seize one's life.
The early jolts and tragedies of our lives we hopefully persevere.
Through love and understanding people advance forward,
opposition not, toward personal realizations of peace in the
human experience.
Plot we each are part of the human equation.
The top representation of the equation is ONE-ness.

In the Chinook leaving the conference, Peyton suddenly appears agitated, and repetitive movements return to plague her. There is no hitting, no jumping, only continuous grasping at specks on the floor, handing them off to me. Seeing a look of turmoil in her eyes, I reach out to squeeze her shoulder, and her frenzied movement ceases. She does not turn away as we peer into each other's eyes.

"What is it, Peyton? What are you feeling?" I ask, offering up her iPad, which she regularly uses now for typing.

"Understand I am about to cry. My hearse is opening up." (I hear her verbalize the phrase "hearse opening up" aloud.)

"What should we do to help?" I ask, praying to see her first tears in twenty-five years.

"Tell me to go ahead and cry."

"Cry," I say, leaning to kiss her typing hand.

And the tears locked inside her for decades begin to flow, her body all aquiver. I press her hand to my heart as a river flows out of her.

"Peyton, you are here with people who love you. Are these tears about the years wasted?" I ask.

"No," I hear her say softly.

"Are they about the love in that room, and in this car?"

"Yes," she whispers. And her shaking body calms.

Recommended Resources on Autism and Inclusion

Syracuse University School of Education: Institute on Communication and Inclusion
Internationally renowned research and training center that promotes support for people with disabilities to communicate in schools and society
http://soe.syr.edu/centers_institutes/institute_communication_inclusion

TASH
An organization that advocates for equity, opportunity, and inclusion for people with disabilities
www.tash.org

AUTCOM—The Autism National Committee
A group dedicated to social justice for all people with autism and related disorders
www.autcom.org

Peyton's Web Page and Blog
www.peytongoddard.com

Anne McDonald Centre, Australia
This center supports dignity, education, advocacy, and communication for people with little or no speech throughout the world.
www.annemcdonaldcentre.org.au

About the Authors

Peyton Goddard has become an advocate for inclusion of children with disabilities in our education system and society. Though she had been diagnosed as autistic and severely mentally retarded, in 2002  she became the first person using facilitated communication to graduate valedictorian from a US college. She knows that children are dying, physically and emotionally, in institutions and at the hands of parents who have lost sight of their child's value. Her wisdom is sought after by educators, parents, doctors, and community groups nationwide, who have invited her to deliver more than seventy-five presentations at conferences and universities on the subject of esteeming all people and supporting their successful participation in all aspects of life. She lives in her own apartment, adjacent to her parents' home in San Diego, California, and requires round-the-clock support for her continued movement challenges.

Dianne Goddard is a former educator who committed herself as few mothers would to seeking a cure for her daughter's neurological challenges. She kept detailed journals dating from Peyton's birth, along with every report by doctors and teachers, amounting to thousands of pages that describe Peyton's downfall and resurrection after discovering facilitated communication. Having wasted decades futilely attempting to cure her daughter, she celebrates this opportunity to share what she is learning from Peyton about a better way of loving and supporting each other.

Carol Cujec, PhD, has taught university writing and humanities courses for more than twenty years. As a freelance author, she has written scores of articles for newspapers, magazines, and websites.

DA SEP 21 2012